Parenting Coordination in Postseparation Disputes

Parenting Coordination in Postseparation Disputes

A COMPREHENSIVE GUIDE FOR PRACTITIONERS

EDITED BY
SHIRLEY ANN HIGUCHI AND STEPHEN J. LALLY

American Psychological Association • Washington, DC

Published by
American Psychological Association
750 First Street, NE
Washington, DC 20002
www.apa.org

To order
APA Order Department
P.O. Box 92984
Washington, DC 20090-2984
Tel: (800) 374-2721; Direct: (202) 336-5510
Fax: (202) 336-5502; TDD/TTY: (202) 336-6123
Online: www.apa.org/pubs/books
E-mail: order@apa.org

In the U.K., Europe, Africa, and the Middle East, copies may be ordered from
American Psychological Association
3 Henrietta Street
Covent Garden, London
WC2E 8LU England

Typeset in Goudy by Circle Graphics, Inc., Columbia, MD

Printer: Maple Press, York, PA
Cover Designer: Mercury Publishing Services, Rockville, MD

Library of Congress Cataloging-in-Publication Data

Parenting coordination in postseparation disputes: a comprehensive guide for practitioners / [edited by] Shirley Ann Higuchi and Stephen J. Lally.
pages cm
Includes bibliographical references and index.
ISBN 978-1-4338-1739-7 — ISBN 1-4338-1739-X 1. Children of divorced parents—Psychology. 2. Parenting, Part-time. 3. Custody of children. I. Higuchi, Shirley Ann. II. Lally, Stephen J.
HQ777.5.P3737 2014
306.89—dc23
2013046893

British Library Cataloguing-in-Publication Data
A CIP record is available from the British Library.

Printed in the United States of America
First Edition

http://dx.doi.org/10.1037/14390-000

To Linda E. G. Campbell, PhD,
for teaching me the value and efficacy of this service,
and to my children, who benefited from her help.
—*Shirley Ann Higuchi*

To Jennifer, Sam, Will, and Emma;
you are my foundation,
bringing meaning and joy to my life.
—*Stephen J. Lally*

CONTENTS

CONTRIBUTORS

Debra K. Carter, PhD, Cofounder and Clinical Director, National Cooperative Parenting Center, Bradenton, FL

Linda A. Delaney, Esq., Partner at Delaney McKinney, L.L.P., Chevy Chase, MD

Robin M. Deutsch, PhD, Director, Center of Excellence for Children, Families and the Law at the Massachusetts School of Professional Psychology, Newton

Giselle A. Hass, PsyD, Private Practice, Washington, DC

Shirley Ann Higuchi, JD, Associate Executive Director, Legal and Regulatory Affairs, Practice Directorate, American Psychological Association, Washington, DC

Jennifer Joyner-Hall, PsyD, Clinical Director, Office of the Parenting Coordinator, District of Columbia Superior Court, Washington

Joan B. Kelly, PhD, Lecturer, Consultant, former Executive Director of the Northern California Mediation Center, Corte Madera

Stephen J. Lally, PhD, ABPP, Professor, American School of Professional Psychology at Argosy University, Washington, DC

Margaret J. McKinney, Esq., Partner at Delaney McKinney, L.L.P., Chevy Chase, MD

Alan Nessman, JD, Senior Special Counsel, Legal and Regulatory Affairs, Practice Directorate, American Psychological Association, Washington, DC

Matthew J. Sullivan, PhD, Private Practice, Palo Alto, CA

ACKNOWLEDGMENTS

Hillary Rodham Clinton wrote that it takes a village to raise a child. The birth and development of this book also took a community. The original seed for this book was the parenting coordination program to serve the needs of indigent families in the District of Columbia's Superior Court. That project grew and developed into the Office of the Parenting Coordinator, the first permanent parenting coordination office. Along the way, many of the leaders of parenting coordination and alternative dispute resolution provided training and consultation to the program. The project led to a number of presentations at conferences, a series of advanced workshops held during the Annual Conventions of the American Psychological Association (APA), and to APA's development of parenting coordination guidelines (APA, 2012).[1] The various authors of the chapters of this book have all had connections either directly with the original project or its offspring. However, the community that helped the development of the original project and this book stretches beyond the chapter authors.

[1]American Psychological Association. (2012). Guidelines for the practice of parenting coordination. *American Psychologist*, *67*, 63–71. doi:10.1037/a0024646

APA has played a large role in the genesis of the original parenting coordination program, the development of this book, and the advancement of the field of parenting coordination. Initially Russ Newman, PhD, JD, as the executive director of the APA's Practice Directorate, and later Katherine Nordal, PhD, his successor, provided support that helped establish this court-based program. Thanks are due to Elizabeth Winkelmann, PhD, JD; Stacey Larson, PsyD, JD; Javier Aquino; Ieshia Haynie; and Charlene Harvey for their assistance with this book and work on this important topic.

Former Chief Judge of the District of Columbia Superior Court Rufus King III's initial support, and the support as well of his successor, Chief Judge Lee Satterfield, were crucial for the initial parenting coordination program. Although there was broad support throughout the family court, the efforts of then–Presiding Family Court Judge Anita Josey-Herring were critical for spearheading the efforts to adopt this program as a court-based initiative. Judge Judith Bartnoff, who served on the advisory committee, was particularly notable as a pioneer in advocating for the efficacy of parenting coordination services in the DC court system. A number of attorneys in both the family law and pro bono sections of the District of Columbia Bar supported this work, including Joan Strand, JD, of George Washington University Law School, who served on the advisory committee. The editors thank the leadership of the Annie E. Casey Foundation for their invaluable support and financial assistance on the programmatic and research aspects of the DC parenting coordination program.

The American School of Professional Psychology at Argosy University in Washington, DC, was an early partner in the project, and individuals there have continued to provide support for the various parenting coordination trainings. Robert Barrett, PhD, chair of the clinical program, has been a consistent supporter and helped guide the project as a member of the advisory committee. Paul Berman, PhD; Michele Parker, PhD; and Bruce Copeland, PhD, JD, parenting coordinators in independent practice, greatly helped the project during different stages of its development. The editors also want to express their appreciation to Dr. Berman and Neil Ribner, PhD, for sharing their insights on PC developments in Maryland and San Diego, CA. Dr. Ribner is the director of the clinical psychology program of Alliant University, San Diego, where he is spearheading the development of a PC program in the San Diego court system.

Parenting Coordination in Postseparation Disputes

INTRODUCTION

SHIRLEY ANN HIGUCHI AND STEPHEN J. LALLY

In the past 30 years, there has been increasing evidence of the detrimental effects of parental conflict on children from divorced families (e.g., Kelly, 2000) as well as the potential benefits of increased involvement of the father (e.g., Lamb, 1981). This evidence has moved courts and other advocates away from adversarial models in making custody decisions and toward joint custody and more collaborative models (Katz, 1994). With these changes, families have often benefited from court-sponsored parent education that focuses on the needs of children and the impact of conflict as well as mediation both before and after divorce. For some families, however, the custody decisions continued to be litigated after the divorce and when education and mediation did not prove effective. Parenting coordination was developed independently in several locations as a means to address this situation (see Chapter 1, this volume, for a detailed review of the history in the United States; see Fidler, 2012, and Fidler & Epstein, 2008, for the history of

http://dx.doi.org/10.1037/14390-001
Parenting Coordination in Postseparation Disputes: A Comprehensive Guide for Practitioners, S. A. Higuchi and S. J. Lally (Editors)

its development in Canada). A parenting coordinator (PC) is a professional, either appointed by the court or jointly agreed on by the parents, who uses mediation and education techniques to resolve disputes regarding parenting plans but who also has the ability to arbitrate and make decisions when mediation efforts are not successful. The current thinking of many judges who have worked with PCs is to view them as behavioral change consultants or referees for the court. Lawyers, psychologists, and other professionals provide this unique service in many jurisdictions.

Over the past 25 years, parenting coordination has developed into an innovative, cutting-edge service to help families resolve high-conflict custody disputes. Through court-based programs and increased research, practice, and awareness, parenting coordination services have evolved into a recognized and respected practice. Two major national organizations have developed guidelines to assist practitioners. In 2006, the Association of Family and Conciliation Courts (AFCC) Task Force on Parenting Coordination[1]—a respected interdisciplinary organization of professionals dedicated to improving the lives of children and families through the resolution of family conflict—developed the first set of guidelines. Subsequently, in 2012, the American Psychological Association (APA) published a set of parenting coordination guidelines. APA is the largest scientific and professional organization representing psychology in the United States. Its mission is to advance the creation, communication, and application of psychological knowledge to benefit society and improve people's lives.[2] Along with these guidelines, in the last decade there has been a significant increase, both nationally and internationally, in presentations, trainings, and publications in the area of parenting coordination.

In addition, over the last several years PC services have been increasingly recognized by the courts. A number of states in the United States and provinces in Canada have enacted legislation and court rules that recognize the role of the PC and define the training and requirements for parenting coordination work (see Chapter 2 for a detailed review of the laws in the United States). Despite the potential of the PC to help children and their caregivers struggling with the many challenges related to custody disputes, cost has often limited the ability to provide such services. In 2004, the DC Superior Court, the APA Practice Directorate, Argosy University, and the DC Bar Family Law Section worked collaboratively to launch a pilot parenting coordination program to make services more widely available. In 2009,

[1]AFCC members are the leading practitioners, researchers, teachers, and policymakers in the family court arena.
[2]APA is the world's largest association of psychologists, with more than 137,000 researchers, educators, clinicians, consultants, and students as its members.

this pilot program was funded by the court and became the first official Office of the Parenting Coordinator (see Chapter 4 for additional details). In a landmark case, *Jordan v. Jordan* (2011), the use of parenting coordination services within this court-based program was affirmed by the District of Columbia Court of Appeals.

Clearly, the field of parenting coordination has matured to the point where there is a need to consolidate the current body of information in a comprehensive handbook. In this growing practice area, however, there is a dearth of resources to assist individuals practicing or contemplating practice as a PC. The editors of this book look to fill that gap by bringing together authors who are at the forefront of parenting coordination practice, training, publication, and research. The goal of this book is to provide a resource that comprehensively reviews the theory and practice of parenting coordination, grounds this review in APA's (2010) *Ethical Principles of Psychologists and Code of Conduct* as well as the field's newly developed practice guidelines (AFCC, Task Force on Parenting Coordination, 2006; APA, 2012), and summarizes the existing evidence base for parenting coordination. In addition, this book addresses areas of parenting coordination practice that have not been covered in depth in the existing literature. These areas include the provision of parenting coordination to economically challenged parents and to diverse populations, the handling of domestic violence issues within parenting coordination, and the use and involvement of children by PCs.

This book can serve as an introduction to parenting coordination for graduate students in the fields of mental health and law who are interested in working in this area of family law. It also provides an introduction for currently practicing mental health professionals and attorneys who are seeking to move into this area of practice. In particular, the initial chapters, with their coverage of the history of the field, the competencies needed to function effectively as a PC, and an overview of the practice, provide a foundation for individuals contemplating a parenting coordination practice. The book also is designed to be a valuable resource for individuals already engaged in the practice of parenting coordination. The latter part of the book addresses managing a parenting coordination practice, advanced parenting coordination skills, and special topics, all of which should be useful to individuals practicing parenting coordination.

This book brings together the leading psychologists and attorneys in the United States within parenting coordination practice, most of whom have worked in a variety of ways to better define and provide guidance on the role of the PC. Although many of the authors are psychologists, and the book is grounded within psychologists' ethics and APA's emphasis on evidence-based practice, this book is a valuable resource regardless of the reader's professional background. As surveys of PCs have found (e.g., Kirkland & Sullivan, 2008), parenting coordination is an area of practice for psychologists, counselors, social workers, mediators, and attorneys that requires advanced skills and knowledge. With that in mind, this book was written to be relevant across these various disciplines.

ORGANIZATION OF THE BOOK

This book is divided into four sections. Part I provides background and foundational information on parenting coordination. Part II covers the knowledge and skills necessary for intermediate and advanced parenting coordination. Part III comprises chapters that focus on special issues and populations within parenting coordination, and the final section, Part IV, addresses the future of parenting coordination, both the developing body of evidence that supports the efficacy of the practice and predictions of where the practice will evolve.

Foundational Information

Part I of this book provides the foundation for the book's coverage of parenting coordination. In Chapter 1, "Origins and Development of Parenting Coordination," Joan B. Kelly describes the societal, legal, and family context in which parenting coordination developed. She maps out the independent development of this intervention in different areas of the country and the work of leaders in the field as well as legislative efforts, publications, and related programs that resulted in the formal recognition of parenting coordination services. As one of the leading researchers in divorce and its effects on children, and one of the country's first PCs, Kelly is uniquely situated to offer this historical review. She has been involved in the growth of this area of practice and has served on the AFCC and APA task forces that helped craft the two organizations' current guidelines.

Chapter 2, "Legal Standards and Issues Associated With Parenting Coordination," was written primarily by individuals from the law firm of Delaney and McKinney, with additional contributions from APA legal and regulatory staff. Linda A. Delaney and Margaret J. McKinney have substantial experience representing parents and children while litigating and negotiating complex child custody and divorce cases. Their chapter outlines the legal authority for appointing a PC and reviews a number of important legal issues that PCs should consider (e.g., when to appoint a PC—either prejudgment or postjudgment, the issue of quasi-judicial immunity).

In Chapter 3, "Competencies Required for Conducting Parenting Coordination," Stephen J. Lally and Robin M. Deutsch review the basic knowledge, skills, training, and attitudes that are required to function effectively as a PC. This chapter is grounded in the current competency movement that has guided professional psychology training as well as psychology accreditation and licensure. Both authors are professors at APA-accredited doctoral clinical psychology programs. Lally is also past president of the National Council of Schools and Programs of Professional Psychology and was one of the authors of the council's developmental achievement levels. Deutsch is the director for the Center of Excellence for Children, Families and the Law at the Massachusetts School of Professional Psychology. In that role, she directs one of the first PC certification programs to have been established. She is a former AFCC president, has served as a member of both AFCC's and APA's task forces that crafted the organizations' PC guidelines, and is a nationally recognized PC who is one of the leading authors and trainers in the field of parenting coordination.

Chapter 4, "Parenting Coordination: Basic Approaches and Strategies," was written by Robin M. Deutsch. This is the final chapter in Part I and serves as a primer for parenting coordination practice. Deutsch describes the hybrid role of a PC, including the various functions associated with the role (e.g., assessment of disputes, parent education, conflict management, mediation and arbitration). She takes readers through this process, beginning with the start of a case and setting the stage for ongoing work, ranging from establishing a communication structure between the parents and between parents and their children to the crafting and documenting of written agreements.

Intermediate and Advanced Topics

The four chapters that make up Part II cover topics relevant to both beginning and experienced PCs. In Chapter 5, "Creation, Development, and Management of a Parenting Coordination Practice," Matthew J. Sullivan provides background information in setting up and developing a PC practice. He describes the special skills needed in this practice area and provides several practice tips and sample materials to assist practitioners setting up a PC practice. Sullivan is an experienced PC who has written and presented widely about parenting coordination practice. He was instrumental in developing the AFFC PC guidelines.

In Chapter 6, Robin M. Deutsch and Stephen J. Lally explore "Ethical Issues and Risk Management in Parenting Coordination." They offer guidance regarding how to ensure one practices in an ethical manner with appropriate risk management measures in place. They also discuss various ethics codes and guidelines and highlight specific parenting coordination scenarios that create ethical dilemmas. In addition to her earlier noted experience, Deutsch brings to the chapter her experience serving on and chairing APA's

Ethics Committee. Lally's experience on APA's Committee for Professional Practice and Standards as well as with the District of Columbia Psychological Association informed his coauthorship.

Chapter 7, "Strategies for Working With Difficult Clients," by Matthew J. Sullivan, deals with special issues and concerns in parenting coordination practice. Certain situations and difficult clients provide unique challenges and may require modification on how a PC would typically handle a case. Sullivan brings his experience not only as a PC but also as a trainer and supervisor of PCs to describe the challenges of working with parents who have personality disorders (e.g., histrionic, narcissistic, borderline, and antisocial).

Chapter 8, "Setting Up a Parenting Coordination Project in the Courts: The District of Columbia Program," describes a cutting-edge collaborative parenting coordination project established in the District of Columbia Superior Court that currently serves low-income families. This collaborative model involved APA, the Family Law section of the DC Bar, a local university, and the court. Chapter authors Stephen J. Lally, Shirley Ann Higuchi, and Jennifer Joyner-Hall review the history of the establishment of the first office of parenting coordination established in a court. They list the unique challenges associated with such a program as well as efforts to duplicate it in other settings. The first two authors represent some of the initial stakeholders who helped shape this project, with the second author, Higuchi, also bringing to the chapter her experience as a former DC Bar president and a leader helping spearhead APA's involvement with this project and its transfer to other jurisdictions. The third author, Joyner-Hall, is the program's current director.

Special Topics in Parenting Coordination

Part III covers a number of special topics in parenting coordination that are important to both novice and experienced PCs. In Chapter 9, "Including Children in the Parenting Coordination Process: A Specialized Role," Joan B. Kelly draws on her broad research and clinical experience working with children of divorce to describe how and when children should be brought into the PC process. She describes the value of using a structured interview format in obtaining helpful information from the child. The input provided by the child assists parents in putting their differences aside and reaching positive agreements. When done correctly, eliciting the children's views and effectively relaying that information to the parents will help ensure the children's future well-being.

In Chapter 10, "Parenting Coordination and Diversity Issues," Giselle A. Hass, a forensic psychologist who was the clinical director of the District of Columbia PC project as well as a member of the group that authored the APA parenting coordination guidelines, addresses issues that arise when providing parenting coordination services to diverse populations, nontraditional parents, and those who are economically challenged. When working with this population, unique sensitivities based on one's racial, ethnic, social/economic and sexual orientation status may arise. Given the increased awareness toward diversity in today's society, it has become necessary to consider pertinent issues in the practice of parenting coordination. Hass informs readers on the importance of understanding the individual complexity of the client's life.

Giselle A. Hass, who has written and presented extensively on issues of relational violence, explores in Chapter 11, "Parenting Coordination and Domestic Violence," the issue of providing parenting coordination in situations in which domestic violence is suspected, an area of considerable controversy. Hass articulates the critical importance of assessing domestic violence is articulated and reviews the need to assess the nature and type of violence in deciding whether parenting coordination is appropriate and how such services should be delivered.

In Chapter 12, "Collaboration With Attorneys," Margaret J. McKinney, Linda A. Delaney, and Alan Nessman discuss how PCs can most effectively work with attorneys to accomplish the goals of parenting coordination. They describe the PC's involvement in the divorce and custody process, and they suggest ways of dealing with tension between PCs and attorneys and how PCs can educate recalcitrant attorneys about the parenting coordination process. They also address the challenges regarding PCs' testimony on the witness stand.

The Future of Parenting Coordination

The last two chapters make up Part IV and cover the future of parenting coordination. Debra K. Carter, a PC involved in some of the field's pioneering research, and Stephen J. Lally, the research coordinator for the DC parenting coordination program, explore in Chapter 13, "Charting the Challenging Path Toward Establishment of Parenting Coordination's Efficacy," the efficacy of parent coordination practice and review the research available as it relates to parenting coordination practice. They review the relationship between parenting coordination services and court-based activities and the evidence available on validating the parenting coordination process. They also explore related research and discuss what future research is needed to demonstrate positive outcomes and advance parenting coordination.

The final chapter of the book, Chapter 14—"The Future of Parenting Coordination"—is authored by Joan B. Kelly, one of the individuals present at the beginning of parenting coordination and one of the first PCs, and Shirley Ann Higuchi, the driving force behind APA's initiatives in parenting coordination. These two authors bring a unique perspective to a review of the journey that parenting coordination has traveled and their predictions for its future travels. This forward-looking chapter is a springboard for both the novice and experienced parenting coordination readers to explore their future practice and the role PCs will have in the courts.

Online Resources

Readers are encouraged to visit the APA website for additional resources, including links to the APA and AFCC guidelines, relevant court opinions, and appendixes to later chapters at http://pubs.apa.org/books/supp/higuchi.

REFERENCES

American Psychological Association. (2010). *Ethical principles of psychologists and code of conduct (2002; revised June 1, 2010)*. Retrieved from http://www.apa.org/ethics/code/principles.pdf

American Psychological Association. (2012). Guidelines for the practice of parenting coordination. *American Psychologist, 67*, 63–71. doi:10.1037/a0024646

Association of Family and Conciliation Courts, Task Force on Parenting Coordination. (2006). Guidelines for parenting coordination. *Family Court Review, 44*, 164–181. doi:10.1111/j.1744-1617.2006.00074.x

Fidler, B. J. (2012). Parenting coordination: Lessons learned and key practice issues. *Canadian Family Law Quarterly, 31*, 237–273.

Fidler, B. J., & Epstein, P. (2008). Parenting coordination in Canada: An overview of legal and practice issues. *Journal of Child Custody, 5*, 53–87. doi:10.1080/15379410802070393

Jordan v. Jordan, Nos. 09-FM-1152, 09-FM-1337, and 10-FM-375 (District of Columbia Court of Appeals Mar. 10, 2011).

Katz, S. N. (1994). Historical perspective and current trends in the legal process of divorce. *The Future of Children, 4*, 44–62.

Kelly, J. B. (2000). Children's adjustment in conflicted marriage and divorce: A decade review of research. *Journal of the American Academy of Child & Adolescent Psychiatry, 39*, 963–973. doi:10.1097/00004583-200008000-00007

Kirkland, K., & Sullivan, M. (2008). Parenting coordination (PC) practice: A survey of experienced professionals. *Family Court Review, 46*, 622–636. doi:10.1111/j.1744-1617.2008.00228.x

Lamb, M. E. (1981). The development of father–infant relationships. In M. E. Lamb (Ed.), *The role of the father in child development* (rev. ed., pp. 459–488). New York, NY: Wiley.

I

BACKGROUND TO PARENTING COORDINATION

1

ORIGINS AND DEVELOPMENT OF PARENTING COORDINATION

JOAN B. KELLY

The intervention known today as *parenting coordination* first emerged in the mid-1980s in northern California. Several mental health practitioners in adjacent San Francisco Bay Area jurisdictions were asked by family lawyers or the court to accept cases in which high conflict and repeated litigation regarding children persisted in the years following divorce. The objective was to help parents resolve their ongoing child-related disputes through a combination of mediation and decision making as an alternative to the conflict escalation and high expense of the adversarial legal system.

In this chapter, I describe the societal, legal, and family contexts in which the parenting coordination intervention developed in the United States[1] and the evolution of a more defined hybrid practice model over the next two decades. I then summarize the more organized efforts made in

[1]For a review of Canadian developments in parenting coordination, see Fidler (2012) and Fidler and Epstein (2008).

http://dx.doi.org/10.1037/14390-002
Parenting Coordination in Postseparation Disputes: A Comprehensive Guide for Practitioners, S. A. Higuchi and S. J. Lally (Editors)

the 21st century to guide the parenting coordination model toward greater maturity and acceptance through the development of practice guidelines, managing domestic violence concerns, specialized training, legislation, and publications focusing on practice issues and research.

ORIGINS OF THE PARENTING COORDINATION INTERVENTION

Parenting coordination interventions were precipitated in part by the high marital dissolution rates that followed the passage of no-fault divorce laws as well as by shifting demographic trends in the 20th century. Concerns about high levels of parental conflict during divorce and custody cases, and the effect of this conflict on children's well-being, also played a role.

Shifting Demographics, Social Trends, and New Interventions

A confluence of demographic, social, and legal changes led to the development of the parenting coordination intervention. The divorce rate began its sharp increase in 1960 and had more than doubled by the end of the 1970s. By that time, more than 1 million children under age 18 were affected by divorce each year, an increase that overburdened the capacity of courts to handle custody and access matters. Although the divorce rate has trended downward since the 1980s, the number of children affected by parental separation each year has remained relatively stable, in part because of an increase in the number of younger unmarried women with premarital pregnancies, the emerging trend to cohabit rather than marry, and the fragility of cohabitation unions (Furstenberg, 1994; Shiono & Quinn, 1994). The majority of people who separate or divorce do so now in the early years of their cohabitation or marriage, resulting in a greater number of young children affected than was the case in the 1970s and 1980s. Families with young children are more likely to be highly conflicted both legally and in day-to-day parenting (Maccoby & Mnookin, 1992).

Emerging social and legal trends contributed to increases in the number of parents who turned to the adversarial legal system to settle disputes regarding custody and access. The maternal presumption (i.e., the assumption that children should remain with the mother unless she is proven to be unfit) underlying custody decisions was challenged by fathers' claims of sex discrimination, the emergence of fathers' rights groups, constitutional concerns for equal protection, the feminist movement, and the entry of large numbers of women into the workforce (see Kelly, 1994, for a detailed review). Gender-neutral laws slowly replaced the maternal presumption, and The Uniform Marriage and Divorce Act of 1970 provided for a "best interests" standard in its stead. For the first time, the needs and interests of the child, rather than the gender or rights of the parents, were the primary consideration in determining custody and access (Kelly, 1994, 1997).

These developments prepared the way for the emergence of a new and controversial custody arrangement in the 1980s, that of joint physical custody, and joint legal decision making. Lay and scholarly publications described the benefits children gained from greater father involvement after separation (Folberg, 1984; Greif, 1979; Kelly, 1983; Ricci, 1981; Roman & Haddad, 1978; Thompson, 1986; Wallerstein & Kelly, 1980), and states gradually passed statutes that recognized joint custody. This change was supported by new research describing the deficiencies for the majority of children of the traditional visiting pattern of every other weekend (Amato, 1987; Hetherington, Cox, & Cox, 1982; Kelly & Wallerstein, 1977; Wallerstein & Kelly, 1980). Equally important is that the field of child development shifted from a near-exclusive focus on mother–child relationships and began to examine fathers' contributions to the emotional, social, and psychological development of the child and the importance of children's early attachments to their fathers as well as their mothers (Lamb, 1981; Lamb, Ketterlinus, & Fracasso, 1992; Parke, 1981; Thompson, 1994). With these various trends converging in the 1980s and 1990s, litigation between parents increasingly focused on the extent of paternal involvement and shared custody as well as disputes regarding parenting abilities. Mothers opposed to significant paternal involvement were supported by long-standing cultural traditions and advocates for the continuation of the maternal presumption (Carbone, 1994; Fineman & Opie, 1987). Fathers were supported by emerging social science research supporting greater father involvement (Kelly, 1988); the recognition that, given the opportunity, fathers were just as adequate as mothers in parenting skills and sensitivity (Lamb, 1981; Lamb et al., 1992); and fathers' rights groups.

In the 1970s and 1980s, the adversarial legal system was the only option available to assist parents in resolving their disputes in most jurisdictions in the United States. It was, and remains, an expensive, emotionally draining, and protracted process, and mental health and legal professionals, social science researchers, and judges increasingly expressed dismay at the inappropriateness of the adversarial system for resolving custody and access, with particular concern about the apparent negative effects of protracted litigation on parenting capacities and children's adjustment. Considerable interest developed in finding more humane ways for parties to separate and divorce, which coincided with the passing of no-fault divorce legislation to replace fault-based divorce statutes in a number of states (Katz, 1994).

A range of alternative educational, legal, and dispute-resolution interventions emerged over the next two decades (Emery, 1994; Katz, 1994; Kelly,

1994, 2002). For the first time, parents were provided with several non-adversarial opportunities, during and after separation and divorce, to avoid or settle custody and access disputes and enable them to exit the legal system at the earliest possible point.

Divorce education and custody mediation programs were anticipated to reduce legal conflict and interparental hostility and to assist parents in reaching mutually acceptable agreements. By 1998, more than 1,500 U.S. counties had court-connected education programs for separating parents (Geasler & Blaisure, 1999). Additional research-based programs were developed, implemented, and evaluated by social scientists (e.g., Arbuthnot & Gordon, 1996; Haine, Sandler, Wolchik, Tein, & Dawson-McClure, 2003).

Divorce mediation was the first major dispute-resolution process to emerge on the national stage as a viable alternative to the adversarial process for settling all separation and divorce disputes, including custody and parenting, and it gradually gained national recognition. California mandated in 1981 that mediation would be the first step for all custody and access disputes prior to initiating formal adversarial proceedings, and the service was provided free of charge by means of court-connected family mediation services (see Depner, Cannata, & Simon, 1992; Kelly, 2004).

Empirical research demonstrated acceptably high settlement rates, reduced parental conflict, improved parental support and communication, and high client satisfaction, and it considerably reduced expense compared to divorces negotiated using the adversarial system (Depner et al., 1992; Emery, 1994; Kelly, 1991, 1996, 2004; Pearson & Thoennes, 1989). The continuing shift in attitudes within the legal profession by the end of the 20th century was evident in the development of a major innovation within family law: the *collaborative divorce model*, whereby the divorcing individuals and their lawyers resolve conflicts through cooperative methods rather than adversarial litigation and commit themselves to negotiating an outcome. To date, no empirical research has yet evaluated the effectiveness, cost, or benefits to families of this model.

Concerns About Ongoing Parent Conflict

A growing awareness of the detrimental effects of marital conflict on children's adjustment in the 1980s and 1990s (Amato & Keith, 1991; Cummings & Davies, 1994; Emery, 1982; Kelly, 2000; Kline, Johnston, & Tschann, 1991) led to substantial interest in the impact of parent anger following separation. Early small longitudinal studies of divorce reported a surprising amount of parent hostility and acrimony well beyond the divorce decree (Hetherington, 1999; Wallerstein & Kelly, 1980). Although hostility diminished significantly within the first year or two after separation and divorce for the majority of parents, a minority remained very angry and in conflict about their children beyond this normative range of recovery. Two longitudinal studies found that 20% to 25% of parents remained highly conflicted at 3 to 4 years after a separation or divorce (Hetherington, 1999; Maccoby & Mnookin, 1992), whereas King and Heard (1999) reported that between 8% and 12% of parents remained in high conflict by 2 to 3 years after a divorce, differences that are most likely attributable to varying measures of conflict. Contrary to expectations, a final divorce did not always end conflicts; some parents continued to litigate parenting disputes. Clinical studies indicate that these chronically high-conflict and litigating parents were more likely to have mental illness or severe personality disorders, and many remained fixated on perceived injustices and grievances or the other parent's inadequacies (Johnston, 1994; Johnston & Campbell, 1988; Johnston, Roseby, & Kuehnle, 2009; Kelly, 2000, 2003; Wallerstein & Kelly, 1980). They were also more likely to expose their children to verbal and physical aggression and to display hostile attitudes and behaviors toward the other parent in front of the children (Johnston et al., 2009), and noncompliance with court orders and a lack of cooperation were common.

The label *high-conflict parents* presumes that both parents are angry and actively fueling the conflict and litigation. Practitioners in the divorce field now recognize that in a substantial number of cases (perhaps 35%), one parent has emotionally disengaged from the former partner, has attempted to move forward in his or her life, and has no interest in returning to court to litigate parenting disputes (Friedman, 2004; Kelly, 2003, 2012). Like the children, they were victims of the other parent's vindictive rage and irresponsible behaviors, and they reluctantly returned to court to defend or seek compliance with parenting plans and support payments.

Research describing coparenting patterns 2 to 3 years after a divorce contributed to a better understanding of parents who are likely to need professional or court assistance. Maccoby and Mnookin (1992) reported that 24% of the families engaged in *conflicted coparenting* (low communication and high discord), 41% of parents engaged in *disengaged coparenting* (low communication and low discord), and 29% engaged in *cooperative coparenting* (high communication and low discord). Hetherington (1999) reported that 20% of parents remained highly conflicted 2 to 3 years after a divorce, nearly 50% engaged in parallel parenting, and 25% to 30% had cooperative coparenting relationships (involving joint planning, flexibility, sufficient communication, and coordination of schedules). The parenting coordination process is intended for these highly conflicted parents, who disproportionately consume the resources and time of family courts in the years after divorce and drain personal financial resources and emotional energy that could be more effectively directed toward the children's well-being.

High Conflict and Children's Adjustment After Separation and Divorce

A large body of research documents that continued intense conflict following separation and divorce is associated with a substantially greater risk of children developing behavioral, social, and emotional problems (Amato, 2000; Emery, 1999; Johnston, 1994; Johnston et al., 2009; Kelly, 2000, 2003). Because not all outcomes were negative, research that differentiated types of conflict associated with child adjustment was deemed valuable in that it helped provide an understanding of which children are more likely to be at risk and in developing strategies for addressing parental conflict (Birnbaum & Bala, 2010; Buchanan, Maccoby, & Dornbusch, 1991; Grych, 2005). The amount of legal conflict during separation and divorce was not associated with child adjustment (Goodman, Bonds, Sandler, & Braver, 2004). Frequency of conflict also was found to not be a particularly good measure of child outcomes. The most detrimental conflict was intense and volatile (rather than frequent), focused on the child (as opposed to financial and property disputes), and remained unresolved by the parents (Grych, 2005). Furthermore, the type of parent conflict most consistently associated with negative outcomes after a divorce was when parents used their child to express their anger. When parents asked their children to carry hostile messages to the other parent, asked intrusive questions about the other parents, and/or created a need in the child to hide information or conceal positive feelings about the other parent, their children were more likely to be depressed and anxious, compared to high-conflict parents who did not put their children in the middle in this manner (Buchanan et al., 1991). Hetherington (1999) reported that when parents encapsulated their conflict—that is, shielded their children from angry confrontations and arguments and did not demean the other parent—then high conflict was not in itself detrimental.

College students who had experienced high levels of parental conflict over time reported more stress, distress, and painful feelings and a greater likelihood of self-identification as a child of divorce, compared with college students with low-conflict parents (Fabricius & Luecken, 2007; Laumann-Billings & Emery, 2000). For the majority of youngsters, feelings of being caught between parents generally diminishes in the decade following divorce (Amato & Afifi, 2006), but not necessarily for those whose parents continue to be high in conflict (Johnston et al., 2009). Demeaning or putting down the other parent in the presence of children or adolescents is associated with increased anger, stress, and less close parent–child relationships in later years (Amato & Afifi, 2006; Fabricius & Hall, 2000).

THE DEVELOPMENT OF AN INTERVENTION FOR HIGH-CONFLICT PARENTS

Beginning in the late 1980s, overburdened court systems and the subsequent frustration led to the development and formalization of two programs to help deal with high-conflict divorce cases: (a) mediation–arbitration and (b) Special Masters.

Mediation–Arbitration and Special Masters: Two Early Interventions

In California and Colorado, two innovative interventions for litigious high-conflict parents were initiated in the late 1980s and early 1990s in response to burgeoning family court caseloads and the frustration of judges and family court personnel about their inability to stem the flow of repeated postdecree litigation among high-conflict parents and the growing awareness of detrimental outcomes reported for children in chronically high-conflict families. It became apparent that this group of parents needed something quite different from the adversarial system offered: a more efficient, timely, less expensive, and less destructive process removed from the court and adversarial system. These observations led to the beginnings of the Special Master program in California and the mediation–arbitration model in Colorado, each developed independently of the other.

In California, before the introduction of the Special Master program, parents could return to family court mediation services for resolution of postdecree parenting disputes; however, mediators, lawyers, judges, and mental health professionals observed that when parents returned to court five to 10 times a year, mediation was rarely effective and instead constituted a waste of family court resources. It is important to note, however, that litigating child matters after a decree is sometimes necessary and appropriate as, for example, with repeated noncompliance with visitation and support court orders, problems with substance abuse, instances of child abuse, or contested relocations. The type of disputes brought for adjudication by repeat litigators most often involved child rearing and scheduling, which have no real basis in law or psychology for resolution (Kelly, 2002).

In northern California, several independent mental health practitioners with well-established forensic, divorce, and custody mediation practices were referred parents with repeated postdecree litigation and continued high conflict. Each practitioner initially worked in isolation without any defined template about role and function or guiding court orders. In 1986, two lawyers, at the parents' request, asked me, a clinical child psychologist, divorce and custody mediator, custody evaluator, and divorce and mediation researcher, to accept a case in which I would arbitrate any future child-related disputes if the parents could not settle them on their own. The parents were described as angry; weary of litigation; economically depleted; and as having different child-rearing values, styles, and objectives. After some consideration about the implications of this role shift, I agreed to work with the parents on the condition that efforts would first be made to mediate such disputes and arbitration occur only if those efforts were unsuccessful. There was no written agreement, only a verbal understanding that processes characteristic of divorce and custody mediation would be followed. Two months later, the parents called with a significant dispute about whether their 14-year-old daughter would attend a private or public high school. When mediation was not successful, I obtained the parents' permission to talk with their daughter to understand her views. I had prior experience interviewing children for their views in my capacity as a divorce researcher and custody mediator. (See Chapter 9, this volume, for more discussion of including children in the parenting coordination process.)

Articulately expressing her views, and concerned about her parents' reaction should she chose either alternative, the daughter agreed to attend a mediation session with her parents to express her perspectives and preference, with the assurance of my assistance as needed. As a result of the daughter's input and the subsequent discussion, the parents reached an agreement that reflected her desires, and arbitration was not necessary. Other subsequent disputes occasionally required arbitration.

The story unfolding in Colorado at about the same time was remarkably similar: A well-regarded lawyer mediator, Christine Coates, first accepted a case to provide mediation–arbitration services for several re-litigating high-conflict parents in the late 1980s. The parenting coordination model was further developed in collaboration with a group of other mental health and legal professionals in the early 1990s in the Boulder area.

Over the next several years, practitioners in California discovered other professionals engaged in similar work. By 1990, the term *Special Master* was adopted, based on a California statute describing the power and role of a category of experts for court cases. Special Masters in Marin County first received referrals from Family Court Mediation Services in 1991, and a monthly case consultation and support group of six to eight mental health professionals was formed. In 1992, this group expanded to include family lawyers with extensive custody litigation experience, and an interdisciplinary framework for thinking collaboratively about these difficult cases was adopted. The early Special Masters were mental health professionals, but over time the consultation group recognized that experienced family lawyers would also be effective Special Masters. The monthly meetings highlighted the fact that each Special Master was using a different agreement or court order (if any) without consistency as to authority or procedures. The group asked the Marin Bar Family Law Section to petition the family court judge to appoint a task force with a goal of standardizing the model, procedures, and court order for appointing a Special Master. Collaboration with Special Masters providing similar services in two other Bay Area counties was also initiated.[2]

The acceptance and refinement of the Special Master model in California benefited from the existence of a state chapter of the Association of Family and Conciliation Courts (AFCC), an interdisciplinary organization of judges, lawyers, mental health professionals, and mediators involved in family law and custody work. Frustration with postdecree litigating parents ("frequent flyers") was often discussed at annual conferences, as was research on the effects of divorce, including high-conflict divorce, on children's well-being.

Interdisciplinary Working Groups Refine the Model and Develop Court Orders

In 1993, the Marin Superior Court Family Judge appointed an interdisciplinary task force, composed of family lawyers and several mental health practitioners and mediators providing Special Master services. Their charge was to explore the development of a more formalized intervention; evaluate potential statutory authorities for the role of Special Master; discuss acceptable procedures; and develop a consistent order for Special Masters, lawyers, and parents in the jurisdiction to use. The first uniform Special Master Order was adopted by the Marin Superior Court in 1994 after months of discussion and negotiations, including addressing and resolving opposition from several family lawyers to various aspects of the court order. Working in parallel, but independently, a second Bay Area county (Santa Clara) developed and approved a consistent order in the same year.

From the beginning, based on research and experience regarding which parents were unlikely to use mediation productively, it was understood that the Special Master intervention would be a hybrid of mediation and arbitration. Mediation was perceived as the primary and preferred process, with arbitration to be used as a backup as necessary. Parenting coordinators (PCs) have often commented that the latent threat of arbitration, or a recommendation to court, serves as a strong incentive for parents to resolve their disputes in the initial exploration and mediation stages of the process. In California jurisdictions, experienced Special Masters stressed the importance of the following core features that enhance the effectiveness of the process:

- The flexibility to use mediation and arbitration as appropriate for resolving child-related disputes

[2]Matthew Sullivan, PhD, in Santa Clara County, had his first Special Master case 1991, and Jeanne Ames, an experienced mediator in San Francisco, started at about the same time.

- The understanding that the Special Master was not providing psychotherapy, counseling, or legal representation
- The process should be nonconfidential.
- Ex parte communications (meetings conducted over the phone and in person) were essential to assess, mediate, and arbitrate disputes in an expeditious manner.
- Authority should be given to the Special Master to talk with all essential parties to any particular dispute, including parents; children; extended family; new partners; child care providers; and relevant school, legal, mental health, and medical professionals.
- Fees should be shared in a percentage determined in advance by lawyers or the court.
- The court would provide backup in the event a parent did not comply with the original custody-and-access decree or subsequent agreements and decisions reached within the Special Master process.

At this early stage of development of the model, the Special Master did not have specific limitations on the type of child-related disputes that could be decided, nor was the issue of the improper delegation of judicial authority to a Special Master addressed. The task force revisited the Special Master court order 4 years later and made substantial revisions based on accumulated experience. At this time, a three-tier structure was developed that specified (a) a group of minor parenting and child-rearing disputes that a Special Master could decide and that were not subject to parent appeal, (b) a group of disputes for which the Special Master could make recommendations and that became orders if a parent did not appeal within a specified period of time, and (c) a third category of disputes involving substantial changes in time sharing and custody for which the Special Master could make recommendations only for the consideration of the court.

In Colorado, an interdisciplinary group of professionals who studied high-conflict parents began meeting in 1992 and continued refining a similar model for dealing with the type of high-conflict parents described above. The first case within this group was in 1993, after which the term *parenting coordination* was coined, and several members began providing parenting coordination trainings soon thereafter.

The Need for Specialized Training

Recognizing the complexities and challenges of being a Special Master, and the extent to which functioning as a Special Master deviated from the

AFCC – Assoc of Family + Conciliation Courts

usual services provided by clinical and forensic psychologists, two Special Masters in Marin County, California—myself and M. Margaret Lee—offered a 1-day specialized training course in 1994, attended by nearly 100 mental health professionals and family lawyers. The training described the unique hybrid model of the PC, the absence of confidentiality, how the court order initiated and governed the parenting coordination process, and the authority to make decisions in working with parents on child-related disputes. In that same year, Santa Clara County offered its first Special Master training conference.

The California Special Master and Colorado parenting coordination models began to receive national attention and interest among those working in the family law and divorce area. Marin County professionals, including myself and Margaret Lee, offered a workshop describing the Special Master role and function at the AFCC annual conference in Hawaii in 1994. The Colorado colleagues presented their model of parenting coordination later in 1994 at the first AFCC Child Custody Evaluation Conference and at that time learned of the Special Master model in California. In 1995, I presented a 1-day Special Master Institute at the AFCC annual conference. Thereafter at annual AFCC conferences and regional conferences, preconference institutes and conference workshops were presented on the Special Master and parenting coordination models to increasingly large audiences of mental health professionals, lawyers, mediators, and judges. Starting in the early 2000s, 2-day introductory parenting coordination trainings were offered by the AFCC in different regions of the United States, and advanced parenting coordination trainings followed.

PARENTING COORDINATION IN THE 21ST CENTURY

Parenting coordination has come a long way since its inception a few decades ago. Both the AFCC and the American Psychological Association (APA) have appointed task forces and developed formal guidelines for PCs. Training of PCs has expanded, and the field has addressed concerns about domestic violence as well as ensuring access to parenting coordination by low-income parents.

Formal Recognition of the Parenting Coordination Model: Practice Guidelines

In response to growing national interest and the increasing practice of parenting coordination, in 2001 the AFCC appointed an interdisciplinary task force to discuss the creation of model standards of practice. The task force decided the PC role was too new to have standards developed for it and instead focused on issues associated with the role and how jurisdictions in the

United States were addressing these issues. The task force published a report on implementation issues 2 years later (AFCC, Parenting Coordination Task Force, 2003). A second interdisciplinary task force was appointed in 2003 and developed model standards of practice for the United States and Canada, a draft of which was posted on the AFCC website for comments. The revised final document, retitled "Guidelines for Parenting Coordination," reflected the recognition that creating standards at this early stage in the development of the parenting coordination process was problematic (AFCC, Parenting Coordination Task Force, 2006). It included 12 guidelines focused on practice, ethics, qualifications, and training, with four appendixes that detailed recommendations for training, best judicial and program practices, the Canadian parenting coordination perspective, and members of the task force. Approved by the AFCC in May 2005, the guidelines were published in *Family Court Review* in April 2006. These guidelines were discussed and disseminated at PC trainings and continue to guide the parenting coordination practice of AFCC members as well as many other professionals not affiliated with the AFCC.

In recognition of the growing number of psychologists serving as PCs, APA appointed a Task Force for the Development of Parenting Coordination Guidelines in 2008. These guidelines were intended to provide a specific framework and direction for psychologists in regard to professional conduct and decision making as PCs, as distinct from traditional psychological practices. Two of the psychologists appointed—Robin M. Deutsch and myself—were previous members of the AFCC task force and experienced PCs. The draft guidelines were made available for comment in 2010, revised and approved in February 2011, and published in 2012 (APA, 2012). Both the AFCC and APA guidelines are aspirational in nature rather than standards of practice per se and are similar in that they focus on training and professional competence, ethical guidance, and role functions (including arbitration).

Formal Recognition of the Parenting Coordination Model: Domestic Violence Concerns

As parenting coordination emerged in the family law field in the late 1990s as an increasingly visible model for managing high-conflict postdecree cases, domestic violence advocates for women became active in expressing opposition to its use. The development of legislation for parenting coordination mobilized these concerns, as did the work of AFCC and APA in developing parenting coordination guidelines for practice. The primary reasons for opposition were similar to earlier advocacy against divorce and custody mediation, which were viewed as dangerous and disadvantageous processes for women. Because parenting coordination was framed as an alternative dispute-resolution process, it was similarly viewed as posing more risks to the victims of violence in the years after separation and divorce than was repeated litigation. The fears were that parenting coordination would facilitate inappropriate engagement between the two parents and focus on cooperation between coparents, therein continuing to subject victims of domestic violence to ongoing emotional and financial abuse. The other major concerns raised were insufficient knowledge and competence on the part of PCs, including the failure to do appropriate screening and assessment.

To effectively address these major issues, the AFCC task force (2003–2005) charged to develop guidelines included a member with extensive legal, practice, and policy experience with domestic violence: Billie Lee Dunford-Jackson, codirector of the Family Violence Department of the National Council of Juvenile and Family Court Judges. Dunford-Jackson sensitized task force members to the many issues germane to the parenting coordination process for victims of domestic violence. The AFCC guidelines reflect these deliberations in an extensive paragraph in the first section, which reads in part, "The alternative dispute resolution process described above as central to the parenting coordinator's role may be inappropriate and potentially exploited by perpetrators of domestic violence who have exhibited patterns of violence, threats, intimidation and coercive control over their coparent" (AFCC, Parenting Coordination Task Force, 2006, p. 165). Additional training recommendations for PCs were addressed in Appendix A of the AFCC guidelines. The APA (2012) guidelines for parenting coordination practice were similarly influenced by concerns about the safety of families and the need for professional knowledge, competence, and responsibilities on the part of the PC. Guideline 4 (APA, 2012, p. 67) specifically addresses family violence and the PC's function and role, starting with the professional and ethical responsibilities of psychologist PCs to avoid any harm to participants, to facilitate healthy environments, and to ensure the safety of all family members. The importance of knowledge of extensive empirical and clinical research involving violence between partners, including differentiation of patterns of intimate partner violence, is stressed. As with the AFCC guidelines, the APA guidelines recognize that some cases may not be appropriate for PC intervention and that the scope of parenting coordination may need to be limited or modified, "with an emphasis on monitoring parties' adherence to court orders and facilitating safe implementation of the court orders and parenting plans" (APA, 2012, p. 67).

Parenting Coordination in a Developing Field: Training

The concept and practice of parenting coordination developed rapidly in the 21st century, primarily in the private practice sector, in large part because the AFCC continued to offer regional 2-day core and advanced parenting coordination trainings several times a year, as well as institutes and workshops at annual conferences, and a few state AFCC chapters sponsored trainings or included programs in their conferences. In 2008, the AFCC provided a preconference parenting coordination institute in Vancouver, British Columbia, Canada, with combined Canadian and American faculty, and other trainings have been provided in British Columbia and Ontario by experienced Canadian PCs in the past decade (Fidler, 2012; Fidler & Epstein, 2008).

APA has begun to recognize the potential of parenting coordination for its members. In 2008, an interview with two psychologist PCs describing the PC's role and practice opportunities appeared in APA's practice organization magazine, *Good Practice* (APA Practice Organization, 2008). The Practice Directorate also worked with three psychologists—Robin M. Deutsch, Matthew J. Sullivan, and myself—to develop a curriculum for an online course explaining the parenting coordination model for psychologists interested in learning more about it. APA sponsored its first 1-day preconvention parenting coordination training in Toronto in 2009 with a Canadian psychologist[3] joining the American faculty, and in 2011 the first 2-day core training was offered prior to the annual APA conference in Washington, DC, an expansion of a 2-day core parenting coordination training that paralleled the 2-day AFCC core trainings. These intensive trainings were consistent with APA PC guidelines that listed substantive areas in which PCs need to gain knowledge and competency and stated that trainings would be of "sufficient duration and intensity to enable psychologists to function competently in the PC role and to meet statutory requirements" (APA, 2012, p. 65).

Formal Recognition of the Parenting Coordination Model: Legislation

In the United States, the first parenting coordination statute was enacted in 2001, in Oklahoma and, at the time of this writing, 11 states have statutory authority specifically for parenting coordination. Ten states have authorized parenting coordination through a related statute (e.g., arbitration, parenting time) or by local jurisdictional rule. In states or local jurisdictions that have no authorizing language or mechanism for appointing a PC, PCs are authorized by signed stipulations or private consent agreements between the PC and the parents. In British Columbia the local parenting coordination society developed a Parenting Coordination Agreement in 2009, and in 2012 legislation was introduced to allow judges to appoint parenting coordinators, effective 2013. Many of the private consent agreements contain similar elements, including decision-making authority, to guide the parenting coordination process. PCs operating with private consent agreements have no relationship to the court

[3]Barbara J. Fidler, PhD, also joined Joan B. Kelly, PhD, in several AFCC preconference institutes and began to provide parenting coordination trainings in Toronto and other Canadian locations.

for reporting or backup in the event of noncompliance. (See Chapter 2, this volume, for a more complete discussion of legislation and legal issues relevant to psychologists serving as a PC.)

One result of the piecemeal legislation in the United States is that considerable variations in parenting coordination models and practices have emerged based on local preferences, politics, and the manner in which the issue of the delegation of judicial authority to nonjudges was handled. These variations include the point in the separation or divorce process at which the PC is appointed, the manner of and authority for appointment of the PC, the authority for and scope of recommendations and decision making, whether the parenting coordination process is nonconfidential or confidential, the relationship of parenting coordination to court and reporting requirements, the PC's qualifications and expertise, whether the PC is restricted to one professional group or is interdisciplinary, and whether children and other parties to the dispute may be included.

Formal Recognition of the Parenting Coordination Model: Publications and Programs

A brief description of the Colorado mediation–arbitration model for high-conflict parents first appeared in a newsletter (Coates, 1993), followed by a description of the Special Master intervention (Kelly, 1994). Members of the interdisciplinary Colorado group contributed to the first book on parenting coordination (Baris et al., 2001), and a lengthy description of the Special Master intervention followed (Kelly, 2002). Expanded interest in the field in the 21st century has since been reflected in books and articles focusing on models, practices, ethics, opportunities for practice, statutory authorities, legal issues, inclusion of children in the parenting coordination process, and training (Bailey, 2005; Boyan & Termini, 2004; Carter, 2011; Coates, Deutsch, Starnes, Sullivan, & Sydlik, 2004; Deutsch, Coates, & Fieldstone, 2008; Greenberg, 2010; Kelly, 2008; Kirkland, 2008; Kirkland & Kirkland, 2006; Kirkland & Sullivan, 2008; Shear, 2008; Sullivan, 2004, 2008).

Although still quite limited, research projects and surveys of PCs also reflect the maturation and acceptance of parenting coordination in the past decade and include research on efficacy (Henry, Fieldstone, & Bohac, 2009), the development and evaluation of a new program and model (Lally & Higuchi, 2008), and surveys of PCs on practice similarities and differences (Beck, Putterman, Sbarra, & Mehl, 2008; Brewster, Beck, Anderson, & Benjamin, 2011; Hayes, 2010). More detailed findings from these studies are described in Chapter 13.

One of the ongoing concerns among family courts and independent PCs is the expense of the parenting coordination process, which at times excludes lower income parents. Without economic resources, but similarly entrenched in high conflict about their children, many of these parents returned to court, unrepresented by legal counsel, to continue their litigation. In a striking innovation and an alternative to private sector parenting coordination, the APA Practice Directorate began collaborating in 2003 with the District of Columbia Family Law Section and the Pro Bono Program of the Washington, DC, Bar to develop a pro bono parenting coordination service for low-income litigants in the District's Family Court (see Chapter 8, this volume).

PARENTING COORDINATION: SUMMARY AND THOUGHTS FOR THE FUTURE

Parenting coordination intervention has taken 20 to 25 years from its earliest origins to become a nationally recognized, specialized model of service for separated and divorced parents who are characterized by continuing high conflict, repeated litigation, and loss of focus on their children's psychological and developmental needs. At the time of this writing, parenting coordination is recognized and practiced in more than 30 states. Because the United States has 50 states with independent jurisdiction over family law matters, widespread implementation has been slow and has proceeded in a piecemeal fashion. For the same reason, programs and statutes in different states have resulted in increasingly varied practices and scopes of authority. There is no uniformity of parenting coordination models with respect to the point at which the PC is appointed; what entity provides and describes the authorization for the PC's role and function; whether recommendations, arbitration, or decision making are permitted in addition to mediation of parental disputes; and whether the PC has a formal relationship to the court as a result of a court order, or stipulation and order, or whether he or she functions privately with consent agreements signed by the parents and the PC.

To determine which models are most effective and generate more compliance with parenting plans, considerably more sophisticated empirical research is needed. Such research would include pre and post measures of parent conflict, coparent relationship characteristics, the number and type of parenting disputes regarding children brought to the court, the manner in which those disputes were settled, PC ratings of nature and degree of complexity of disputes, and measures of parent satisfaction. Also needed are comparisons of different models on a number of dimensions, including the following: whether the PC has the authority to make certain recommendations or decisions that are binding unless a parent files a motion with the court, as compared to models that rely only on mediation or some form of parent counseling; the scope of that authority; the number of disputes settled by PCs (who have broad authority) using only mediation or mediative techniques, using a recommendation to the court, or arbitration of the dispute; the value of confidential versus nonconfidential models; and having the court as a backup for noncompliance versus parenting coordination with no relationship to the court. Such research will greatly enhance our understanding of the implications of variations in parenting coordination models, if any; influence parenting coordination training; and encourage professionals who provide parenting coordination services to shape their practices in the most effective manner possible.

REFERENCES

Amato, P. (1987). Family processes in one-parent, stepparent and intact families: The child's point of view. *Journal of Marriage and the Family*, *49*, 327–337. doi:10.2307/352303

Amato, P. (2000). The consequences of divorce for adults and children. *Journal of Marriage and the Family*, *62*, 1269–1287. doi:10.1111/j.1741-3737.2000.01269.x

Amato, P., & Keith, B. (1991). Parental divorce and adult well being: A meta-analysis. *Journal of Marriage and the Family*, *53*, 43–58. doi:10.2307/353132

Amato, P. R., & Afifi, T. D. (2006). Feeling caught between parents: Adult children's relations with parents and subjective well-being. *Journal of Marriage and the Family*, *68*, 222–235. doi:10.1111/j.1741-3737.2006.00243.x

American Psychological Association. (2012). Guidelines for the practice of parenting coordination. *American Psychologist*, *67*, 63–71. doi:10.1037/a0024646

American Psychological Association Practice Organization (2008, Fall). In the best interests of children. *Good Practice*, 9–12.

Arbuthnot, J., & Gordon, D. (1996). Does mandatory divorce education for parents work? A six-month outcome evaluation. *Family Court Review*, *34*, 60–81. doi:10.1111/j.174-1617.1996.tb00400.x

Association of Family and Conciliation Courts, Parenting Coordination Task Force. (2003). Parenting coordination: Implementation issues. *Family Court Review*, *41*, 533–564.

Association of Family and Conciliation Courts, Parenting Coordination Task Force. (2006). Guidelines for parenting coordination. *Family Court Review*, *44*, 164–181. doi:10.1111/j.1744-1617.2006.00074.x

Bailey, D. S. (2005). A niche that puts children first: Psychologists in many states are becoming parent coordinators to help divorcing parents focus on their children's needs. *Monitor on Psychology*, *35*(1), 46–48.

Baris, M., Coates, C., Duvall, B., Garity, C., Johnson, E., & LaCrosse, E. (2001). *Working with high conflict families of divorce: A guide for professionals*. Lanham, MD: Jason Aronson.

Beck, C. J. A., Putterman, M. D., Sbarra, D. A., & Mehl, M. R. (2008). Parenting coordinator roles, program goals and services provided: Insights from the Pima County, Arizona program. *Journal of Child Custody, 5*, 122–139. doi:10.1037/1076-8971.6.4.989

Birnbaum, R., & Bala, N. (2010). Toward the differentiation of high-conflict families: An analysis of social science research and Canadian case law. *Family Court Review, 48*, 403–416.

Boyan, S. M., & Termini, A. (2004). *The psychotherapist as parent coordinator in high conflict divorce: Strategies and techniques*. New York, NY: Haworth Clinical Practice Press.

Brewster, K., Beck, C., Anderson, E., & Benjamin, A. (2011). Evaluating parenting coordination programs: Encouraging results from pilot testing a research methodology. *Journal of Child Custody, 8*, 247–267. doi:10.1080/15379418.2011.620926

Buchanan, C. M., Maccoby, E., & Dornbusch, S. (1991). Caught between parents: Adolescents' experience in divorced homes. *Child Development, 62*, 1008–1029. doi:10.2307/1131149

Carbone, J. R. (1994). A feminist perspective on divorce. *The Future of Children, 4*, 183–209. doi:10.2307/1602484

Carter, D. K. (2011). *Parenting coordination: A guide for family law professionals*. New York, NY: Springer.

Coates, C. (1993). Using mediation–arbitration: It's time to settle our differences. *AFCC Newsletter, 12*(4).

Coates, C. A., Deutsch, R., Starnes, H., Sullivan, M. J., & Sydlik, B. L. (2004). Parenting coordination for high conflict families. *Family Court Review, 42*, 246–262. doi:10.1177/1531244504422006

Cummings, E., & Davies, P. (1994). *Children and marital conflict*. New York, NY: Guilford Press.

Depner, C., Cannata, K., & Simon, M. (1992). Building a uniform statistical reporting system: A snapshot of California Family Court Services. *Family Court Review, 30*, 185–206.

Deutsch, R. M., Coates, C. A., & Fieldstone, L. (2008). Parenting coordination: An emerging role to assist high conflict families. In L. Fieldstone & C. A. Coates (Eds.), *Innovations in interventions with high conflict families* (pp. 187–221). Madison, WI: Association of Family and Conciliation Courts.

Emery, R. (1999). *Marriage, divorce, and children's adjustment* (2nd ed.). Thousand Oaks, CA: Sage.

Emery, R. (1994). *Renegotiating family relationships: Divorce, child custody, and mediation*. New York, NY: Guilford Press.

Emery, R. E. (1982). Interparental conflict and the children of discord and divorce. *Psychological Bulletin, 92*, 310–330. doi:10.1037/0033-2909.92.2.310

Fabricius, W. V., & Hall, J. (2000). Young adults' perspectives on divorce: Living arrangements. *Family Court Review, 38*, 446–461. doi:10.1111/j.174-1617.2000.tb00584.x

Fabricius, W. V., & Luecken, L. J. (2007). Post-divorce living arrangements, parent conflict, and long-term physical health correlates for children of divorce. *Journal of Family Psychology, 21*, 195–205. doi:10.1037/0893-3200.21.2.195

Family Law Act (Canada) R.S.O. 1990, Chapter F.3

Fidler, B. J. (2012). Parenting coordination: Lessons learned and key practice issues. *Canadian Family Law Quarterly, 31*, 237–273.

Fidler, B. J., & Epstein, P. (2008). Parenting coordination in Canada: An overview of legal and practice issues. *Journal of Child Custody, 5*, 53–87. doi:10.1080/15379410802070393

Fineman, M., & Opie, A. (1987). The uses of social science data in legal policymaking: Custody determination at divorce. *1987 Wisconsin Law Review*, 107–121.

Folberg, J. (Ed.). (1984). *Joint custody and shared parenting*. Washington, DC: Bureau of National Affairs and Association of Family and Conciliation Courts.

Friedman, M. (2004). The so-called high-conflict couple: A closer look. *The American Journal of Family Therapy, 32*, 101–117. doi:10.1080/01926180490424217

Furstenberg, F. F. (1994). History and current status of divorce in the United States. *The Future of Children, 4*, 29–43. doi:10.2307/1602476

Geasler, M. J., & Blaisure, K. R. (1999). 1998 Nationwide survey of court-connected divorce education programs. *Family and Conciliation Courts Review, 37*, 36–63. doi:10.1111/j.174-1617.1999.tb00527.x

Goodman, M., Bonds, D., Sandler, I., & Braver, S. (2004). Parent psycho-educational programs and reducing the negative effects of interparental conflict following divorce. *Family Court Review, 42*, 263–279. doi:10.1177/1531244504422007

Greenberg, E. (2010). Fine tuning the branding of parenting coordination: " . . . You may get what you need." *Family Court Review, 48*, 206–201. doi:10.1111/j.1744-1617.2009.01301.x

Greif, J. B. (1979). Fathers, children, and joint custody. *American Journal of Orthopsychiatry, 49*, 311–319. doi:10.1111/j.1939-0025.1979.tb02612.x

Grych, J. H. (2005). Interparental conflict as a risk factor for child maladjustment: Implications for the development of prevention programs. *Family Court Review, 43*, 97–108. doi:10.1111/j.1744-1617.2005.00010.x

Haine, R. A., Sandler, I. N., Wolchik, S. A., Tein, J.-U., & Dawson-McClure, S. R. (2003). Changing the legacy of divorce: Evidence from prevention programs and future directions. *Family Relations, 52*, 397–405. doi:10.1111/j.1741-3729.2003.00397.x

Hayes, S. W. (2010). "More of a street cop than a detective": An analysis of the roles and functions of parenting coordinators in North Carolina. *Family Court Review, 48*, 698–709. doi:10.1111/j.1744-1617.2010.01343.x

Henry, W. J., Fieldstone, L., & Bohac, K. (2009). Parenting coordination and court relitigation: A case study. *Family Court Review, 47*, 682–697. doi:10.1111/j.1744-1617.2009.01281.x

Hetherington, E. M. (Ed.). (1999). *Coping with divorce, single parenting, and remarriage*. Mahwah, NJ: Erlbaum.

Hetherington, E. M., Cox, M., & Cox, R. (1982). Effects of divorce on parents and children. In M. E. Lamb (Ed.), *Nontraditional families: Parenting and child development* (pp. 233–288). Hillsdale, NJ: Erlbaum.

Johnston, J. R. (1994). High-conflict divorce. *The Future of Children, 4*, 165–182. doi:10.2307/1602483

Johnston, J. R., & Campbell, L. (1988). *Impasses of divorce: The dynamics and resolution of family conflict*. New York, NY: Free Press.

Johnston, J. R., Roseby, V., & Kuehnle, K. (2009). *In the name of the child: A developmental approach to understanding and helping children of conflict and violent divorce* (2nd ed.). New York, NY: Springer.

Katz, S. N. (1994). Historical perspective and current trends in the legal process of divorce. *The Future of Children, 4*, 44–62. doi:10.2307/1602477

Kelly, J. B. (1983). Further observations on joint custody. In J. Folberg (Ed.), *Joint custody and shared parenting* (pp. 55–62). Washington, DC: Bureau of National Affairs and Association of Family and Conciliation Courts.

Kelly, J. B. (1988). Longer-term adjustment in children of divorce: Converging findings and implications for practice. *Journal of Family Psychology, 2*, 119–140. doi:10.1037/h0080489

Kelly, J. B. (1991). Parent interaction after divorce: Comparison of mediated and adversarial divorce processes. *Behavioral Sciences & the Law, 9*, 387–398. doi:10.1002/bsl.2370090404

Kelly, J. B. (1994). The determination of child custody. *The Future of Children, 4*, 121–142. doi:10.2307/1602481

Kelly, J. B. (1996). A decade of divorce mediation research: Some answers and questions. *Family Court Review, 34*, 373–385. doi:10.1111/j.174-1617.1996.tb00427.x

Kelly, J. B. (1997). The best interests of the child: A concept in search of meaning. *Family Court Review, 35*, 377–387. doi:10.1111/j.174-1617.1997.tb00480.x

Kelly, J. B. (2000). Children's adjustment in conflicted marriage and divorce: A decade review of research. *Journal of the American Academy of Child & Adolescent Psychiatry, 39*, 963–973. doi:10.1097/00004583-200008000-00007

Kelly, J. B. (2002). Psychological and legal interventions for parents and children in custody and access disputes: Current research and practice. *The Virginia Journal of Social Policy & the Law, 10*, 129–163.

Kelly, J. B. (2003). Parents with enduring child disputes: Multiple pathways to enduring disputes. *Journal of Family Studies*, 9, 37–50. doi:10.5172/jfs.9.1.37

Kelly, J. B. (2004). Family mediation research: Is there support for the field? *Conflict Resolution Quarterly, 22*, 3–35. doi:10.1002/crq.90

Kelly, J. B. (2008). Preparing for the parenting coordination role: Training needs for mental health and legal professionals. *Journal of Child Custody, 5*, 140–159. doi:10.1080/15379410802070476

Kelly, J. B. (2012). Risk and protective factors associated with child and adolescent adjustment following separation and divorce: Social science applications. In K. Kuehnle & L. Drozd (Eds.), *Parenting plan evaluations: Applied research for the family court* (pp. 49–84). New York, NY: Oxford University Press.

Kelly, J. B., & Wallerstein, J. (1977). Part-time parent, part-time child: Visiting after divorce. *Journal of Clinical Child Psychology, 6*, 51–54. doi:10.1080/15374417709532764

King, V., & Heard, H. E. (1999). Nonresident fathers' visitation, parental conflict, and mother's satisfaction: What's best for child well-being? *Journal of Marriage and the Family, 61*, 385–396. doi:10.2307/353756

Kirkland, K. (2008). Parenting coordination (PC) laws, rules, and regulations: A jurisdictional comparison. *Journal of Child Custody, 5*, 25–52. doi:10.1080/15379410802070377

Kirkland, K., & Kirkland, K. E. (2006). Risk management and aspirational ethics for parenting coordinators. *Journal of Child Custody, 3*, 23–43. doi:10.1300/J190v03n02_02

Kirkland, K., & Sullivan, M. (2008). Parenting coordination (PC) practice: A survey of experienced professionals. *Family Court Review, 46*, 622–636. doi:10.1111/j.1744-1617.2008.00228.x

Kline, M., Johnston, J., & Tschann, J. (1991). The long shadow of marital conflict: A model of children's postdivorce adjustment. *Journal of Marriage and the Family, 53*, 297–309. doi:10.2307/352900

Lally, S. J., & Higuchi, S. A. (2008). The American Psychological Association Parenting Coordination Project: Development of the project and initial review of the first two years. *Journal of Child Custody, 5*, 101–121. doi:10.1080/15379410802070435

Lamb, M. E. (1981). The development of father–infant relationships. In M. E. Lamb (Ed.), *The role of the father in child development* (rev. ed., pp. 459–488). New York, NY: Wiley.

Lamb, M. E., Ketterlinus, R., & Fracasso, M. (1992). Parent–child relationships. In M. Bornstein & M. Lamb (Eds.), *Developmental psychology: An advanced textbook* (3rd ed., pp. 465–518). Hillsdale, NJ: Erlbaum.

Laumann-Billings, L., & Emery, R. E. (2000). Distress among young adults in divorced families. *Journal of Family Psychology, 14*, 671–687. doi:10.1037/0893-3200.14.4.671

Maccoby, E. E., & Mnookin, R. H. (1992). *Dividing the child: Social and legal dilemmas of custody.* Cambridge, MA: Harvard University Press.

Parke, R. (1981). *Fatherhood.* Cambridge, MA: Harvard University Press.

Pearson, J., & Thoennes, N. (1989). Divorce mediation: Reflections on a decade of research. In K. Kressel & D. Pruitt (Eds.), *Mediation research: The process and effectiveness of third party intervention* (pp. 9–39). San Francisco, CA: Jossey-Bass.

Ricci, I. (1981). *Mom's house–Dad's house*. New York, NY: Macmillan.

Roman, M., & Haddad, W. (1978). *The disposable parents: The case for joint custody*. London, England: Penguin.

Shear, L. (2008). In search of statutory authority for parenting coordinator orders in California: Using a grass-roots, hybrid model without an enabling statute. *Journal of Child Custody*, 5, 88–100. doi:10.1080/15379410802070419

Shiono, P. H., & Quinn, L. S. (1994). Epidemiology of divorce. *The Future of Children*, 4, 15–28. doi:10.2307/1602475

Sullivan, M. J. (2004). Ethical, legal, and professional practice issues involved in acting as a psychologist parent coordinator in child custody cases. *Family Court Review*, *42*, 576–582. doi:10.1177/1531244504042003l3

Sullivan, M. J. (2008). Coparenting and the parenting coordination process. *Journal of Child Custody*, 5, 4–24. doi:10.1080/15379410802070351

Thompson, R. A. (1986). Fathers and the child's "best interests": Judicial decision-making in custody disputes. In M. E. Lamb (Ed.), *The father's role: Applied perspectives* (pp. 61–102). New York, NY: Wiley.

Thompson, R. A. (1994). The role of the father after divorce. *The Future of Children*, 4, 210–235. doi:10.2307/1602485

The Uniform Marriage and Divorce Act of 1970 (amended 1973), 9A U.L.A. 446 (Supp. 2010).

Wallerstein, J., & Kelly, J. B. (1980). *Surviving the breakup: How children and parents cope with divorce*. New York, NY: Basic Books.

2

LEGAL STANDARDS AND ISSUES ASSOCIATED WITH PARENTING COORDINATION

MARGARET J. McKINNEY, LINDA A. DELANEY, AND ALAN NESSMAN

Across the nation, parenting coordinators (PCs) play a vital and growing role in resolving high-conflict custody cases and protecting children from exposure to parental conflict. In this chapter, we explain our perspective on key legal issues for PCs. That view is based on our many combined years as attorneys working with PCs in District of Columbia and Maryland courts. Our perspective may reflect the particular ways that PCs are appointed and used in those courts, including the fact that most of the PCs in those jurisdictions are psychologists or other mental health professionals.

http://dx.doi.org/10.1037/14390-003
Parenting Coordination in Postseparation Disputes: A Comprehensive Guide for Practitioners, S. A. Higuchi and S. J. Lally (Editors)

LEGAL AUTHORITY FOR APPOINTING A PARENTING COORDINATOR

The appointment of PCs and the rules governing the parenting coordination process vary from state to state. Some states have formal statutes in place, others use parenting coordination guidelines, and others operate without the guidance of specific rules.

States With Statutes or Rules

A number of states, including Colorado, Florida, Idaho, Louisiana, Maine, North Carolina, North Dakota, Oklahoma, South Dakota, and Texas, have passed statutes specifically providing for the appointment of a PC.[1] Other states, including Arizona, Illinois, Indiana, Kentucky, Maryland, Missouri, North Dakota, Ohio, Oregon, Pennsylvania, Utah, and Vermont appoint PCs pursuant to a court rule.[2] New Jersey is currently operating under a pilot parenting coordination program (Carchman, 2007). Several New York State counties are operating under parenting coordination guidelines ("Eighth Judicial District Guidelines," 2008).

Jurisdictions Without a Specific Parenting Coordination Statute or Rule

Courts in California and the District of Columbia appoint PCs although they do not have specific statutes or rules concerning parenting coordination. In California, the family courts in certain counties have crafted a stipulation and order allowing for the appointment of PCs. In the District, the long-standing practice of appointing PCs under a general court rule for Special Masters was recently approved by the District's highest court.[3] Despite the lack of a specific rule for PCs, the District has been at the forefront of the parenting coordination movement with an innovative program for serving diverse, low-income families (Lally & Higuchi, 2008; see also Chapter 18, this volume). Several other states without a specific parenting coordination statute or rule, such as

[1]Colo. Rev. Stat. § 14-10-128.1 (2009); Fla. Stat. § 61.125 (2009); Idaho Code Ann. § 32-717D (2010); La. Rev. Stat. Ann. § 9:358.1 to 358.9 (2007); Me. Rev. Stat. tit. 19-A, § 1659 (2009); N.C. Gen. Stat. Ann. § 50-90 to 50-100 (West 2005); N.D. Cent. Code Ann. § 14-09.2-01 to -08 (West 2009); Okla. Stat. Ann. tit. 43, § 120.1 to 120.7 (West 2010); S.D. Codified Laws § 25-4-63 (2008); Tex. Fam. Code Ann. § 153.601 to 153.611 (West 2009).

[2]Ariz. R. Fam. L. Proc. 74; Idaho R. Civ. P. 16(l); Ill. Cook Co. Cir. Ct. R. 13.10; Ind. Lake Co. R. Fam. L. 8; Ind. Wayne Co. R. Fam. L. 11; Ky. Jefferson Fam. Ct. Dom. Rel. R. 705; Md. Rule 9-205.2; Mo. 31st Cir. R. 6.9(d)(6); N.D. R. Ct. 8.11; Ohio Fulton Cnty. Dom. Rel. R. 14.01; Pa. Allegheny Cnty. Civ. Fam. R. 1915.17; Pa. Erie Cnty. R. Civ. Proc. 1940.10 to .16; Utah Jud. Admin. R. 4-509; Vt. Fam. Proc. R. 4(s).

[3]*Jordan v. Jordan*, 14 A 3rd 1136 (D.C. 2011, approving the use of Dom. Rel. R. 54, which generally allows for the appointment of Special Masters in domestic relations cases).

Georgia and New York, have condoned or allowed the appointment of a PC (or its equivalent) under appropriate conditions and circumstances.[4] In states that do not have a specific parenting coordination statute or rule and where the courts have not specifically approved of the use of PCs, it is common for PCs to be appointed by mutual agreement of the parents.

When to Appoint a Parenting Coordinator: Prejudgment Versus Postjudgment

In many jurisdictions, PCs are appointed at the end of divorce or custody litigation (whether by settlement or court order) to help the parties implement a court order or agreement and to help resolve disputes that arise after the court case ends. This is called a *postjudgment appointment* because it comes after the court's judgment that finalizes the resolution of the case after settlement or trial. Although this certainly is a valid use for PCs, we have found that PCs can be extremely useful and can help a family avoid more conflict, if there is a *prejudgment appointment*, whereby they are employed at the very beginning of the separation and divorce process.

A PC who is employed early in the process can help the parties develop and implement a parenting plan while providing an alternative dispute-resolution option that helps the parties defuse conflict, resolve interim issues amicably, and focus on the child's best interests. During that process the PC would also observe the parties' ability to cooperate and coparent and could report to the judge on his or her observations, if the parents are unable to reach an agreement. A PC can help keep the parents out of court by resolving their issues early in the divorce process, by applying his or her training in handling the complexities of high-conflict parents, child development, mental health issues, and the psychological nuances of custody disputes.

Proponents of prejudgment appointment argue that such early involvement by the PC reduces the substantial harm that parental conflict inflicts on children during the divorce litigation, increases the likelihood that the parents can settle without litigation, and focuses the parents' and the PC's attention on the children's issues and needs during this difficult phase.

Opponents of prejudgment appointment argue that the court's judgment on custody and the associated parenting plan give necessary structure and focus to the PC process. For example, it is difficult for a PC to determine which parent should pick up the child after soccer practice at

[4]See *McGarrah v. Posig*, 635 S.E.2d 219, 220 (Ga. 2006; parents sought "postdivorce parent coordinating" from a therapist who referred the parents' child to psychological counseling after the mother raised allegations of abuse), and *K. R. v. K. R.*, 237 N.Y.L.J. 56 (N.Y. Fam. Ct. 2007; in an appropriate case, the court has authority to appoint a case manager or PC to oversee the day-to-day details of visitation for the purpose of carrying into effect the determinations and directives of the court).

5:00 p.m. on Friday, when the court has not even decided how custody will be divided between the parents and what the basic schedule should be. Opponents argue that the decision is more properly made in the context of a court order and parenting plan providing, say, for joint custody with alternating weeks, with the transfer at 3:00 p.m. on Friday. Opponents also note that although there is always the possibility that one parent may try to relitigate the custody issue after judgment, a custody battle is much more likely prior to judgment. This imminent custody battle increases the risk that parents will use the parenting coordination process to gain advantage in that battle (e.g., by setting the other parent up to appear uncooperative) rather than using the parenting coordination process to benefit of the child.[5]

Whether employed postjudgment or at the beginning of the separation process, a PC can provide insight to the court on a number of factors that must be considered in resolving a custody dispute. For example, the PC can provide information about the source(s) of the parental conflict, the role of each party in creating or perpetuating the conflict, the temporal boundaries of the conflict (i.e., whether it is a fixable, short-term conflict as a result of the fresh separation or an intractable, interminable conflict), whether and to what extent the parental conflict affects the parents' ability to make joint decisions regarding the child (i.e., whether, despite the conflict, the parents can come to an agreement regarding the child's health, education, and welfare), the quality of each parent's decisions and decision-making process, whether each parent solicits and considers the input of the other parent in making decisions, whether the involvement of a third-party professional can facilitate joint decision making and coparenting, and what limits or conditions on custody are in the child's best interest.

LEGAL ISSUES TO CONSIDER

Several legal issues must be taken into consideration when parenting coordination agreements are being set up, before they are formally implemented. Most notable among these are the scope and structure of the formal agreement, specific rules concerning confidentiality and privilege, and whether PCs should be given immunity (i.e., from lawsuits) when acting in their professional capacity.

[5]Other opponents argue that after years of trying to clarify the PC role with lawyers, judges, and others, prejudgment appointment of PCs will muddy those waters again.

Scope and Structure of PC Agreements

Three pertinent factors to consider when constructing a parenting coordination agreement are (a) the degree of authority the PC will have; (b) the power given the PC to compel parents, third parties, and children to participate in the parenting coordination process; and (c) specific guidelines regarding who can initiate issues for discussion and resolution, and the process of doing so.

Defining the Parenting Coordinator's Authority

How much authority does the parenting coordinator have? A good agreement between a PC and the parents must define, with specificity, the authority that is granted to the PC. There are several questions to consider: Is the PC limited to assisting the parents in developing or implementing a parenting plan and methods for better communication and decision making? Is the PC authorized to mediate disagreements between the parents? When the parents are unable to resolve day-to-day issues in a timely manner, can the PC make the decisions? If so, is the decision binding (i.e., are the parents required to follow it), or is it to be considered simply a recommendation? Is a binding decision subject to court review (i.e., can a parent go back to the court to have that decision reconsidered by the judge)?

An important limitation is that the PC is generally not authorized to resolve issues that usurp the ultimate authority of the court to determine custody. Examples of issues that may be resolved by a PC without usurping the court's authority include the dates, time, and method of transition between the parents' homes; logistics and transition times for sharing vacations and holidays; the setting of daily routines to be applied in both homes, such as mealtimes and diet, bedtime, and homework; and discipline strategies and methods.[6] Parents may also agree to give the PC additional control, for example, the authority to resolve disputes such as choice of school and choice of medical provider. Although the court may be limited in what authority it can give a PC, parents are generally free (in private PC agreements where the court is not involved) to give the PC as much (or as little) authority as they like.

Specifying the Parenting Coordinator's Power to Compel Participation

What power does the parenting coordinator have or need to compel participation by the parents, third parties, and the children? The parenting

[6]Other examples are health care coordination and management, alterations in the residential schedule that do not substantially alter the basic custody agreement (e.g., changes to accommodate special events or travel by a parent), introduction of new significant others, manner and schedules of communication between the children and each parent, and TV/computer time limitations and parameters.

coordination agreement should specify the authority of the PC to compel the parties to participate in the process. A typical agreement provides that the parents are required to participate in whatever manner the PC requests. Parents typically are also required to facilitate the involvement of their children, significant others, extended family, and service providers for the family (e.g., child care providers, pediatricians, therapists, teachers). The parenting coordination agreement should specify whether parents are required to provide consent for release of information by service providers if such consent is required by law. Without such provisions, a PC may be extremely limited in his or her ability to adequately perform the PC role.

Identifying Who Can Initiate Discussion or Resolution of Issues

It is very helpful for parenting coordination agreements to specify who can bring issues to the PC for resolution and by what method. In typical cases, either parent may raise an issue, or the PC may raise an issue. It is generally helpful to require parents to raise issues in writing, such as by e-mail, so there is a record of the specific issue and when it was raised. The PC can be given authority to determine how each issue should be resolved, either generally or on a case-by-case basis. For example, some agreements require that the parents meet with the PC for a specific number of sessions to try to resolve an issue. Other agreements allow issues to be resolved without meetings.

Confidentiality and Privilege

Parenting coordination agreements should cover both confidentiality and privilege. The latter is particularly important to address when a PC must speak with a family member's therapist.

No Privilege With Parents

As stated in the American Psychological Association's (APA's, 2012) *Guidelines for the Practice of Parenting Coordination*, parenting coordination is generally not a confidential process. There is no mental health privilege created between the PC and the parent.[7] This should be specified in parenting coordination agreements and orders. Standard language would be, for example, "No therapist–patient privilege is created by this appointment or otherwise exists between the PC and any of the parties or children."

[7]Privilege and confidentiality are related concepts that are often confused. A very simplified explanation is that, for psychologists, *confidentiality* refers to a standard of professional conduct that obligates them not to discuss patient information with anyone. *Privilege* refers more narrowly to protection against disclosure in a variety of legal settings from responding to a subpoena to testifying at trial (Keith-Spiegel & Koocher, 1980).

The APA parenting coordination guidelines also recognize that PCs are frequently authorized to speak with other professionals involved with the family, and the court may require the PC to document parenting coordination interventions and outcomes. However, the APA guidelines state that PCs must not disclose clients' records or information except as relevant to the parenting coordination process, in emergencies, or as authorized by court order or written agreement of the parties. This language is also typically included in parenting coordination agreements and orders.

Limited Waiver for Talking to Therapists

Family members' discussions with their therapists are generally protected by privilege. When a PC seeks information from a therapist, a legal question arises as to whether the therapist's disclosure to the PC will act as a complete waiver of the privilege, eliminating it altogether (for a more complete discussion of ethical issues and parenting coordination, see Chapter 6, this volume). Most PC agreements or orders address this issue by providing that the therapist's disclosure of information to the PC creates only a limited waiver of privilege; this means that it does not impair the family member's privilege in any other setting (e.g., if a parent became involved in a personal injury lawsuit).

This is an important issue to resolve in a PC agreement or order because a complete waiver could severely undermine the treatment of the relevant party and lead to the unnecessary disclosure of highly confidential information. Some states do not recognize a limited waiver of the mental health privilege. It is important to know whether a limited waiver is permitted in your jurisdiction and, if it is not generally recognized by the law, whether parties can make a binding agreement creating a limited waiver. A sample of parenting coordination agreement/order language on this topic is as follows: "The releases required by this agreement are solely for the purpose of allowing the PC to obtain relevant information to assist in her work with the family and shall not be deemed a waiver of any applicable privilege."

Immunity: Is Quasi-Judicial Immunity Available in Your Jurisdiction?

An important question for PCs is whether they are entitled to immunity from lawsuits when acting in the capacity as officers of the court, or persons carrying out functions delegated by the judge. Judges have immunity from civil liability for acts done within the scope of their authority; this allows them to impartially decide cases before them without fear that a party who does not like the decision will sue them. Similarly, quasi-judicial officers, such as Special Masters to whom the court may delegate some of its responsibility for fact finding or decision making, are typically granted quasi-judicial immunity. (For more information on Special Masters, see Chapter 1, this volume.) This grant is for the same reason: so they can perform those functions impartially without their findings or decisions being swayed by the fear that they may be sued. Kirkland (2008) observed that court-appointed PCs have consistently been granted quasi-judicial immunity. This typically means suits are dismissed before the necessity of a trial.

Quasi-judicial immunity may be specified in a PC statute or in the court rules permitting the appointment of PCs. It may also it flow from the mere fact that the PC has been appointed by the court as a Special Master or simply as a PC. It should be noted, however, that quasi-judicial immunity generally does not necessarily mean that a PC will be protected from licensing board complaints, unless that additional immunity is specifically granted in a PC statute. In other contexts, such as child custody evaluations, courts have held that quasi-judicial immunity does not protect a professional playing a quasi-judicial role from complaints of negligent or unethical behavior that a disgruntled parent may bring to a licensing board.

REFERENCES

American Psychological Association. (2012). Guidelines for the practice of parenting coordination. *American Psychologist, 67*, 63–71. doi:10.1037/a0024646

Carchman, P. S. (2007, April 2). *Notice to the Bar: Parenting coordinator pilot program—Program guidelines and related material.* Retrieved from http://www.judiciary.state.nj.us/notices/2007/n070403a.pdf

Eighth Judicial District guidelines for parenting coordination. (2008, April 25). Retrieved from http://test.nycourts.gov/courts/8jd/pdfs/ADR/Parent_Coord_Guide.pdf

Keith-Spiegel, P., & Koocher, G. P. (1980). *Ethics in psychology.* New York, NY: Oxford University Press.

Kirkland, K. (2008). Parenting coordination (PC) laws, rules, and regulations: A jurisdictional comparison. *Journal of Child Custody, 5*, 25–52. doi:10.1080/15379410802070377

Lally, S. J., & Higuchi, S. A. (2008). The American Psychological Association Parenting Coordination Project: Development of the project and initial review of the first two years. *Journal of Child Custody, 5*, 101–121. doi:10.1080/15379410802070435

3

COMPETENCIES REQUIRED FOR CONDUCTING PARENTING COORDINATION

STEPHEN J. LALLY AND ROBIN M. DEUTSCH

From early on, parenting coordinators (PCs) have come from diverse professional backgrounds; they may be licensed psychologists, attorneys, professional mediators, or other mental health professionals. Individuals from all of these fields bring a unique skill set and knowledge that informs their work as PCs; however, some of the earliest publications (e.g., Association of Family and Conciliation Courts, Task Force on Parenting Coordination [hereafter AFCC], 2003) recognized that these professionals need to have additional experience and training to function effectively as PCs. The two sets of parenting coordination guidelines approved by professional associations (AFCC, 2006; American Psychological Association [APA], 2012) both formally articulated the qualifications one needs to be a PC. In addition, in the United States a number of states have laws and regulations in place that govern parenting coordination and specify the experience and training that are required before one can be qualified as a PC (see Fidler, 2012; Fidler &

http://dx.doi.org/10.1037/14390-004
Parenting Coordination in Postseparation Disputes: A Comprehensive Guide for Practitioners, S. A. Higuchi and S. J. Lally (Editors)

Epstein, 2008, for a review of Canadian laws and regulations). Finally, several authors (e.g., Kelly, 2008; Sullivan, 2004) have written extensively about the experiences and qualifications required for parenting coordination. In this chapter, we review these recommendations and requirements.

In the general field of education, and more specifically within the education and training of professional psychologists, there has been a move to describe the competencies that provide the foundation for effective practice. This is a move away from listing hours of required training in specific topic areas to a developmentally sensitive identification of the knowledge, skills, and attitudes that underpin the profession's core competencies. This focus on competencies helps guide the current accreditation process in psychology (APA, 2009) and shapes the licensure process in psychology (Association of State and Provincial Psychology Boards [ASPPB], Task Force on Guidelines for Practicum Experience, 2009). In this chapter, we identify and describe these foundational competencies to enrich the currently published literature of PC qualifications.

REVIEW OF PARENTING COORDINATION QUALIFICATIONS

PCs have a variety of professional backgrounds, usually based in the fields of mental health and law. Formal qualifications to practice as a PC vary from state to state, and two sets of competency guidelines have been published, by the AFCC (2006) and APA (2012). In the sections that follow, we describe education, licensure, training, and competencies as they relate to formal parenting coordination practice.

Diversity of Professional Backgrounds

PCs have a wide variety of professional experience and training, spanning the professions of psychology, law, mediation, and other mental health professions. This variety was evident in the early years, when psychologists (e.g., Joan Kelly, Matthew Sullivan), mediators (e.g., Jeanne Ames), and attorneys (e.g., Christine Coates) were all pioneers in the development of parenting coordination in California and Colorado (see Chapter 1, this volume, for a detailed review of the early history). Recent surveys of PCs (e.g., Beck, Putterman, Sbarra, & Mehl, 2008; Hayes, 2010; Kirkland & Sullivan, 2008; see also Chapter 13 for a review of these surveys) have shown that this professional diversity is still evident in current parenting coordination practice.

Qualifications Listed in Professional Guidelines

In 2003, the AFCC Task Force on Parenting Coordination issued a report on parenting coordination implementation issues that reviewed different states' qualifications and requirements to function as a PC. In addition to noting that jurisdictions vary in regard to the formality and extent of the required education and training, the report also listed six areas of required expertise for PCs:

> a) conflict resolution theory and techniques, including mediation; b) child development and psychology, including adjustment to divorce; c) family dynamics, family systems theory; d) domestic relations law; e) familiarity with the dynamics of domestic violence and associated safety and intervention considerations; and f) parenting education and techniques. (AFCC, 2003, p. 25)

Three years after publishing the report, the task force (2006) published parenting coordination guidelines. Guideline I states that a PC needs to be qualified by education and training before undertaking the role. The guideline goes on to specify that a PC needs education and training in family mediation (and, in jurisdictions that have certification, should be a certified mediator); should be a licensed mental health or legal professional in an area related to families, or a certified family mediator; should have "extensive practical" experience with "high conflict or litigating parents" (p. 166); and should have training in a variety of areas relevant to parenting coordination. These areas include "parenting coordination process, family dynamics in separation and divorce, parenting coordination techniques, domestic violence and child maltreatment, and court specific parenting coordination procedures" (p. 166). In addition, the AFCC guidelines include an appendix with a model training program consisting of four modules covering the parenting coordination process, family dynamics in separation and divorce, parenting coordination techniques and issues, and court-specific parenting coordination procedures.

APA's (2012) guidelines also address the necessary competencies to function effectively as a PC. It is notable that the guidelines clearly state that the "competencies for standard psychological practice are generally insufficient for competent functioning as a PC" (p. 66). The guidelines also acknowledge that state and local laws may have specific requirements, including a mental health or law degree, training on domestic violence, and mediation training. The APA guidelines list competencies from general psychology practice that are relevant to PCs, including the use of research- and practice-based knowledge, writing skills, the ability to practice in a culturally competent manner, and an understanding of ethical and legal responsibilities. The guidelines also specify professional and personal competencies that are needed for a PC to function effectively. These competencies focus on intrapsychic and interpersonal skills and attitudes and include such things as understanding alternative views, empathy and self-awareness, establishing interpersonal boundaries, and engaging in professional problem solving in a systematic manner. In addition to these competencies, the guidelines note that PCs should endeavor to make decisions that are based on "empirical social science research regarding children's psychological and developmental needs, cultural context, diversity, and best interests" (p. 67).

Qualifications Listed in State Laws and Regulations

In the United States, at least 15 states have passed statutes providing for the appointment of a PC, and a number of other jurisdictions without specific statutes have allowed the appointment of a PC under certain conditions (see Chapter 2, this volume, for a detailed review of parenting coordination statutes and regulations). Many of these states and jurisdictions articulate the required qualifications for individuals to serve as a PC. In some jurisdictions (e.g., the 8th Judicial District of New York; 8th Judicial District, n.d.), the AFCC qualifications are listed as required qualifications, but in many other jurisdictions there are specific requirements that are unique to that jurisdiction. Some of these unique requirements were first summarized in the AFCC's (2003) report on implementing parenting coordination and, more recently, Kirkland (2008) included a listing of jurisdiction-specific qualifications in his review of parenting coordination laws, rules, and regulations. Drawing from these earlier publications and including recently enacted laws and regulations, in this section we review the jurisdictions' requirements in terms of degree and licensure, training experiences, and other requirements.

Degree and Licensure

States vary as to the level and detail of professional background required for one to function as a PC. Many are similar to Louisiana's law, which requires a "master's, Ph.D., or equivalent degree" in a mental health field such as "psychiatry, psychology, social work, marriage and family counseling, or professional counseling" and to hold a Louisiana license in that mental health field (Louisiana Revised Statute, § 358.3, n.d.). North Carolina has similar requirements but also lists the law as one of the areas of study to meet the educational qualifications (§ 50-93; "North Carolina General Statues," n.d.), and Florida Statute 61.125 (n.d.) also includes a certified mediator (with a master's degree in a mental health field) in its approved qualifications. Texas ("Texas Family Code 153.606," n.d.) allows attorneys and mental health professionals with graduate degrees as well as individuals with bachelor's degrees in "counseling, education, family studies, psychology, or social work" to serve as PCs. Some states (e.g., Colorado, Idaho, Oregon, Vermont) do not specify any required educational background or licensure for PCs.

At the time of this writing, no state has yet approved a separate licensure or certification for parenting coordination (however, at least one Canadian province—Alberta—appears to require PCs to be a "Registered Parenting

Coordinator and Arbitrator," and have their qualifications approved by the Alberta Family Mediation Society, n.d.), although Louisiana's law does list having such a certification from a "legal or mental health association whose focus includes resolution of child-related conflicts" (La. Revised Statute, §358.3, n.d.) as a qualification in lieu of the other qualifications required by the state. Since 2010, the Pennsylvania-based Professional Academy of Custody Evaluators (PACE; see http://www.pacehelp.com) has offered certification as a "Nationally Certified Parenting Coordinator," a term the group has apparently trademarked. PACE has separate application forms for attorneys and mental health professionals, and lists minimum number of years of experience as well as hours of training in a variety of areas (although their website notes that the Committee on Certification has the "authority to be flexible" in accepting alternative subjects). There is no evidence from PACE, or any other sources, that their certificate has been recognized by any jurisdiction.

The Massachusetts School of Professional Psychology (n.d.) also offers a certification in parenting coordination for 2 academic credits or 28 continuing education credits. This certification is based on 28 hours of training over 5 weeks (13 hours online and 15 hours on site) and covers much of the material listed in the AFCC guidelines, including psychological dynamics of high-conflict families; PC functions and practices; qualifications and areas of knowledge for a PC; procedures for setting up and beginning cases; intervention strategies; techniques to shift conflictual spousal relationships to functional parenting relations; ethical and legal challenges of PCs; writing agreements and drafting decisions; when and how to include children; research on parent education; and parenting coordination in situations of domestic violence, abuse and neglect, mental illness and substance abuse, and alienation. The program is designed to expand mental health practitioners', mediators', and attorneys' skills and requires an advanced degree in law, mental health, or human services.

Training Experiences

Most states specify training requirements for PCs beyond their professional degree and licensure. Some states list the content and number of hours of training. These range from Idaho's requirement of 20 hours of domestic violence training all the way to Vermont's 160 hours of training in seven different areas, with most states setting requirements somewhere in between. Many states list similar content areas for the required training. Some states (Colorado, Florida, Maryland, North Carolina, Texas, and Vermont) require training in mediation or alternative dispute-resolution techniques, and others require the PC to be a "qualified" mediator as defined by their statutes (Idaho, Louisiana, and Oklahoma). Many states require training in domestic violence (Colorado, Florida, Louisiana, Maryland, and Vermont), child development

(Colorado, Florida, Louisiana, Maryland, North Carolina, Oklahoma, Texas, and Vermont), the dynamics of high-conflict families (Colorado, Florida, Maryland, North Carolina, and Oklahoma), effects of divorce on families and children (Colorado, Maryland, North Carolina, Louisiana, and Oklahoma), family dynamics (Colorado, Florida, Louisiana, Texas, and Vermont), specific parenting coordination techniques (Florida, Louisiana, Maryland, North Carolina, Oklahoma, Texas, and Vermont), diagnosis of mental and emotional disorders (Colorado and Oklahoma) and substance abuse (Colorado and Vermont), ethics (Louisiana), and family or parenting coordination law (Colorado, Florida, Louisiana, North Carolina, Oklahoma, Texas, and Vermont).

Other Requirements

In addition to the educational and training requirements, a number of states have additional requirements for qualification as a PC. Several states mandate that the individual has to have a number of years of experience in his or her profession (Louisiana and Maryland, 3 years postdegree; Florida, 3 years of postlicensure or postcertification practice; North Carolina and Oklahoma, 5 years postdegree). Vermont requires 12 hours of parenting coordination training that includes "shadowing" a minimum of two cases. Some states require a certain number of hours of continuing education training (Colorado, 15 hours every 3 years; Louisiana, 20 hours every 2 years; Maryland, 4 hours every year), whereas North Carolina, for example, does not specify a number of hours but instead states that to remain eligible as a PC a person must attend seminars that "provide continuing education, group discussion, and peer review and support" (§ 50-93; "North Carolina General Statutes," n.d.). In Colorado, a statute specifies that the qualifications for *Decision-Makers* (the term for PCs with decision-making authority) will be set forth in chief justice directives. This statute (Office of the Chief Justice, 2008) is notable for its emphasis in the qualification section on the need for PCs to be mindful of and sensitive to diversity issues and to guard against bias. Although areas of training and number of required hours are listed, the statute also emphasizes the importance of attaining competence through education, specialized training, supervision, consultation, and professional experience.

Qualifications in the Published Literature

A number of authors, on the basis of their own experience and—in one case—a survey of the field, have delineated the knowledge and training required to competently perform parenting coordination. In 2004, Sullivan noted that in many jurisdictions PCs are required to have experience with diagnostic evaluations for family court as well as specific knowledge in "psychology (child development, custody schedules, domestic violence, family systems) and law (custody laws, local court rules)" (p. 580). Barsky (2011) referenced Sullivan's work in describing areas of required training for a PC and emphasized the importance of formal mediation training. He argued that general PC training should incorporate process-specific mediation training to ensure that mediation is used effectively and appropriately during parenting coordination.

Fidler and Epstein (2008), in an informal survey of PCs practicing in Canada, found that the PCs' education and qualifications were generally consistent with the recommendations articulated by the AFCC (2006). Specifically, there was recognition of the need for considerable experience with and knowledge of "the impact of separation and divorce, high conflict families, developmental psychology, parenting time schedules, family systems, family violence, mediation and conflict resolution, arbitration, and the relevant legislation and family law rules" (p. 61). Fieldstone, Lee, Baker, and McHale (2012) conducted a survey of judges, magistrates, attorneys, and PCs in Miami–Dade county (the fourth-largest judicial circuit in the United States and the largest in Florida). One of the results was that the majority of respondents from each of the three groups—77% of judges, 91% of attorneys, and 91% of PCs—indicated that further training in parenting coordination would be helpful. The respondents identified parenting coordination skills and techniques, time-sharing and parenting plans, and court-specific procedures as the areas where training was most needed.

Kelly (2008) provided the most comprehensive review of the training and education needs for both mental health and legal professionals preparing to function as PCs. Although acknowledging that licensed mental health professionals and practicing family lawyers bring a wealth of experience and expertise, she argued for the need for additional training, given the hybrid nature of parenting coordination and the risk of professionals drifting to their usual modes of intervention (i.e., shifting into therapy or adversarial representation). Kelly stated that lawyers sometimes struggle to work with both parents in a balanced and objective manner. In addition, she noted that lawyers often need additional training in the developmental aspects of children's expected behavior as well as on the research about the factors that affect adjustment after divorce. Lawyers frequently have little knowledge of or skill in interviewing children. In regard to mental health professionals, Kelly stated that they generally have little practice in drafting concise decisions. She noted that, across all professionals, it is important to have training in the unique aspects of the PC role and the specific processes and challenges associated with that role. She also highlighted the importance of having mediation training and experience as well as knowledge of the separation and divorce literature (including the specific risks and protective factors

I mediate often in fam ?
fx — rite ?
Frene

associated with children's psychosocial outcomes), parenting skills associated with positive adjustment, dynamics of high-conflict families, unique ethical challenges associated with parenting coordination, and the impact of partner violence. In addition, Kelly indicated a number of personal issues of which the PC needs to be aware and guard against. In particular, she described the risk of succumbing to the power of the role, guarding against fostering dependency, and managing one's workload to avoid burnout.

FOUNDATIONAL AND FUNCTIONAL COMPETENCIES OF PARENTING COORDINATION

In the past two decades there has been an increasing movement toward articulating and measuring the underlying skills that are the elements and components of professional competence as well as developing strategies to assess outcomes that measure these skills (Rubin et al., 2007). This competency movement can be seen in a variety of professions (e.g., education, nursing, dentistry, medicine), but here we focus on efforts within psychology (Kaslow et al., 2007; Leigh et al., 2007) because they offer a pathway to describing the competencies that form the basis of a competent PC. Although based in professional psychology practice, this review of competencies is relevant to other professions (i.e., law, mediation, social work, counseling) that may provide the background of a PC.

History of the Competency Movement in Psychology

The National Council of Schools and Programs in Professional Psychology (NCSPP) was an early leader in delineating the curriculum for doctoral-level education that provided the needed competencies for graduates to function effectively as professional psychologists. In 1990, NCSPP officials described the discrete knowledge, skills, and attitudes associated with six competency areas (relationship, assessment, intervention, research/evaluation, consultation/teaching, and supervision/management; Peterson et al., 1991). In 2002, diversity—which had previously been recognized as a core value embedded across the six competencies—was added as a seventh competency. In 2007, NCSPP defined the expected levels of achievement in the seven competency areas across the professional development of students. The result was the Competency Development Achievement Levels (NCSPP, n.d.; see also Kenkel & Peterson, 2010), which describe the expected knowledge, skills, and attitudes for each of the seven NCSPP competencies at the beginning of practicum, the beginning of internship, and the completion of the doctoral degree.

Influenced by the early work of NCSPP, APA's Committee on Accreditation (2009) revised its 1996 guidelines on accreditation to require training programs to articulate the goals and objectives in terms of competencies expected of their graduates. In 2002 (Fouad et al., 2009), APA, along with other training groups sponsored the 2002 "Competencies Conference: Future Directions in Education and Credentialing," which focused on the competencies required for a professional psychologist. One outcome of that meeting was the development of the "Competency Cube," whereby six foundational competencies were graphed with six functional competencies and both were graphed across a third dimension to reflect various developmental stages (Rodolfa et al., 2005). The *foundational competencies* refer to the knowledge, skills, attitudes, and values that serve as the foundation for psychologists' professional practice. They include reflective practice/self-awareness, scientific knowledge and methods, relationships, ethical and legal standards/policy issues, individual and cultural diversity, and interdisciplinary systems. The *functional competencies* involve the major functions that a psychologist is expected to perform and include assessment/diagnosis/conceptualization, intervention, consultation, research/evaluation, supervision/teaching, and management/administration. They involve an integration of foundational competencies. The third axis, *the developmental stages*, includes doctoral education, doctoral internship/residency, postdoctoral supervision, residency/fellowship, and continuing competency. This work has been further expanded in a comprehensive report and a series of articles on competency assessment (Kaslow et al., 2007; Leigh et al., 2007; Lichtenberg et al., 2007). Building on this work, the Assessment of Competency Benchmarks Workgroup (Fouad et al., 2009) identified benchmarks for 15 core competency areas at three different levels of education and training. Each competency is defined and broken down into its essential components. Behavioral anchors were described for these components at different training levels. Later, a work group (Campbell et al., 2012; Competency Benchmarks in Professional Psychology, n.d.) produced a guidebook to the benchmarks document to aid educational and training programs in applying the benchmarks. To assist in this process, the competencies in the original document were organized into six clusters, and the 16 competencies (an additional competency was added to the original 15) were grouped within these six clusters (with competencies located in the cluster given in parentheses):

1. Professionalism (Professional Values and Attitudes; Individual and Cultural Diversity; Ethical, Legal Standards, and Policy; Reflective Practice/Self-Assessment/Self-Care)
2. Relational (Relationships)
3. Science (Scientific Knowledge and Methods, Research/Evaluation)

4. Application (Evidence-Based Practice, Assessment, Intervention, Consultation)
5. Education (Teaching, Supervision)
6. Systems (Interdisciplinary Systems, Management/Administration, Advocacy)

These efforts to identify the competencies for professional psychology have recently been applied to various specialty areas of psychology practice. Specifically, authors have used this general framework to highlight the unique knowledge, skills, and attitudes in clinical health psychology (France et al., 2008), geropsychology (Molinari, 2012), clinical neuropsychology (Rey-Casserly, Roper, & Bauer, 2012), clinical child psychology (Jackson, Wu, Aylward, & Roberts, 2012), group-specialty practice (Barlow, 2012), and forensic psychology (Varela & Conroy, 2012). These efforts provide a model for our effort in this chapter to identify the underlying competencies for parenting coordination practice.

Competencies for Parenting Coordinators

Using the competency cube (Rodolfa et al., 2005) as a framework, and drawing freely from the NCSPP's Competency Developmental Achievement Levels (NCSPP, n.d.) and the competency benchmark (Fouad et al., 2009), in this section we describe the necessary knowledge, skills, attitudes, and values in both foundational and functional competencies associated with parenting coordination. These competencies comprise the elements and components of a competent PC. Foundational competencies are the building blocks that provide a foundation for all of the functional competencies. The functional competencies are the knowledge and skills that a PC uses to provide day-to-day services.

Foundational Competencies

Relationship skills. One of the most important foundational skills that underpins the work of a PC is the ability to relate effectively and meaningfully with a wide variety of individuals, both adults and children. For PCs who are not mental health professionals, this may mean seeking additional experience and training in what are referred to as the *nonspecific therapeutic factors* (i.e., rapport building, empathy). However, it is particularly important that PCs are able to maintain clear boundaries and remain objective in their interactions. For mental health professionals, this means guarding against the drift to move into a therapeutic stance (see Chapter 6, this volume, for additional discussion of this issue). An important skill is being able to tolerate and work effectively with the intense emotions and conflict that may be present between the parents. The PC must be able to allow and facilitate the exploration of emotionally difficult issues but remain clearly within the objective frame of parenting coordination. In addition, the PC must be comfortable shifting from education and consulting to an adjudicative role. As Beck et al. (2008) noted, PCs' professional backgrounds may lead them to be more comfortable in certain roles, but to effectively operate as a PC an individual must be comfortable with and competent in all of the roles associated with parenting coordination.

Knowledge of ethical–legal standards. The hybrid role of a PC calls for specialized knowledge in the areas of ethics and the law. PCs must have thorough knowledge of their profession's (e.g., psychology, social work, counseling, law) ethical code and the standards and guidelines of practice for their profession. This knowledge, along with both the holding of ethical values and the ability to use ethical-decision-making models in professional practice, set the foundation for a PC's ethics. However, given the unique nature of the work, there is a need for additional knowledge and training in the areas of ethical practice. Familiarity with the two guidelines published by the AFCC (2006) and APA (2012) is a starting point, but a competent PC needs an even more detailed understanding of PC-specific challenges with such issues as informed consent, confidentiality, role clarity, problems with conflicts of interests, and record keeping (see Chapter 6 for a detailed review of these topics). In addition to receiving formal training in workshops or classes, both sets of published guidelines recommend using consultation, and North Carolina's parenting coordination statute lists the need for peer review and support (North Carolina General Statutes, n.d.). Such consultation is consistent with psychology's ethical code, which explicitly lists such an action when a professional is encountering an ethical challenge (APA, 2010).

Training in family law and the local laws regarding parenting coordination is required in a number of states (Colorado, Florida, Louisiana, North Carolina, Oklahoma Texas, and Vermont), and even when not required is a minimum expectation for a competent PC. Attorney PCs have an obvious advantage in this area over PCs with a mental health background; however, even an attorney with a legal background must be knowledgeable about current laws, rules, and regulations covering PC practice (see Chapter 2, this volume, for additional discussion of legal issues). The goal is not to have the knowledge and training equivalent to that of an attorney but to have sufficient knowledge to operate ethically within the PC role. In addition to the knowledge of the relevant laws, PCs need to have the skills to effectively operate within this hybrid role. As Kelly (2008) noted, PCs with a mental health background may need practice in drafting concise decisions as well as in other court-related skills.

Familiarity with scientific knowledge and method. PCs need to have an in-depth knowledge of the scientific literature in a number of areas relevant to parenting coordination. Some of the areas identified in state regulations and laws are child development, family dynamics, effects of divorce on children and families, domestic violence, and dynamics of high-conflict families. Although PCs who are mental health practitioners may have some advantage in this area over attorney PCs, the level of knowledge required in this area goes beyond what is typically presented within graduate studies (see Chapter 9, this volume, for a more detailed review of the knowledge of child development needed). In other words, many mental health professionals may have a well-informed general understanding of normal development, but rarely are they comprehensively exposed to the literature on the impact of divorce on children and factors that affect that impact. In addition, scientific knowledge is not static but dynamically shifts and changes with additional research. Although some PCs (e.g., doctoral-level psychologists) may have the training to be able to evaluate the adequacy of a published study's methods and outcomes, such knowledge and skills are not required for a competent PC. However, when PCs are not able to evaluate the adequacy of study's methods and outcomes, it is important that they establish channels that will allow them to access such knowledge and skills (e.g., study groups, consultations, workshops) so that their PC-specific scientific knowledge is not dated.

Sensitivity to individual–cultural diversity. The United States is becoming an increasingly more diverse country, and the skills and knowledge needed to work with various individuals and groups are an important foundational competency in parenting coordination practice. A PC may be working with parents who were never married or never even lived together. A child's "parents" may not be the biological parents (e.g., but instead a stepparent, or a grandparent), and the "family" may not be the traditional nuclear family (e.g., same-sex couples, extended families). Competency in the area of cultural diversity includes not just knowledge of varying individuals', groups', and communities' cultural and individual backgrounds and characteristics but also an awareness of one's own cultural identity and its impact within the parenting coordination relationship. The skills needed to effectively operate in diverse settings start with an openness to be informed by the other and include the knowledge of self and others as cultural beings within the parenting coordination process (see Chapter 10 for an in-depth discussion of this and related issues).

Reflective practice and self-assessment. The term *reflective practice* refers to a foundational competency whereby a practitioner demonstrates personal and professional self-awareness and reflection, including an awareness of his or her competencies and the ability to self-monitor to ensure appropriate self-care. Kelly (2008) noted that there are a number of personal issues of which PCs need to be aware and guard against that relate to this competency. Specifically, she indicated that PCs need to be aware of the danger of being seduced into the potential power inherent in the PC role as well as the risk of fostering dependency in the parents involved in the parenting coordination process. She and other authors (see, e.g., Chapter 7, this volume) also warn of the dangers of the PC taking on too many cases and thus experiencing burnout. The ability to monitor one's workload and emotional resources is key in providing effective and ethical parenting coordination services.

Functional Competencies

Intervention. Although training in the delivery of psychotherapy may provide useful skills to PCs (see the above discussion of nonspecific therapy skills in the relationship competency), it is not essential for competent parenting coordination. In fact, such training can cause a PC to drift more toward therapy and adopt a less objective stance. What both the state regulations and the published guidelines (AFCC, 2006; APA, 2012) make clear is that PCs need to be knowledgeable of and skilled at mediation. This training is typically not provided within mental health professionals' curriculum of study, and gaining the knowledge in a postgraduate mediation workshop is necessary but may not be sufficient to make one competent. In particular, Kelly (2008) recommended that in addition to knowledge individuals should also have experience in mediation prior to undertaking parenting coordination. Other nontraditional intervention skills that a PC needs include knowledge and skill in helping parents learn conflict management and communication techniques as well as teaching parenting skills. Some of these skills may have been learned within a mental health professional's formal training, but some mental health PCs and, likely, all PCs with no mental health education background, will need training in this area. Additional related skills include those involved in case management, whereby PCs may be helping coordinate the delivery of services for children or adults, and skill in interviewing and working with children (see Chapter 9 for a more detailed review of working with children). A basic understanding of the nature and effectiveness of these services (including psychotherapy) also is needed.

Assessment and diagnosis. This competency does not refer to the administration and interpretation of psychological tests with the PC's families. Such a dual role may present a number of conflicts (see Chapter 6, this volume, for a discussion of the issue of dual roles). Instead, a competent PC needs to be able to assess the family's functioning and dynamics and have a good understanding of potential mental health problems. This needed knowledge is recognized in some state laws and regulations that require training in the diagnosis of mental and emotional disorders (Colorado and Oklahoma), substance abuse (Colorado and Vermont), and family dynamics (Colorado, Florida, Louisiana, Texas, and Vermont). In addition, PCs need to be alert to and able to assess for the presence and differentiation of types of interpersonal violence. The assessment and diagnosis of the individuals and the larger system inform PCs' work. In situations where a family member has a specific physical or psychological disorder (e.g., a child with autism), PCs need to ensure they have sufficient understanding of the condition and its impact on functioning so they can work effectively with the family. In some cases, this means a PC must seek additional training or knowledge.

Consultation. In the role of a PC, individuals will need to provide consultation to the court as well as consult with other agencies. In the former role, PCs must have a good understanding of the court system, the rules of the court, and the appropriate means of communicating information in their jurisdiction. In particular for PCs with a background in mental health, this needed understanding may mean training on what should and should not be included with communications to the court as well as the manner in which such communications should be crafted. In addition, competencies in consultation often overlap with the case management, because PCs may need to work with a variety of different service providers to assist the families. Case management includes both gathering information from other providers (e.g., psychotherapists, teachers, doctors) and, at times, helping the family make sure needed services are accessed (e.g., testing for a child with special needs).

Teaching. Although much of what has been written about parenting coordination focuses on the mediation and adjudication functions, the role of education at times is the most important function. For many parents, learning about the impact of their conflict on their children's development and the children's developmental needs plays a crucial role in helping move them toward effective coparenting. PCs not only need to have the knowledge of the impact of parental conflict on children and the developmental needs of children in the short term and long term, (see the above-listed scientific knowledge and method competency), but they also need to be able to effectively educate the parents. This means being aware of diverse learning styles and having the ability to disseminate information using varied didactic strategies that are sensitive to developmental and individual differences.

Management and administration. Parenting coordination, whether provided within a court system or as part of an independent practice, requires a variety of management and administrative skills. Within a larger system, individuals need to be able to effectively operate in the organization to ensure that parenting coordination is delivered in an effective and ethical manner. This may include advocacy for the services being provided. Within an independent practice, the skills of scheduling, billing, and maintaining records are all involved in this competency. The knowledge and skills related to managing such a practice are articulated in greater detail in Chapter 5.

Research and evaluation. There is a need for more research regarding parenting coordination in general and specifically on the efficacy of this intervention with families. There is still relatively little information about what types of interventions (e.g., parallel parenting vs. cooperative coparenting) are most effective in different situations as well as what types of problems parenting coordination most effectively impacts (e.g., reducing conflict between parents, reducing use of the court, improving children's adjustment; see chapter 9, this volume, for a detailed review of these issues). However, to be effective, PCs are not required to be competent researchers. It is recommended that, given the need for such research, PCs who are not directly engaging informal studies consider how they can facilitate and participate in others' projects. This collaborative model is evident in Florida, where data have been collected by a research team from a variety of PCs' practices (e.g., Fieldstone et al., 2012; Fieldstone, Carter, King, & McHale, 2011). Although conducting research and collaborating with researchers is an optional competency, the skills and knowledge to engage in practice in a scientific manner are not. The model of the local clinical scientist (Stricker & Trierweiler, 1995; Trierweiler & Stricker, 1998) describes a method of practice whereby interventions are informed by the evidence in the literature and practitioners evaluate the effectiveness of interventions in their practice. In a form of hypothesis testing, practitioners attempt an intervention, assess its success, and, on the basis of the results, either modify or continue with the intervention. This model of clinical practice—and the skills, knowledge, and values associated with it—can be applied to competent parenting coordination. This requires that PCs evaluate their actions in a manner similar to that of a scientist and then evaluate and modify these actions depending on the results. It is a model and perspective that may be familiar to many mental health PCs, but for others it may be a place where training is needed.

CONCLUSIONS AND IMPLICATIONS

Drawing on the AFCC (2006) and APA (2012) guidelines, state laws and statutes, and the published literature, and using the framework of competencies developed for the practice of psychology, in this chapter we have articulated both the foundational and functional competencies needed to be an effective PC. The assumption in these competencies, and the regulations in most states, is that an individual entering practice as a PC is a trained and licensed mental health professional (e.g., psychologist, social worker, counselor), a certified mediator, or a practicing attorney. We have described the advanced-level competencies that build on the foundation of skills and knowledge acquired in the underlying or initial profession of the PC.

A focus on competencies, rather than number of hours of training, suggests that what is important is whether the knowledge is attained, the skill learned, or the value and attitude appreciated. It is easy to measure hours of workshop attendance but much more difficult to assess whether a competency has been achieved. In the evolution of parenting coordination, the next stage may be to move toward models of assessing the attainment of competencies necessary to be a qualified PC. This is the direction that has occurred, and is continuing to occur, in professional psychology as well as other mental health professions, and it is proposed in legal education. The focus on competencies also suggests a closer examination of how the knowledge, skills, and attitudes are acquired. Kelly (2008) described a variety of learning activities that could be used within a workshop format. However, many of these skills may best be learned by either shadowing an experienced PC or being supervised by one. This model of learning is listed in the Colorado directive, and Vermont requires the shadowing of at least two cases. Finally, the knowledge acquired is not static, and it is important that PCs continue to receive education so they remain competent and current in the different areas. Participation in continuing education activities is recognized in a number of state laws and regulations as well as in the professional guidelines published by the AFCC (2006) and APA (2012). In conclusion, a move to a competency-based model of parenting coordination will broadly influence education and qualification standards and is a needed step at this point in the field's evolution.

REFERENCES

Alberta Family Mediation Society. (n.d.). *Requirements for registered parenting coordinator and arbitrator.* Retrieved from http://afms.ca/index.php?pid=31

American Psychological Association. (2009). *Guidelines and principles for accreditation of programs in professional psychology.* Retrieved from http://www.apa.org/ed/accreditation/about/policies/guiding-principles.pdf

American Psychological Association. (2010). *Ethical principles of psychologists and code of conduct (2002; revised June 1, 2010).* Retrieved from http://www.apa.org/ethics/code/principles.pdf

American Psychological Association. (2011). *Competency benchmarks in professional psychology.* Retrieved from http://www.apa.org/ed/graduate/benchmarks-evaluation-system.aspx

American Psychological Association. (2012). Guidelines for the practice of parenting coordination. *American Psychologist, 67,* 63–71. doi:10.1037/a0024646

American Psychological Association, Committee on Accreditation. (2009). *Guidelines and principles for accreditation in professional psychology.* Retrieved from http://www.apa.org/ed/accreditation/about/policies/guiding-principles.pdf

Association of Family and Conciliation Courts, Task Force on Parenting Coordination. (2003). Parenting coordination: Implementation issues. *Family Court Review, 41,* 533–564. doi:10.1111/j.174-1617.2003.tb00914.x

Association of Family and Conciliation Courts, Task Force on Parenting Coordination. (2006). Guidelines for parenting coordination. *Family Court Review, 44,* 164–181. doi:10.1111/j.1744-1617.2006.00074.x

Association of State and Provincial Psychology Boards, Task Force on Guidelines for Practicum Experience. (2009). *ASPPB guidelines on practicum experience for licensure*. Retrieved from http://www.asppb.net/files/public/Final_Prac_Guidelines_1_31_09.pdf

Barlow, S. (2012). An application of the competency model to group-specialty practice. *Professional Psychology: Research and Practice*, *43*, 442–451. doi:10.1037/a0029090

Barsky, A. E. (2011). Parenting coordination: The risks of a hybrid conflict resolution process. *Negotiation Journal*, *27*, 7–27. doi:10.1111/j.1571-9979.2010.00290.x

Beck, C., Putterman, M., Sbarra, D., & Mehl, M. (2008). Parenting coordinator roles, program goals and services provided: Insights from the Pima County, Arizona program. *Journal of Child Custody*, *5*, 122–139. doi:10.1080/15379410802070468

Campbell, L., Fouad, N., Grus, C., Hatcher, R., Leahy, K., & McCutcheon, S. (2012). *A practical guidebook for the competency benchmarks*. Retrieved from http://www.apa.org/ed/graduate/benchmarks-guide.aspx

8th Judicial District (n.d.). *Parenting coordination: Guidelines for parenting coordination*. Retrieved from http://www.nycourts.gov/courts/8jd/parentcoordapp.shtml

Fidler, B. J. (2012). Parenting coordination: Lessons learned and key practice issues. *Canadian Family Law Quarterly*, *31*, 237–273.

Fidler, B. J., & Epstein, P. (2008). Parenting coordination in Canada: An overview of legal and practice issues. *Journal of Child Custody*, *5*, 53–87. doi:10.1080/15379410802070393

Fieldstone, L., Carter, D. K., King, T., & McHale, J. (2011). Training, skills, and practice of parenting coordinators: Florida statewide study. *Family Court Review*, *49*, 801–817. doi:10.1111/j.1744-1617.2011.01415.x

Fieldstone, L., Lee, M. C., Baker, J. K., & McHale, J. P. (2012). Perspectives on parenting coordination: Views of parenting coordinators, attorneys, and judiciary members. *Family Court Review*, *50*, 441–454. doi:10.1111/j.1744-1617.2012.01459.x

Florida Statute 61.125: Parenting coordination. (n.d.). Retrieved from http://www.leg.state.fl.us/statutes/index.cfm?App_mode=Display_Statute&Search_String=&URL=0000-0099/0061/Sections/0061.125.html

Fouad, N. A., Grus, C. L., Hatcher, R. L., Kaslow, N. J., Hutchings, P. S., Madsen, M. B., . . . Crossman, R. E. (2009). Competency benchmarks: A model for understanding and measuring competence in professional psychology across training levels. *Training and Education in Professional Psychology*, *3*, S5–S26. doi:10.1037/a0015832

France, C. R., Masters, K. S., Belar, C. D., Kerns, R. D., Klonoff, E. A., Larkin, K. T., . . . Thorn, B. E. (2008). Application of the competency model to clinical health psychology. *Professional Psychology: Research and Practice*, *39*, 573–580. doi:10.1037/0735-7028.39.6.573

Hayes, S. W. (2010). "More street cop than a detective": An analysis of the roles and functions of parenting coordinators in North Carolina. *Family Court Review*, *48*, 698–709. doi:10.1111/j.1744-1617.2010.01343.x

Jackson, Y., Wu, Y. P., Aylward, B. S., & Roberts, M. C. (2012). Application of a competency cube model to clinical child psychology. *Professional Psychology: Research and Practice, 43*, 432–441. doi:10.1037/a0030007

Kaslow, N. J., Rubin, N. J., Bebeau, M. J., Leigh, I. W., Lichtenberg, J. W., Nelson, P. D., . . . Smith, I. L. (2007). Guiding principles and recommendations for the assessment of competence. *Professional Psychology: Research and Practice, 38*, 4441–4451. doi:10.1037/0735-7028.38.5.441

Kelly, J. B. (2008). Preparing for the parenting coordination role: Training needs for mental health and legal professionals. *Journal of Child Custody, 5*, 140–159. doi:10.1080/15379410802070476

Kenkel, M. B., & Peterson, R. L. (Eds.). (2010). *Competency-based education for professional psychology*. Washington, DC: American Psychological Association. doi:10.1037/12068-000

Kirkland, K. (2008). Parenting coordination (PC) laws, rules, and regulations: A jurisdictional comparison. *Journal of Child Custody, 5*, 25–52. doi:10.1080/15379410802070377

Kirkland, K., & Sullivan, M. (2008). Parenting coordination (PC) practice: A survey of experienced professionals. *Family Court Review, 46*, 622–636. doi:10.1111/j.1744-1617.2008.00228.x

Leigh, I. W., Smith, I. L., Bebau, M. J., Lichtenberg, J. W., Nelson, P. D., Portnoy, S., . . . Kaslow, N. J. (2007). Competency assessment models. *Professional Psychology: Research and Practice, 38*, 463–473. doi:10.1037/0735-7028.38.5.463

Lichtenberg, J. W., Portnoy, S. M., Bebeau, M. J., Leigh, I. W., Nelson, P. D., Rubin, N. J., . . . Kaslow, N. J. (2007). Challenges to the assessment of competence and competencies. *Professional Psychology: Research and Practice, 38*, 474–478. doi:10.1037/0735-7028.38.5.474

Louisiana Revised Statute, §358.3: Qualifications. (n.d.). Retrieved from http://legis.la.gov/lss/lss.asp?doc=451646

Massachusetts School of Professional Psychology, Center for Excellence for Children, Families and the Law. (2012). *Certificate in parenting coordination*. Retrieved from http://www.mspp.edu/community/children-families-law/certificate-parenting-coordination.php

Molinari, V. (2012). Application of the competency model to geropsychology. *Professional Psychology: Research and Practice, 43*, 403–409. doi:10.1037/a0026548

National Council of Schools and Programs in Professional Psychology. (n.d.). *Competency Developmental Achievement Levels (DALs) of the National Council of Schools and Programs in Professional Psychology (NCSPP)*. Retrieved from http://www.ncspp.info/DALof%20NCSPP%209-21-07.pdf

North Carolina General Statutes—Chapter 50, Article 5 (Parenting Coordinator), §50-90-100. (n.d.). Retrieved from http://www.ncleg.net/gascripts/statutes/StatutesTOC.pl?Chapter=0050x

Office of the Chief Justice. (2008). *Supreme Court of Colorado: Directive concerning court appointments of decision-makers pursuant to §14-10-128.3, C.R.S. Chief*

Justice Directive 08-01. Retrieved from http://www.courts.state.co.us/Courts/Supreme_Court/Directives/08-01.pdf

Peterson, R. L., McHolland, J. D., Bent, R. J., Davis-Russell, E., Edwall, G. E., Polite, K., . . . Stricker, G. (1991). *The core curriculum in professional psychology*. Washington, DC: American Psychological Association and National Council of Schools of Professional Psychology.

Rey-Casserly, C., Roper, B. L., & Bauer, R. M. (2012). Application of a competency model to clinical neuropsychology. *Professional Psychology: Research and Practice, 43*, 422–431. doi:10.1037/a0028721

Rodolfa, E. R., Bent, R. J., Eisman, E., Nelson, P. D., Rehm, L., & Ritchie, P. (2005). A cube model for competency development: Implications for psychology educators and regulators. *Professional Psychology: Research and Practice, 36*, 347–354. doi:10.1037/0735-7028.36.4.347

Rubin, N. J., Bebeau, M., Leigh, I. W., Lichtenberg, J. W., Nelson, P. D., Portnoy, S., . . . Kaslow, N. J. (2007). The competency movement within psychology: An historical perspective. *Professional Psychology: Research and Practice, 38*, 452–462. doi:10.1037/0735-7028.38.5.452

Stricker, G., & Trierweiler, S. J. (1995). The local clinical scientist: A bridge between science and practice. *American Psychologist, 50*, 995–1002. doi:10.1037/0003-066X.50.12.995

Sullivan, M. J. (2004). Ethical, legal, and professional practice issues involved in acting as a psychologist parenting coordinator in child custody cases. *Family Court Review, 42*, 576–582. doi:10.1177/1531244504042003l3

Texas Family Code § 153.606: Authority of parenting coordinator. (2007). Retrieved from http://law.onecle.com/texas/family/153.606.00.html

Trierweiler, S. J., & Stricker, G. (1998). *The scientific practice of professional psychology*. New York, NY: Plenum Press. doi:10.1007/978-1-4899-1944-1

Varela, J. G., & Conroy, M. A. (2012). Professional competence in forensic psychology. *Professional Psychology: Research and Practice, 43*, 410–421. doi:10.1037/a0026776

4

PARENTING COORDINATION: BASIC APPROACHES AND STRATEGIES

ROBIN M. DEUTSCH

The role of the parenting coordinator (PC) is not a traditional therapeutic or legal role but, rather, a hybrid one that includes a number of functions, such as assessment of disputes; parent education; conflict management and reduction; case management and coordination; mediation; and, usually, arbitration (American Psychological Association, 2012; Association of Family and Conciliation Courts [AFCC], Task Force on Parenting Coordination, 2006; Deutsch, Coates, & Fieldstone, 2008). In the continuum of alternative dispute-resolution processes, the PC role involves a significant degree of intervention and, ultimately, decision-making power. The PC works proactively with the parents to anticipate areas that may result in dispute and helps the parents come to agreement about the many issues that may be silent in their parenting plan. Building structures and protocols to avoid dispute is the bulk of the beginning phase of the parenting coordination process.

http://dx.doi.org/10.1037/14390-005
Parenting Coordination in Postseparation Disputes: A Comprehensive Guide for Practitioners, S. A. Higuchi and S. J. Lally (Editors)

PCs do not have the confidentiality requirements that mediators do. The most important distinction between a PC and a mediator is that the latter does not make decisions. If the divorce process does not result in resolution, an impasse is declared. A PC, on the other hand, has the option of making a recommendation and, in most agreements and orders, a decision. For families who are involved in long-term, chronic conflict, even impasse-directed mediation (Pruett & Johnston, 2004) is not effective for approximately 25% of them, suggesting that a different model may be necessary. This new mediation–arbitration model guarantees resolution of the disputes.

Although parenting coordination includes elements of education and case management, it is not psychotherapy. The differences between a PC and a psychotherapist are apparent in the separate agreements each makes to provide services. Agreements made by psychotherapists note that the process is confidential, whereas agreements made by PCs note that the role is not confidential. Whether by court order or private consent agreement, a PC may provide a report to the court at its request; testimony per subpoena; or, with appropriate releases, information to or from other parties (e.g., children's therapists, school counselors) that will help the parties come to agreement or the PC to make an informed decision. Confidentiality is waived both for the court and between the parents. Other differences take into account the differences in the stance: A therapist has a supportive, empathic stance consistent with a helping relationship, whereas a PC has a neutral stance that supports the resolution-focused management relationship. In addition, therapists obtain most of their information from the client, but PCs obtain their information from diverse other sources (e.g., therapists, teachers, health care providers, attorneys).

Often, parents seek therapeutic services as they go through a difficult separation or divorce process. Although therapists have knowledge and be available, they do not have any authority to step in when a dispute is occurring. The court, on the other hand, has the authority (and the knowledge), but the wait for a court date may be quite long. While parents are waiting to be heard by the judge, the conflict often escalates and generalizes to other areas of interaction. PCs are in the unique position of having the knowledge and skills, the availability, and the authority to settle disputes and minimize ongoing conflict. They thus become the coparenting link between the parents.

Objectives of the Parenting Coordination Process

The objectives of the parenting coordination process are, first, to implement the parenting plan, that is, those agreements and orders that define the parenting time and the decision-making responsibilities of the parents, including the regular schedule, vacation and holiday schedule, communication processes, travel and appointment notifications, extracurricular activities, and educational and medical decisions. Often that means focusing on the details of the plan that are missing and that will result in conflict. No detail is too small for parents in conflict. Monitoring compliance with the parenting plan also is an objective of this process. Conflict results when one parent believes, realistically or not, that the other parent is not adhering to the plan. Throughout the process, the PC assesses the origins of the parenting disputes, and his or her task is to resolve them while focusing on the best interests of the child, thereby reducing opportunities for conflict between the parents. By providing education, the PC helps the parents shift to a primary focus on the developmental and psychological needs of their children. The PC operates as a functioning manager of the relations between the parents, as they develop a new kind of coparenting relationship. In addition to reducing conflict, a successful parenting coordination process will improve the parents' communication and problem-solving skills.

PCs are typically appointed in cases in which parents have persistently been unable to resolve conflicts about their children without the assistance of attorneys or the court. Other processes have typically failed, and the parents, their attorneys, and the court are all concerned about the significant negative repercussions on the children's short- and long-term adjustment when exposed to the chronic conflict of their parents. In general, a PC is appointed postdecree after the parenting plan has been incorporated into the stipulation or court order. However, a PC is also used at times to help the parents implement a temporary parenting plan by resolving disputes while the divorce is pending. PCs are particularly helpful when there is a need for evolving parenting plans because the children are young, there are substance abuse or mental health compliance issues, or there is resistance to contact with a parent. A PC can be particularly helpful in managing the case and avoiding ongoing litigations for complex and high-risk situations in which a child has complex mental health or medical conditions; where there are allegations of abuse or neglect, or domestic violence concerns; or when coordination of multiple professionals is required.

Functions of the Parenting Coordinator

A PC's functions reflect the hybrid role. Because a PC's primary objective is to reduce conflict, an ongoing function is to assess the impasses that contribute to the conflict. The PC assesses whether the conflict is the result of one or more of the following factors:

1. personality problems of one or more of the parents, including difficulty shifting their focus from their own needs to that of their children, trouble taking another person's point of view, and being hypersensitive to criticism;

2. difficulties separating from the ex-spouse or partner or from seeing the other in a nuanced way, as opposed to through a primarily negative lens;
3. problems in thinking whereby one or both parents make errors of misperception, misinterpretation, and misattribution; and/or
4. the triggers for each parent, which may originate from earlier separation, relationship, or trauma experiences.

Most important, the PC as assessor must determine the extent to which the conflict affects the children, and the necessary or helpful structures and processes to reduce the conflict. Over time, the PC observes patterns of conduct and relationship, and then shares his or her observations with the parents. The PC should note whether and how these repeated patterns build confidence in either negative or positive responses that may affect the shifting coparenting relationship. This assessment function informs the parenting coordination process as the PC attempts to understand how to help the parents implement and comply with their parenting plan and resolve disputes.

Education

Educating parents comprises three main components: (a) the needs of the children, (b) the changing coparenting relationship, and (c) coparenting strategies. Embedded in these three functions are multiple and varied opportunities for broadening parents' perspectives; helping them consider other points of view; and learning about processes for better, more predictable communications. The PC refocuses the parents on the short- and long-term needs of the children and the developmental consequences of the choices the parents are making. When the parents are in dispute about something, the PC ascertains whether the dispute has any effect on the children and, if it does, considers with the parents how the needs of the children may be taken into consideration, thus modeling for them a process for taking the children's interests into account.

It is typical for the parents engaged in a parenting coordination process to need a road map for changing their relationship from a spousal or intimate partnership to a business relationship focused on coparenting. The transition from a nuclear (both parents and children living together) to bi-nuclear (two separate households with one parent heading each; Ahrons, 1995) family involves each subsystem of the family functioning separately and adequately with a functional connection through the access schedule and a feasible means of communication. By setting up structures for communication, expectations for responses, and rules of behavior regarding contact, the PC can educate the parents with a new template for how they will separate, engage, and adjust. Some of these strategies include creating structures for e-mail—including content, frequency, templates, and response time—as well as policies for emergencies, including the definition of an emergency. When parents are both present at an event, expectations for contact, or not, are articulated. A timeline to create a schedule for the school year or summer, with cutoff dates for identifying vacations, changes in parenting schedule, holiday structures and transfers, birthdays, and rules for change in the regular parenting plan is developed with the PC. That process becomes the template for future parent-to-parent communications about scheduling issues.

Conflict Management

Conflict management is closely tied to the education function of a PC. It is often the case that attempts to coparent are clouded by the sense of hurt, betrayal, or anger they feel about the separation. It is often difficult for parents to move into a new role that focuses primarily on the children. Some parents feel desperate to save the marriage or to understand the separation, other parents do not trust the caretaking capacities of the other parent, and still others are in a struggle to prove their parenting superiority. The PC's task is to acknowledge the parents' feelings but to shift the focus from the spousal relationship to the children's needs. This requires both skill and focus. The issues of the couple that are often at the forefront for the parents cannot sidetrack a PC. Modeling respect and dignity, refocusing on the children, and emphasizing the parents' common interest in raising healthy, well-adjusted children should be the ongoing message.

Managing disputes through mediation and negotiation is the mainstay of PC's role. Parents who engage a PC's services typically are unable to agree on day-to-day as well as longer term issues. Parents who wait to get into court to resolve these issues could wait weeks or even months. One of the benefits of a PC is that disputes are managed in a timely manner.

Case Management

For the PC, case management has two goals: (a) to coordinate the educational, medical, therapeutic, and other professionals involved with the family and (b) to help the parents disengage by creating an interface between them. When there is a dispute, the PC as the interface gathers relevant information from the professional team and shares it with the parents in order to educate them or help them to come to agreement, or the PC uses it to make a decision. The PC may also find that members of the family may benefit from psychotherapy; psychological testing; or medical consultations or evaluation, including educational or neuropsychological testing, and substance abuse assessment and testing; parent guidance, or specific medical consultation for a child. It is generally within the scope of the PC's authority to refer family members for such services.

Decision Making

When the parents are unable to come to an agreement with the assistance of the PC, the decision-making function is activated. This function separates the PC role from any other therapeutic, educational, or mediation function. The parent raising a particular issue provides to the PC and the other parent a written statement of the disputed issue. The parents demonstrate how they have attempted to resolve the issue themselves, or the PC acknowledges that they have been unable to come to agreement. The PC then resolves the issue in a timely way and such that the decision is binding, although the court always retains its authority to overturn that decision.

Beginning the Case

Setting up the case requires first and foremost a review of the court order or stipulation to determine the PC's scope of authority, confirmation of payment arrangements, and anything that may fall outside of the standard PC agreement. An agreement signed by both of the parents and the receipt of a retainer check signals the beginning of the parenting coordination process and the time to set up first interviews.

The parenting coordination process is often generated by disputes, so the PC should set the stage by meeting with the parents to review the parenting plan and proactively help them set up protocols to manage any lack of structure. This will provide a template for managing disputes as they arise. If a custody evaluation has been completed, the PC should review that before the first meetings.

The parents have an initial individual interview with the PC so that the PC may become familiar with the parents and the parameters of the case. Initially it is best practice to have individual meetings with each of the parents so the PC can hear about any issues of power and control without fear of repercussion from the other parent (see Chapter 11, this volume, for more on this issue). This initial screening may be mandated by law or statute in some jurisdictions. In the first interview, whether individual or joint, the PC gets the relevant history of the breakdown of the marriage, elicits information and concerns about the children, and identifies the parenting issues and concerns that may result in disputes. The PC establishes a positive atmosphere; reviews the parenting coordination agreement, including terms of payment and the limits of confidentiality; and obtains formal consent for the process.

Setting the stage for the ongoing work should be modeled in the first joint session (after the initial intake and review session). The PC may commence with an overview of how the parenting coordination process can be an opportunity for the parents to together resolve their disputes and manage the care of their children, as opposed to using the court to parent their children.

The PC should set up expectations that each parent will be heard and his or her perspective considered and should explain that the process is solution focused. This should be emphasized through expectations for behavior and ground rules such as only one person talks at a time, all communications to the PC are shared with the other parent, the main concern is the children, and the focus is on present- and future-oriented concerns.

The PC should reflect on the goal of reducing conflict between the parents and provide relevant research to support that goal. He or she will then be able to review the objectives of the process, including development of a communication structure between the parents and the PC, the parents with each other, and the parents with the children; implementation of the parenting plan, including compliance with the plan; reframing of the coparent relationship with a focus on the needs of the children; and resolution of child-related disputes. In this discussion the PC can candidly describe how low-conflict and effective parenting are the two variables that can protect the children from poor outcomes associated with divorce and that the work to come will focus on managing disputes to ensure the best outcomes for their children. The PC should review at this time how and when children will be interviewed and whether other professionals will be contacted. In general, the PC will meet each child at some point during the process, and the expectations for that contact can be discussed ahead of time with the parents.

Meetings with the PC are generally initiated by the parents or agreed on at the most recent meeting. Meetings are most effective if they begin with an agenda that models the businesslike structure of the meetings. Sometimes the agenda is a disputed issue. Ways to manage that issue are to have parents share their agendas within a certain timeline (e.g., 24 hours before the meeting) and then alternate the order in which the agenda items are discussed. Parents may come up with other ways to manage disputes about the agenda, but the PC should use this as a concrete demonstration of problem solving when there is a difference of opinion. The PC should ensure that the agenda items fall within the scope of his or her authority. Each issue should be discussed with the goal of coming up with a solution. Although expression of emotions and interests is part of the process, the PC will want to set limits so that the focus remains on generating and assessing the options in a child-focused manner.

Using a problem-solving model is often helpful. The parents define the problem, and the PC may help them reframe it as a goal. The next step may be to identify obstacles to that goal or to resolving the problem. After brainstorming ideas to meet the goal, the PC should help facilitate a discussion of the pros and cons for each idea, with an eye toward what are unacceptable options, what are acceptable options, and then the best solution.

There are times when parents appear to be stuck, and at such times it may be helpful for the PC to meet briefly with each parent individually to caucus about the disagreement, brainstorm, cool off, and present compromises. Each parent then will have the opportunity to share his or her view, knowing that confidentiality for each parent will be maintained for that part of the session, unless the parents together come to a different agreement about the kinds of information that will be shared between them.

It is not unusual for the discussions to become heated or for people to make disparaging, snide comments or show distress. The PC is in a position to respond to the former with a simple question, such as "What was your intention in saying that?" or "What was it that made you say that?" The purpose of the question is to bring the person back to the agenda and to find out whether something is preventing the parent from being engaged in the problem-solving process. When it appears one of the parents is upset, the PC may want to ask that parent whether he or she is angry or upset about something. The response can be explored as it pertains to the agenda at hand. The PC should consistently try to set limits and boundaries so that his or her role is not compromised and does not spill over into therapy or advocacy. It is well within the PC's scope of authority to recommend a therapist, parent coach, or other professional, but not to take on that role. When an agreement is reached, the PC should carefully record it in the notes, using the parents' own words as much as possible, and making it bilateral, even if the issue most generally pertains to one parent.

Writing Agreements

At the end of each meeting, the PC should document the agreements reached at that meeting. Agreements will cover a range of issues that are within the PC's scope of authority. An initial goal is to review the existing parenting plan, to tighten it so that undefined areas that may result in conflict are eliminated. Areas to cover include things such as parenting time cancellation policies and child-exchange rules; transportation and location for transition of the child from one parent to the other; all holidays; special days, such as child and parent birthdays and vacations; unforeseen emergencies; children's activities; clothing and equipment; scheduling of routine medical and dental care and how information is shared regarding these appointments; how parent–teacher meetings are scheduled and who attends; significant others and dating; supervision and disciplinary interventions; and travel rules (see Appendix 4.1 for a detailed review; located at http://pubs.apa.org/books/supp/higuchi).

Agreements are then written in clear language, using the parents' words as much as possible. Agreements need to be specific and cover who will do what, when, where, how, and how much. The following is an example:

> Parents agree that choice of summer vacation will be alternated so the mother has first choice of her first week in even-numbered years and father has first choice of his first week in odd-numbered years. The first-

> choice parent identifies his or her week by April 1 of each year. Parents then alternate choices week by week by April 8, 15, and 22. If a parent does not identify his or her choice of vacation week by midnight of his or her date to choose, the choice immediately defaults to the other parent.

The PC would include the details of a vacation week in a separate agreement; for example:

> Summer vacation weeks begin at 5:00 p.m. on Friday and end at 5:00 p.m. on Friday. The vacationing parent will pick the children up from camp or the other home. The non-vacationing parent will have the previously agreed to packing list available by 6:00 p.m. on Thursday, the night before the vacation commences, at the previously designated dropoff spot.

Agreements are documented in two ways. They are (a) kept in a running list by date that (b) serves as an addendum to the parenting plan. Some PCs may want to have the parties sign the agreements each time they are appended in order to document the contractual agreement. Each time the agreements are updated, they are sent to the parties in a letter, generally e-mailed, that states something along the following lines:

> This letter documents the agreements that have come from our meeting of 7/1/13. Please review for accuracy and inform me within 48 hours, replying all, if you have questions. In the absence of modification, you have agreed to follow the directives contained in this letter.

Decision Making

In most jurisdictions and private consent agreements the PC is given the authority to make a decision if the parents are unable to do so. It is critical that the PC confirm that the disputed issue is within his or her scope of authority to decide, as delineated in the court order and/or private consent agreement. In no case does the PC have the authority to "make any decision which substantially alters the parties' time sharing arrangements, changes the designation of legal or physical custody, or substantially interferes with a party's contact with his/her children" (AFCC, Task Force on Parenting Coordination, 2006, p. 172).

In some jurisdictions and private consent agreements, the PC may make a recommendation that is nonbinding; in others, it is binding and subject to court review. Although the role of an arbitrator is often confidential, in this role of parenting coordination the decision of the PC is not confidential and is subject to subpoena and testimony. It is up to the PC to know the relevant statutory provisions of his or her jurisdiction of practice.

The PC should explain the decision-making process to the parents during the first joint interview. The process for how and when the arbitration function is activated also is explained and agreed on at that time. Some parties identify a period of time that can elapse between stalled negotiations and the commencement of the decision-making process. If that process is used, there must be an exception made for emergency or time-sensitive resolutions. Other parents determine that either party can invoke the decision-making process when that parent believes negotiations have failed and the parties are at an impasse. The benefit of moving into the next phase is that a decision can be made in a timely way on an issue that may have significant consequences for the children. For example, resolution of the dispute in a timely way may ensure that a child has plans for the summer or appropriate medical care for asthma. Of course, the longer term benefits for the children occur when children can see their parents with a frequency and in a manner that focuses on their safety and well-being.

The process of rendering a decision in a dispute involves adequate gathering of information. The parent raising the dispute typically provides a written statement of the dispute to the other parent and the PC. The PC then asks both parents to provide their preferred solution to the dispute, with their rationale, copied to the other parent. The PC may request more information or clarification from either parent, may choose to interview collateral sources of information, or may choose to meet with any of the children. In this phase the goal is to gather enough information to make an informed, impartial decision.

The PC then issues a decision that summarizes each parent's thinking about the issue; any other sources of information, including records reviewed and conversations with people; the PC's decision; and the rationale for that decision. If the decision is an amendment to previous agreements or decisions, or court orders, they should be referenced and the decision should note that it supersedes the previous order or agreement. The decision is written so that it is comprehensive; addresses all the relevant issues in the dispute; and covers the who, what, where, when, and how aspects. The decision should be unambiguous and written clearly and concisely, with the expectation that parents will comply and conflict will be reduced. To orient and focus the parents, PCs will find it helpful to write the decision with clear headings, brief paragraphs, and bulleted lists. The decision should be titled, signed, and dated. Before distributing the agreement, the PC should review the document to make certain that it covers every detail, there is no ambiguity, and that the decision and rationale are defensible.

Reporting to the Court

The court always retains authority to review the PC's decisions. PCs must be aware of the standard of review that a court would use to review their decisions. In some jurisdictions the parent who objects to the PC's decision files a motion with the court and it is then reviewed *de novo*, that is, without the presence or testimony of the PC. In other jurisdictions the PC is called on to testify about the rationale behind the decision and whether it meets the best interests of the children.

In addition, some jurisdictions require that PCs periodically report to the court about the progress of the parenting coordination process, including compliance, agreements, and decisions. In other jurisdictions, PCs must regularly file all decisions and agreements with the court, and in still others there are no filing or reporting requirements. PCs must know what the reporting requirements are within their jurisdiction and what the PC's standing is before the court.

CONCLUSION

Approximately 10% to 15% of families remain in high conflict a year or two years after their divorce (Maccoby & Mnookin, 1992). Children's adjustment in the short and long term is negatively affected by exposure to their parents' conflict (Deutsch & Pruett, 2009). They are often asked to carry hostile messages back and forth, feel they are in the middle of their parents' conflict, and are prone to anxiety and depression (Grych, 2005; Johnston, Roseby, & Kuehnle, 2009; Kelly & Emery, 2003). PCs can assist parents who remain in high conflict after their divorce to implement their parenting plan, monitor compliance with the details of the plan, and resolve conflicts in a timely manner, with the goal of protecting and sustaining safe, healthy, and meaningful parent–child relationships.

PCs are hired by order of the court or by private consent agreement. They function in a neutral, hybrid role to help with assessment, education, coordination/case management, dispute resolution, and decision making. A PC generally has jurisdiction over almost any child-related issue that is identified in the court order or private consent agreement, except anything that substantially modifies the parenting access and responsibilities awarded by the court. The goal of this process is to help high-conflict parents settle their disputes in a timely manner, reduce conflict, and learn to coparent effectively through the structured parenting coordination process. When conflict is reduced and effective parenting is provided, the children are more likely to experience positive adjustment.

REFERENCES

Ahrons, C. (1995). *The good divorce*. New York, NY: William Morrow.

American Psychological Association. (2012). Guidelines for the practice of parenting coordination. *American Psychologist, 67*, 63–71. doi:10.1037/a0024646

Association of Family and Conciliation Courts, Task Force on Parenting Coordination. (2006). Guidelines for parenting coordination. *Family Court Review, 44*, 164–181. doi:10.1111/j.1744-1617.2006.00074.x

Deutsch, R., & Pruett, M. K. (2009). Child adjustment and high conflict divorce. In R. M. Galatzer-Levy & L. Kraus (Eds.) *The scientific basis of child custody decisions* (2nd ed., pp. 353–375). New York, NY: Wiley.

Deutsch, R. M., Coates, C. A., & Fieldstone, L. (2008). Parenting coordination: An emerging role to assist high conflict families. In L. Fieldstone & C. A. Coates (Eds.), *Innovations in interventions with high conflict families* (pp. 187–221). Madison, WI: Association of Family and Conciliation Courts.

Grych, J. H. (2005). Interparental conflict as a risk factor for child maladjustment: Implications for the development of prevention programs. *Family Court Review, 43*, 97–108. doi:10.1111/j.1744-1617.2005.00010.x

Johnston, J. R., Roseby, V., & Kuehnle, K. (2009). *In the name of the child* (2nd ed.). New York, NY: Springer.

Kelly, J. B., & Emery, R. E. (2003). Children's adjustment following divorce: Risk and resilience perspectives. *Family Relations, 52*, 352–362. doi:10.1111/j.1741-3729.2003.00352.x

Maccoby, E., & Mnookin, R. (1992). *Dividing the child*. Cambridge, MA: Harvard University Press.

Pruett, M. K., & Johnston, J. R. (2004). Therapeutic mediation with high-conflict parents: Effective models and strategies. In J. Folberg, A. L. Milne, & P. Salem (Eds.), *Divorce and family mediation: Models, techniques, and applications* (pp. 92–111). New York, NY: Guilford Press.

II

THE PRACTICE OF PARENTING COORDINATION

5

CREATION, DEVELOPMENT, AND MANAGEMENT OF A PARENTING COORDINATION PRACTICE

MATTHEW J. SULLIVAN

The practice of parenting coordination has burgeoned, due to a combination of its fulfillment of a much-needed niche in the family courts and its attractiveness to mental health and legal professionals as a lucrative practice activity. Parenting coordination is now established in various jurisdictions across the United States and Canada, supported by legislative statutes, case law, and state and local rules of court (Kirkland, 2008; see also see Chapter 2, this volume).

In this chapter, I address issues related to setting up, developing, and managing a parenting coordination practice. In addition to practical advice about the business of doing parenting coordination work in private practice (see Chapter 8 for a discussion of parenting coordination within the public sector), I provide recommended procedures and methods to help parenting coordinators (PCs) ensure that their practice is consistent with ethical standards and risk management processes.

http://dx.doi.org/10.1037/14390-006
Parenting Coordination in Postseparation Disputes: A Comprehensive Guide for Practitioners, S. A. Higuchi and S. J. Lally (Editors)

A survey of PCs across jurisdictions in 2008 provided an important snapshot of professionals who work in this role (Kirkland & Sullivan, 2008). First, PCs come from both family law and mental health backgrounds, with the majority—almost half—being psychologists. Mental health PCs typically need to augment their psychology education and training with legal knowledge and skill, which requires considerable experience in the family courts (Kelly, 2008; see Chapter 3, this volume, for further discussion of the necessary knowledge and skills). The survey validated this, finding that the average PC has been in forensic practice for 18 years, while practicing as a PC for 8 years. Prior to beginning their parenting coordination work, these professionals had specialized in other roles in the family court, such as mediation, custody evaluation, and court-involved treatment. The basic message from the survey is that parenting coordination is a very specialized role that requires extensive experience and training.

The PCs who responded to the survey (Kirkland & Sullivan, 2008) also stated that, on average, they spent about 40% of their total practice time devoted to PC work (range: 5%–70%). This finding supports the recommendation that psychologists should be cautious if their parenting coordination caseload exceeds half of their total practice activities. The difficulty of the work, combined with the fluctuations in case demands, makes caseloads that exceed this total percentage of practice more likely to create two negative consequences in PCs' practice: (a) the lack of flexibility across one's day-to-day work flow to deal proactively with active cases—which tends to escalate their conflict, requiring even more time and attention to de-escalate the case—and (b) the broader negative effects in one's practice involving increased professional practice risk and long-term burnout. Mental health PCs who sustain their involvement in this area of practice typically balance the stress of their parenting coordination case work with other practice roles, such as mediation, therapy, consultation, and other professional activities that are not connected with parenting coordination. Another critical practice management requirement, self-care, also helps sustain a PC's longevity in the practice. I focus on self-care later in the chapter.

Parenting coordination caseloads are also affected by the typical phasing, flow, and development of individual cases. Parenting coordination cases tend to be quite demanding as the case begins and can require several hours a week for the first 1 to 3 months to structure the coparenting process and address what is often a backlog of issues related to the implementation of the parenting plan (Sullivan, 2008). If this work is effective, parenting coordination work on a case often moves into a maintenance phase. In this phase, there are less frequent scheduled contacts and fewer disputes, and issues that have not been previously addressed are managed with the procedural structures established in the earlier phase. Because coparenting conflict is often more about the process of dealing with issues, rather than substantive differences, when the PC establishes protocols to handle issues related to the implementation of parenting plans (e.g., the selection of summer vacation periods), these protocols often continue to manage most future issues during which coparenting conflict can escalate. Finally, the PC can often reduce the parents' direct reliance on contact with the PC, assuming a more symbolic management role (which takes no time commitment and provides no compensation), with the PC and parents meeting only perhaps twice a year for check-in meetings. Total parenting coordination caseloads, therefore, should be sensitive to where the PC's combination of individual parenting coordination cases are in this typical case trajectory.

> **Practice Tip:** Don't take multiple parenting coordination referrals at the same time. Give yourself time to work through the initial, labor-intensive phase of a case before accepting additional cases.

To illustrate how a PC's work on a case can result in a positive case trajectory from more intensive PC involvement to a gradual reduction of direct PC involvement, I offer the following example, which demonstrates how PCs can effectively work with the implementation of the court-ordered regular time-share arrangements, holidays, and vacation periods. More often than not, the parenting plan PCs receive from the court when they begin a case has insufficient detail to guide and structure the implementation of regular, holiday, and vacation time share. Assuming that high-conflict parents require as much detail as is possible in their parenting plan, the first task of the PC as it relates to the custody schedule is to work with the parents to create provisions in the parenting plan that address every aspect of the regular time-share, holiday, and vacation schedule. The goal of this initial work is to have enough specificity in this part of the parenting plan to be able to calendar in which parent's custody the minor children will be every hour of every day. This calendaring should occur for parenting coordination cases early enough so that they are completed before the school year begins and in mid-spring (to calendar the summer period). The summer period necessitates calendaring of the regular time share, designated vacation periods, and any child-related activities (e.g., camp) that might affect the time share. Initial work on the parenting plan may require several meetings to create agreements (or make parenting coordination decisions, if this is within the scope of the PC's authority) about each and every holiday and vacation period. The allocation of these holiday periods (which is usually equal, even if the regular time share is not) is essential to the task of calendaring the time-share schedule each year. Once the work on the holiday and vacation parenting plan is complete, the PC assists the parents in implementing their plan (to create the calendar). This work typically requires more direct parenting coordination work the first time a calendar is created. Then, the PC uses the subsequent calendaring exercises, supporting more independent work constructing the summer schedule, including agreement on vacation periods and camp selection for the children, to reduce the parents' dependence on the parenting coordination process. Helping the parents manage this calendaring with increasing independence from the PC is accomplished by setting up expected time frames during which the parents must complete the components of the calendaring task, monitoring these steps, and having parents bring any disputed parts of the overall calendar to the parenting coordination process for resolution. The calendaring process typically becomes more manageable for the parents over time such that they become fully independent in this task and simply provide the PC with the completed calendar as a documented agreement of their day-to-day timeshare schedule. The calendar goes into the PC's file as a document that can be referred to if scheduling issues arise during that time period. Having the time-share schedule calendared greatly reduces the PC's involvement in cases because scheduling disputes account for a significant percentage of coparenting disputes in high-conflict shared custody cases.

A GUIDE TO PARENTING COORDINATION CASEWORK

In this section, I provide a step-by-step set of considerations to guide PCs in their work with individual cases. I address the referral and intake process, setting up cases, and casework functions once the case has been effectively set up.

Several considerations should guide a PC's consideration of whether to accept or reject a referral. Some cases are inappropriately referred and should not be accepted. PCs cannot assume that referral sources (judges, attorneys, clients) understand what appropriate referrals are or the expectations of the service a PC provides to clients. High-conflict family law cases tend to be quite frustrating and difficult for professionals who have been involved (often for months or years), and the tendency to look for a process by which to dump them is high. The PC should gather information that can help determine whether the case is appropriate for any PC. This can best be accomplished by considering four important questions. First, is there a custody order in place, even a temporary one? If the answer is no, I believe it is not an appropriate parenting coordination case. This is because parenting coordination is a role developed to implement parenting plans, not to create them. Second, are there expectations in the referral that push beyond the PC's scope? For example, does the court expect the PC to provide recommendations about custody, relocation, or financial issues? If so, other court processes, such as mediation, custody evaluation, or litigation, are needed to address these issues. Third, are there domestic violence or child abuse aspects to the case that would make the PC process inappropriate? Refer to the discussion of domestic violence and the PC process in the AFCC parenting coordination guidelines (Association of Family and Conciliation Courts [AFCC], Task Force on Parenting Coordination, 2006) as well as Chapter 11 of this volume. Fourth, do the parents lack the financial means to afford PC services (and you are not willing to do the work pro bono or adjust your fee on a sliding scale)? If clients cannot afford the service, accepting the case is a setup for failure.

Another issue to consider is whether there are aspects of the case referral that make it inappropriate for you to accept the referral, even if it is an appropriate PC referral. These might include aspects of the case that are both outside your scope of competence and in which you cannot address this shortcoming by using a consultant or a collaborative team approach (Greenberg & Sullivan, 2012). Examples of this issue may be a lack of knowledge and expertise about adult issues in the case (substance abuse, domestic violence, serious mental illness, physical or sexual abuse), child issues (e.g., serious psychiatric issues such as autism or serious learning disabilities), or other issues requiring specialized knowledge and skill (e.g., cultural differences, long-distance shared custody). An essential component of a PC's appointment order is the parents' agreement that the PC can consult with any professional (e.g., child psychiatrist, mental health professional from another cultural background, physician) whenever the PC determines it is appropriate to work on the case.

Other considerations in accepting a referral should be the history of the case and the professionals involved. A case that has had previous PC appointments is a red flag that requires additional investigation beyond the report of the referral source. Obtaining information, directly from previous PC, which will require a written authorization from the parents, is essential in determining whether you want to accept the case. A history of multiple failed parenting coordination interventions raises the likelihood that the case is not appropriate for the parenting coordination process (as opposed to the referral source's pitch that you are the only PC in the jurisdiction who has the exceptional competence to succeed with this case). The attorneys involved in the case should be a relevant consideration in whether to accept a referral. If you do not know of them, do the necessary investigation to assess their reputation. The attorneys will be part of your collaborative team, and you should consider their practice style and whether it is more collaborative or litigious, how strongly they tend to identify with and blindly advocate for their clients versus having a more child-focused, or at least a more hands-off, stance as the case moves into the parenting coordination process. Having collaborative relationships with attorneys who represent parents in parenting coordination cases can assist with the containment of clients, who at times may be inclined to move the case back into litigation. Unfortunately, clients can switch attorneys during the course of your parenting coordination work, so you cannot always address these issues for the long term. Similarly, knowledge and assessment of other mental health professionals who are involved in the case should be a consideration. Previous negative experiences with child, adult, and family therapists may lead you to decline the referral because the anticipated teamwork with them may be more challenging than you are willing to undertake (Greenberg & Sullivan, 2012).

Most important, do not accept a parenting coordination case because you need to pay the rent. Financially driven decisions about your professional work, in particular high-risk parenting coordination casework, more often than not lead to negative professional consequences. Similarly, do not accept parenting coordination work because, despite it being full of the negative considerations above, you have received the referral from a very attractive referral source (e.g., the best family law firm in the jurisdiction, the supervising family law judge). Using the referral process to educate the referral source about your reasons for declining the case is likely to be more helpful to your long-term reputation than the concern about the immediate disappointment to the referral source that might be communicated.

Commencing Work on a Case

Never begin work on a parenting coordination case until you have the following three things: (a) the filed custody order, (b) the filed appointment order (or signed informed consent service agreement, if you are working without a court order), and (c) your retainer in the bank. This advice may seem obvious, but it is quite common for PCs to begin work before all of these have been obtained. These cases are often presented with a sense of urgency (if not emergency) and the child's precarious welfare is highlighted in this presentation. This is often despite, or because of, the fact that the referral has taken months to come to your office door. Psychologists' child-focused helping orientation can lead to violations of this three-pronged requirement, and your professional risk is elevated if you begin work without these requirements satisfied.

Having the file custody order assures that there is a parenting plan and usually has a specific reference to the parents being ordered into a parenting coordination process. The definition of the PC's role is to assist with the implementation of the parenting plan (AFCC, Task Force on Parenting Guidelines, 2006), so it follows that verification that there is a parenting plan is essential. Having your appointment order as the PC filed with the court ensures that you have the court-sanctioned authority to engage in the PC role in this case. A careful review of the order is critical. It should specifically address the following points:

- what authority you may have and where your authority is derived from (e.g., legislative statute, rule of court, local rule);
- your scope of authority—what specific domains of legal custody you have authority to address (e.g., time-share, health, and educational issues; holidays and vacations; activities);
- parenting coordination procedures (e.g., meeting protocols, decision-making protocols, access to information about the parents and child, review by the court, grievance processes, quasi-judicial immunity);
- parenting coordination fees (e.g., retainer requirement and replenishment procedures, amount to be charged per hour, what work is covered, allocation); and
- grievance procedures, term of appointment, and termination of or withdrawal by the PC.

Practice Tip: You can find sample appointment orders on the following website: http://www.californiaparentingcoordinator.com

Working to have your jurisdiction, or at least your own practice policy, mandate the use of a standard order of appointment helps your confidence that if a standard order is executed in a case, it contains the necessary components provided above.

Having client fees collected is the third requirement to start work on a case. "The check is in the mail" does not meet this requirement; neither does having only one client's paid retainer satisfy a strong recommendation to have 10 hours of fees in hand prior to commencing work. Keeping interested parties informed about the status of retainer payment will provide the likely pressure to make this requirement happen. Starting work without retainer fees collected communicates the relationship rule (contrary to the written rule in the order) that the financial aspect (and likely other aspects) of your relationship with a client is negotiable. This is a recipe for disaster. Expressing disgruntlement about the execution of your role as the case progresses through nonpayment of fees is common, and not having a retainer and firm policies about its replenishment in place from the commencement of the case will often compromise your effective work.

A service agreement (informed consent intake form) is sometimes the only written contract of the agreed-on parameters of your role in a case. Sometimes it is necessary to have a service agreement in addition to the appointment order, to fill in areas that are not addressed. These areas might include that you are a mandated reporter of child abuse, what your hourly fee is, how missed appointments are handled, how lateness for appointments (in particular, joint appointments, are handled), how professional coverage is handled when you are out of the office, and other office procedures. In working with difficult clients in their complicated circumstance, the more detailed and explicit (written) your policies and procedures are, the more likely it will be that you can maintain the appropriate relationship boundaries necessary to do effective parenting coordination work.

Getting the Parenting Coordination Case Started

With the exception of having one individual meeting with each parent as the casework commences, to develop rapport and hear each parent's perspectives, it is better to have all contacts with parents structured so that both parents are involved/present for all those contacts. This means that meetings (face to face or by phone) should be conjoint, and other communications—initiated by a parent or you—should be copied to the other parent (by e-mail, letter, or fax). If this is the rule, the work is more efficient; billing for work is straightforward and balanced; and the claims of bias, manipulation, and influence by the other parent are more manageable when no one is excluded from information. This policy of no unilateral communication also precludes the sharing of highly sensitive information that may put you in a difficult position of how to manage it. An example is a call from the parent who shares with you that he or she is planning to move out of state but does not want you to share that information with the other parent. Keeping in mind the recommendation that all contact with clients should include both parents, having highly conflicted parents directly interact, either face to face in your office, over the telephone, or even through e-mail, can be extremely difficult to manage because of the reactivity and hostility between the parents. A highly structured meeting protocol (which I describe below) is essential, and a very active meeting management style (the "referee" model) is often required. If attempts to structure and manage joint contacts fails, you may have to have separate contacts with each parent as the structure of your work.

Domestic violence dynamics may preclude contact between the parents. One parent may assert that he or she will not meet with the other because of intimidation, fear, or an inability to function in that setting due to power and control issues. Domestic violence restraining orders may be in place that preclude any direct contact between the parents. In these circumstances, your work will require a structure that does not violate these no-contact orders (see Chapter 11 for further discussion of these situations).

Assuming you work jointly with parents, the functions of scheduled meetings are multiple. Meetings are used in conjunction with e-mail (which usually is the primary mode of communication between the parents) to functionally exchange child-related information and to make decisions. These are the two essential components of coparenting—child-related information exchange and decision making—and therefore these components are the focus of parenting coordination. More specifically, the PC becomes the functional link between parents, constructing an enhanced parallel-parenting model. This model supports the coparenting functions while keeping the parents as disengaged as possible (to manage and minimize the likely conflict that occurs with engagement; Sullivan, 2008). Regular, predictable meetings (with the intervals of time in between determined by the case's current needs) channel coparenting-related business into a manageable and more constructive format. This helps contain conflict, and the structure encourages parents to be more proactive about addressing child-related issues. Seasonal activities, such as sports, should be on the agenda for a meeting that allows a discussion of the child's possible enrollment prior to the deadline for registration. Many coparenting conflicts arise out of the poor planning and last-minute or after-the-fact disclosure of unilateral action ("I signed Mary up for ballet and want you to share the cost") that could have been avoided by training the parents to be more proactive and planful with child-related decisions that need to occur.

PCs work in the following manner to establish and maintain the structures that support functional coparenting meetings. These meetings can be held face to face or via conference call. Sometimes a conference call is necessary because one parent may live in a remote area, or the meeting may need to be by phone because of other circumstances. In addition to these reasons, using a conference call format, even when a face to face meeting is feasible, may have the benefit of reducing the engagement of the parents. This is because a conference call does not have the intensity of nonverbal cues between the parents that may promote more intensely negative and reactive interactions. In some cases, a conference call is the preferred meeting modality. Regardless, several structural components of conjoint meetings help PCs train the clients in more functional coparenting practices, often despite themselves. These structures include handling scheduling of appointments, requiring agendas, handling air time, and documentation of meetings.

Anticipating that scheduling appointments will be a forum for power struggles between the parents, the scheduling of meetings requires protocols that reduce conflict between the parents over scheduling. For the first phase of the work, meetings typically occur at least twice a month, and that should be the expectation. E-mail is the most efficient manner to schedule appointments, and having clients e-mail all parties their availability, copied to the other parent, allows the PC to confirm a meeting time. If there is no match between each parent's availability, then a good strategy is to mandate an appointment time (which should be part of your authority under the court order), with the understanding that you will alternate each parent's preference for appointments to make the system fair. Remind parents to bring their calendars, and always schedule the next meeting (or meetings) before they leave your office. If a parent needs to reschedule, he or she has the burden of informing the PC and the other parent with as much notice as possible and providing as many options to reschedule as possible.

Parents should be required to submit agendas (by e-mail, which has a date and time stamp) to the other parent, copied to the PC, 48 hours prior to any meeting. The agenda should identify the issue as a topic and rank the agenda by its priority to that parent. If time management has become an issue in conducting meetings, then parents should provide a time estimate after agenda items.

Sample Meeting Agenda

The following protocol prevents a parent from being blindsided by an issue and makes the likelihood of constructive dialogue more probable. If a parent does not provide an agenda, his or her agenda is addressed after the other parent's list of agenda is addressed. Although the enforcement of this rule usually is met with protest, it prompts quick compliance to the protocol (a form of one-trial learning). Alternating addressing each parent's agendas with some consideration for balancing the overall time allotted to each in the meeting maintains fairness in the process. Because they have prioritized their agendas, if all agenda items are not addressed they have at least addressed their most important item. The problem of lateness for conjoint meetings can be handled by setting an up-front policy about this (ideally in your service/informed consent agreement) that anticipates and manages this occasional (sometimes frequent) occurrence. The rule should be that the parent will pay the full rate for the percentage of time he or she was late for the scheduled meeting.

You should make clear at the onset of your work that you are responsible for the process of the meetings and that you expect that meetings will be businesslike and that parents will conduct themselves respectfully. Simply stating this rule rarely is sufficient to ensure this goal, but you must make this expectation explicit in order to have any chance of maintaining the rule. As escalations predictably occur—a roll of the eyes, or interruption by one parent, elicits a hostile verbal barb by the other, which elicits a provocative comment about the parent's personality disorder diagnosis—you must immediately, actively, and authoritatively (like a referee) intervene to interrupt this escalation and refocus the interaction. This may require precluding eye contact, reorienting the parents' seating position, or directing the parents to speak only to you.

An essential component of structuring the parenting coordination process is the documentation that you provide after parent meetings (or any contact that generates and agreement or decision). A summary letter (sent by e-mail) should follow each and every meeting. The agenda that you followed should provide the structure for the summary. As a rule, less documentation is better than more, but documentation of any agreements, child-related information exchanged, and decisions/recommendations you have made is essential. This documentation constitutes a written record of this information that will preclude disputes arising in the future about what occurred in earlier parenting coordination work. The summary can be used to positively reinforce behavior (praising the parents for a negotiated agreement) or negatively reinforce problematic conduct (e.g., documenting a parent's failure to be appropriately responsible for a child completing his or her homework can have a powerful effect on the parent addressing this issue).

In this summary letter (see Appendix 5.1 for a sample summary letter; located at http://pubs.apa.org/books/supp/higuchi), the first paragraph has several functions. It changes the more court-oriented mind set of the parents to one that is now engaged in a less formal, more collaborative process. I also put the burden of making modifications to the summary on the client, so that no response implies agreement and, therefore, compliance with the written summary is expected. Note that the date and time of the next meeting are provided.

Practice Tip: Do not schedule more than one or two meetings with clients on the same day. Also, provide at least 30 minutes to an hour after a client meeting to complete the summary letter from the meeting (this is a much easier task when the information is fresh) and to provide some time to regroup before you move on to additional client work.

Parenting Coordination in Cyberspace

Much of what needs to occur for high-conflict parents to adequately exchange child-related information, coordinate shared parenting, and make child-related decisions is best handled in cyberspace (over e-mail and through electronic calendars).[1] Cyberspace can facilitate the least amount of direct, unmonitored engagement between parents with an adequate modality to transact coparenting business. When this link is supplemented by an appropriate interval of coparenting meetings, this structure supports a functional model of parallel parenting.

[1]Parents can set up a master calendar that can be accessed by both by using Google Calendars (a free service) or an online shared custody service such as Our Family Wizard (http://ourfamilywizard.com/ofw/). Our Family Wizard has additional tools to assist with shared custody arrangements.

Assuming both parents have the ability to use the Internet, communicating among parties almost exclusively by e-mail has considerable benefits for high-conflict shared custody situations. First, e-mail is an asynchronous communication modality, which means that the sender and receiver are temporally separated (that, combined with their being physically separated, adds to their disengagement). The sender and receiver have control over when they engage in their end of the communication. As long as there are parameters (set by you) about response time, each parent can delay receipt of an e-mail, and delay his or her response after receipt, which allows more deliberation and potential consultation about how to respond. In addition, e-mail communication is a written document. E-mails have text, and a date and time stamp indicating when they were sent. These characteristics allow for accountability in adherence to communication expectations between parents in the parenting coordination process. If e-mails are required to be copied to the PC, this "big brother" function provides a monitoring of the e-mail communication rules. You should specifically explain these rules to the parents before directing them to use e-mail for their communication.

Practice Tip: The following is an example of a PC directive setting rules for e-mail communication from a summary letter:

Here are the suggested guidelines for e-mail communication that I spoke of at our meeting:

1. *Brief*, in that you don't want your e-mail to turn into a rambling tirade that can be used against you. Don't give the other side more ammunition to attack you.
2. *Informative*, in that you want to communicate only facts rather than unhelpful emotions. Focus on the information you want to communicate rather than on the disinformation coming from the other person. Certainly avoid personal attacks, sarcasm, name-calling, ranting and raving, etc. You want concise information that isn't confused by emotional outbursts.
3. *Friendly*, in that you aren't simply responding in anger. You are much more likely to end the conflict by not escalating but rather maintaining a friendly tone, even if you are tempted to respond in anger. Don't overdo it. Just keep the tone relaxed and non-antagonistic.
4. *Firm*, in that you stand your ground in a nonconfrontational way. Simply state your position clearly, and don't leave the door open for more negotiation (unless, of course, that is what you want; Eddy, 2011).

These rules support a business relationship model in that they communicate only about the business that needs to be transacted (e.g., information exchange, coordination or decisions about the children). In addition, the communication should be brief, respectful (in a letter format, including a salutation) and offer no commentary about the conduct of the other parent.

Once you have set the rules, your role is to monitor and "train" the parents in this business model of communication. If necessary (e.g., in the case of a failure to comply with the e-mail rules), you can intervene, first by providing feedback about problems with the e-mail communication and then, if there is a continuing pattern of problems, requiring the parent to send the e-mail first to you for editing so you can make any needed corrections before sending the e-mail. The problem parent, of course should be required to pay for that editing function by the PC, which tends to motivate that parent to address the problems identified.

The volume of e-mails between parents (which can be observed quickly in the parenting coordination process by having a standard directive after the first meeting that they copy you on all of their e-mail communications) is often extreme—literally, 20+ e-mails a day in some cases. From the point of view of the goals of the parenting coordination process, to reduce coparenting engagement to the minimum necessary to support a parallel coparenting model, e-mail communication between the parents rarely needs to occur more than once a day. Once a week is more than likely adequate. See Appendix 5.2 (located at http://pubs.apa.org/books/supp/higuchi) for an example of a weekly e-mail exchange protocol for parents where the father has Wednesday after school until Monday morning on alternate weeks and the mother has the remainder of the time share. These parents began with an e-mail volume of several per day. The once-a-week e-mail provided in the appendix is an example of batching coparenting communication.

The PC e-mail protocol for the case described in Appendix 5.2 required both parents to send only one e-mail per week and, therefore, "batch" child-related requests, discussion items, and other matters into one e-mail, rather than sending them piecemeal. As can be seen, an additional rule was that particular issues specified whether it was a for-your-information e-mail or a communication that requested a response. The response rule was that the receiving parent had to respond within 48 hours. This limited the possible total of four e-mails being exchanged per week. This structure, supported by twice-monthly meetings, worked for these parents, who shared custody of four children (and so lots of logistics).

There are many practice issues for PCs who work in cyberspace. They include reimbursement for time working in cyberspace (e-mail), structuring e-mail communication (bounding, accessibility), and risk management issues of working in cyberspace, such as confidentiality, unsecured networks, informed consent, and protecting electronic case information.

Practice Tip: You may have clients agree that you will estimate time spent on a monthly basis for the e-mail monitoring function that was described above. Even an underestimate of the monthly time spent on this task is preferable to taking the time to record each e-mail read.

When PCs work in cyberspace, creating functional PC–client boundaries through explicit practice procedures and protocols is essential to managing the challenges and violations of those boundaries that are common in parenting coordination work. You must provide clear rules and expectations about your own e-mail availability to clients in order to train them to be more proactive and structured in their approach to coparenting. Client expectations of the PC having open, 24/7 accessibility (e-mail or otherwise) reinforces dysfunctional coparenting patterns. Letting clients know that "your emergency does not make it my emergency" is important training for clients and important self-care for you as the PC. In my view, there is no legitimate reason why a PC should be available during nonregular working hours. True emergencies are more appropriately handled by emergency services (either medical, psychiatric, or law enforcement). Other issues and disputes that are raised as emergencies between parents are nearly always the result of poor planning, avoidance of dealing with the issue, or deliberate attempts to undermine parenting plans and create conflict. For this reason, they are best handled in a deliberate manner in the structured parenting coordination processes described above.

PCs who work in cyberspace face greater permeability in work and nonwork boundaries. The more recent explosion of the Internet, in particular e-mail and the "crackberry" phenomenon[2] has made 24/7 connectivity to clients both possible and seductive, but it should be resisted.

> **Practice Tip:** When you do work, such as summary letters, during nonwork times (evenings/weekends), save them and send them first thing the next workday. This maintains the clarity of availability boundaries.

Using the Internet in parenting coordination work (or in the provision of any psychological services) requires the transmission of confidential client information over the Internet and storing client information on computers, and likely mobile devices and clouds. I address a variety of issues below and offer some management suggestions. The informed consent service agreement should address your intent to use the Internet to transmit information in your work with clients. The example given in Appendix 5.3 (located at http://pubs.apa.org/books/supp/higuchi) of an informed consent provision, which requires the review and agreement of parenting coordination clients, highlights the potential risks of transmitting such information and documents the agreement of clients to use the Internet in their case.

With regard to transmitting case information, two types of information are commonly transmitted: (a) e-mails and (b) attached documents.

[2]The *crackberry phenomenon* is the tendency to be connected at all times by smartphone to clients through e-mail, text, and phone.

Both e-mails and attached documents should be sent on secured (password-protected) networks. E-mail communications should have an accompanying statement such as the following to address the confidentiality of the transmission:

> Notice: This e-mail is covered by Electronic Communication Privacy Act, 18 U.S.C. §§ 2510-2521 and is legally privileged. This e-mail and any file transmitted is confidential and intended only for the person(s) to whom this e-mail message is addressed. Do not rely on e-mail for urgent matters. Any use of e-mail is at your own risk.

An additional protection for attached documents you may send is to pay for a service that allows you to encrypt the document before sending. Encryption provides an added protection in that the receiver is verified before he or she can access the attached document. Though not currently required by standards of practice, encryption will likely be a requirement in the future.

> **Practice Tip:** You should meet or exceed emerging standards of practice that address the security of electronically stored client information.

MANAGING A PARENTING COORDINATION PRACTICE: SELF-CARE AND RISK MANAGEMENT

Parenting coordination is one of the most challenging roles a psychologist can undertake. The combination of working with difficult clients in high-conflict relationships in a court-involved context can feel like trying to captain a ship in a perfect storm. Parenting coordination can be isolating work, particularly in a private practice setting, and strategies to prevent isolation and build professional support are essential to self-care. PCs who have longevity in this practice area must cultivate relationships with trusted colleagues who can be available as mentors and consultants when cases present particular dilemmas and challenges. Utilizing consultative relationships with attorneys and other mental heath professionals increases effective practice, manages role stress, and is an important risk management strategy. The structure of consultation can vary from one-on-one relationships (sometimes across the country, via e-mail, phone, and videoconferencing) and group consultation settings. I have conducted a monthly consultation group via videoconferencing with parenting coordination professionals in another state for several months. Finally, setting up collaborative teams of specialized professionals (e.g., child therapists, adult therapists, family therapists, substance abuse specialists, learning specialists, psychiatrists, school placement specialists) in more complex cases can help share and defuse the stresses and challenges of managing these cases (Greenberg & Sullivan, 2012).

REFERENCES

Association of Family and Conciliation Courts, Task Force on Parenting Coordination. (2006). Guidelines for parenting coordination. *Family Court Review, 44*, 164–181. doi:10.1111/j.1744-1617.2006.00074.x

Eddy, B. (2011). *BIFF: Quick responses to high conflict people, their emails, personal attacks and social meltdowns*. Scottsdale, AZ: High Conflict Institute Press.

Greenberg, L., & Sullivan, M. J. (2012). Parenting coordinator and therapist collaboration in high-conflict custody cases. *Journal of Child Custody, 9*, 85–107. doi:10.1080/15379418.2012.652571

Kelly, J. B. (2008). Preparing for the parenting coordination role: Training needs for mental health and legal professionals. *Journal of Child Custody, 5*, 140–159. doi:10.1080/15379410802070476

Kirkland, K. (2008). Parenting coordination (PC) laws, rules, and regulations: A jurisdictional comparison. *Journal of Child Custody, 5*, 25–52. doi:10.1080/15379410802070377

Kirkland, K., & Sullivan, M. (2008). Parenting coordination (PC) practice: A survey of experienced professionals. *Family Court Review, 46*, 622–636. doi:10.1111/j.1744-1617.2008.00228.x

Sullivan, M. J. (2008). Coparenting and the parenting coordination process. *Journal of Child Custody, 5*, 4–24. doi:10.1080/15379410802070351

Zur, O., Williams, M. H., Lehavot, K., & Knapp, S. (2009). Psychotherapist self-disclosure and transparency in the Internet age. *Professional Psychology: Research and Practice, 40*, 22–30. doi:10.1037/a0014745

6

ETHICAL ISSUES AND RISK MANAGEMENT IN PARENTING COORDINATION

ROBIN M. DEUTSCH AND STEPHEN J. LALLY

In this chapter, we explore the ethical issues that can arise in a parenting coordination case. As an emerging area, the practice of parenting coordination was both inconsistent and varied when first surveyed in 2001 (Coates, Deutsch, Starnes, Sullivan, & Sydlik, 2004). Guidance and best practices have been available only since the development of the first guidelines, initially by the Association of Family and Conciliation Courts, Task Force on Parenting Coordination (hereafter AFCC, 2006) and, more recently, the American Psychological Association (APA, 2012). Initial questions about this hybrid role considered first the question of whether parenting coordinators (PCs) are acting as a licensed professional in their field (e.g., psychologist, social worker, lawyer) and whether they needed to comply with the ethical principles and standards of their field (e.g., the APA Ethics Code; APA, 2010a). There appears to be a consensus among malpractice insurance carriers, active PCs, and the organizations that sponsored the development of

http://dx.doi.org/10.1037/14390-007
Parenting Coordination in Postseparation Disputes: A Comprehensive Guide for Practitioners, S. A. Higuchi and S. J. Lally (Editors)

guidelines for parenting coordination that in fact PCs bring the experiences, training, skills, and expertise of their particular profession to this role and are therefore subject to the ethics code that guides their profession.

Our review of ethics and risk management issues surrounding parenting coordination is informed by the published PC guidelines (AFCC, 2006; APA, 2012) as well as other relevant ethical standards and guidelines (APA, 2003, 2007, 2010a, 2010b, 2013). Although these other standards and guidelines were developed by individuals in the profession of psychology, they are relevant to the risk management practices of nonpsychologist PCs. Within psychology, standards and guidelines are differentiated, with *standards* defined as mandatory, enforceable rules and *guidelines* pertaining to recommended behavior and conduct (APA, 2002). Guidelines are meant to be educational and aspirational in nature. Our discussion in this chapter is informed by a growing literature in this area (e.g., Barsky, 2011; Fidler & Epstein, 2008; Sullivan, 2004) and developing state rules and regulations. We organize our discussion around seven major areas of potential risk for PCs: (a) competence, (b) informed consent, (c) confidentiality, (d) role clarity, (e) conflicts of interest, (f) record keeping, and (g) ethics and risk management.

COMPETENCE

Standard 2.01 of APA's (2010a) *Ethical Principles of Psychologists and Code of Conduct* (hereafter the *Ethics Code*) states that psychologists can provide services only within the boundaries of their competence "based on their education, training, supervised experience, consultation, study, or professional experience." The specialty guidelines for forensic psychology (Guideline 2.01, APA, 2013) similarly note that psychologists consider their relevant training and experience as well as the opportunity to consult a competent colleague in deciding the scope of their practice in forensic matters. In addition, the two published PC guidelines (Guideline I, AFCC, 2006; and Guideline 3, APA, 2012) both emphasize the need to attain training and experience in a variety of areas to function in an ethical and legally responsible manner. As described in Chapters 3 and 4 of this volume, parenting coordination is a hybrid role that requires multiple areas of knowledge. Both sets of guidelines (AFCC, 2006; APA, 2012) emphasize the need for the PC to maintain these competencies with continued training and consultation. This is consistent with APA's ethical standards (Standard 2.03, APA, 2010a) as well as the specialty guidelines for forensic psychologists (APA, 2013). Core competencies include psychological knowledge, applicable legal knowledge, and mediation skills. The ethics standards (Standard 2.01b, APA, 2010a), the specialty guidelines for forensic psychologists (Guideline 2.08, APA, 2013), and APA's

(2003) multicultural guidelines also recognize the importance of having a knowledge and appreciation of the impact of individual and group differences on the services provided. This is especially important as the United States becomes increasingly racially and ethnically diverse. In addition, PCs must have skill and expertise in any special issues specific to the particular case (e.g., if a child has autism, the PC should have knowledge and understanding of the disorder and the needs associated with it).

Competencies can be obtained through education, training, supervised experience, consultation, study, and professional experience, but most essential is specific training in parenting coordination. The APA Ethics Code (Standard 2.01e, 2010a) states that "in those emerging areas in which generally recognized standards for preparatory training do not yet exist, [we] nevertheless take reasonable steps to ensure the competence of their work and to protect clients/patients . . . from harm." Parenting coordination does not have a comprehensive, fully articulated curriculum for training, but the two sets of published guidelines help standardize the training of PCs (AFCC, 2006; APA, 2012; see also Chapter 3, this volume). Specific areas of core training are described in both sets of guidelines. Both guidelines also note the importance of "peer consultation or mentoring" (AFCC, 2006, p. 166) or "case supervision, professional and peer supervision" (APA, 2012, p. 67) in both attaining and maintaining one's competence.

All PCs, regardless of profession, must be familiar with the legal framework within which a parenting coordination case resides. Becoming familiar with the judicial or administrative rules and procedures that govern their role is an ethical and professional responsibility that is noted in APA's Ethics Code (Standard 2.01f, APA, 2010a), the specialty guidelines for forensic psychology practice (Guideline 2b, APA, 2013), and the two sets of parenting coordination guidelines (AFCC, 2006; APA, 2012). In order to practice this role, a PC needs to be familiar specifically with the scope of authority, areas of decision making, and requirements for or prohibitions on reporting to the court. Likewise, attorneys and mediators without a background in mental health may have the familiarity with the legal framework but still need the requisite training, education, and experience with relevant areas of psychological knowledge as listed within the AFCC guidelines (see Appendix A, AFCC, 2006), the APA guidelines (Guideline 3, APA, 2012), and in Chapter 3, this volume.

When a case is referred for parenting coordination services, it is the PC's ethical responsibility to determine whether he or she has sufficient training, education, and experience to take that specific case. For example, if the case includes very young children and the PC's role is to modify the parenting plan as the children develop, the PC should be knowledgeable about pertinent research on attachment and parenting plans for young children. When a case involves experiences or identities that differ from those of the PC, the PC should endeavor to acquire knowledge of the culturally specific issues, seek consultation, or decline the referral (Guideline 5b, APA, 2012).

INFORMED CONSENT

The need to obtain informed consent is recognized in both ethical standards (Standard 3.10, APA, 2010) and guidelines governing PCs (Guidelines V, VIII, and IX, AFCC, 2006; Guidelines 2b, 5a, and 5b, APA, 2012) as well as other relevant guidelines (APA, 2007), and even within state regulations and guidelines (e.g., Oregon). Although some jurisdictions (e.g., Oklahoma, Colorado) allow the appointment of a PC over the objection of one party, even in these situations it is important to provide information about the process and attempt to gain assent from all parties. In gaining consent, or assent, it is important that the information be provided in a manner that is easily comprehended, and the parties need to be competent to agree to participate (see Beck & Frost, 2006, for a discussion of competency to participate in mediation as an example of this process). It is important for the informed consent process to be documented, and it has been suggested that the PC use the court order as a framework for the discussion and documentation of the consent (Sullivan, 2004). Informed consent is an ongoing process that must be reviewed at the outset of the parenting coordination process and revisited as necessary.

It has been articulated in standards and guidelines (APA, 2010a, 2012; AFCC, 2006), as well as by other authors (Barsky, 2011; Sullivan, 2004), that informed consent should include, at a minimum, a discussion of the nature, process, and course of parenting coordination; fees; grievance procedures; record keeping; and confidentiality. Of particular importance is the specific arbitration authority of the PC, which is the sine qua non of the PC role. Explaining to the parties the areas established by court order or private consent agreement in which the PC can and cannot make decisions is a critical part of the informed consent process. The PC's decisions are binding (see Chapter 2, this volume, for a more detailed discussion of this) in some jurisdictions, as well as in some court orders and consent agreements, and in others they are not. That distinction often needs repeated explanation to parent clients as the parenting coordination intervention continues.

The responsibilities of the PC should be discussed throughout the parenting coordination case, but the PC must review his or her functions and duties at the outset and provide clarification as needed. Because parenting coordination is a process that involves decision-making authority, in general, the parties must agree to the PC role and responsibilities at the outset of the process. It is prudent to review the authority of the PC, including the process of decision making, and obtain the signed consent of the parties. Parties need very careful and detailed clarification of the process for resolving disputes. It is typical that one party must trigger the decision-making function. The other party must then be able to respond to proceed, or to offer another resolution. Both parties need to be assured that they will each have the opportunity to respond to the dispute with a proposed resolution and rationale.

PCs are frequently professionals such as psychologists or other mental health workers, lawyers, or mediators whose non-PC roles are confidential and in which confidentiality is an essential feature of the relationship. Parenting coordination does not have that same requirement. Careful initial and ongoing explanation of the nonconfidential nature of the relationship is essential. The PC may receive information from a variety of sources: from within the relationship, from the family, from the professionals involved, and from other persons familiar with the parties or their children. It is important that parents have an understanding of how confidentiality will be handled with these other groups. If the PC is required to make a decision to resolve a dispute in which there are no confidentiality protections, it is unnecessary for the PC to obtain further authority or permission to offer a decision based on information from others.

Parties involved in parenting coordination may be confused about the PC's role because of its hybrid nature. It is essential that the PC describe the limits of the role at the beginning of the process and throughout as the role is challenged and the expectations may exceed the functions of the PC. This potential ethical conflict was noted as a frequent problem in a survey of Florida PCs, attorneys, and judges (Fieldstone, Lee, Baker, & McHale, 2012). It is not uncommon for clients to request legal advice from the PC, including whether they should change lawyers, whom they should get for a lawyer, or whether they should take an issue to court. These questions are beyond the scope of the PC's authority. The PC can remind the parents that a disputed issue can be heard by the court if one or both parties do not agree with the PC's decision. The parents' ability to return to the court is written into the PC's agreement as a due process protection. PCs should not provide therapeutic assistance. As noted earlier in this volume, because parenting coordination is an intervention with multiple functions (see, e.g., Chapter 2), it is easy for a PC to slip into the role of therapist. Explaining the different functions a PC can provide, as well as those the PC cannot provide, is part of the informed consent process at the beginning and, as necessary, throughout the process.

CONFIDENTIALITY

An important part of the informed consent process is to provide information about the limits of confidentiality (Guideline V, AFCC, 2006; Guideline 5b, APA, 2012). Parenting coordination is not a confidential process in that the circle of people who know about the content and process of the work with a family includes both the parents, and potentially other professionals involved with the family, their lawyers, and the court. There is no PC–client privilege, unlike in mediation, where confidentiality applies and extends to the court, or in psychotherapy or legal representation, where the therapist–client or attorney–client privilege applies (see Chapter 2, this volume, for additional discussion of these issues). The PC may be subpoenaed to court to testify, and in some jurisdictions it is part of the court order for the PC to provide information to the court.

Although the PC must explain to the parents that the parenting coordination process is not confidential, there may be some communications within the PC process that the parties involved agree can be confidential. For example, if the PC is meeting individually with a parent at either the parent's request or as part of the PC's caucusing during a session, the PC should first discuss whether the parents agree to caucus or to have individual meetings. With the parents' agreement, the PC then discusses with both parents what, if anything, will remain confidential between the parties. The parties may agree that the general themes of the separate sessions are not confidential (e.g., discussing concerns about a parent's drinking, or frustrations with the process, or an attempt to reach compromise) but that the specific disclosures will not be shared. In these separate meetings, the parties must be informed about the exceptions to confidentiality (e.g., child abuse reporting).

Mental health professionals are mandated reporters and so are required by state laws and regulations to report certain events (i.e., abuse or neglect of children, elderly individuals, or incapacitated adults; imminent danger to readily identifiable others). Some states, and many experienced PCs, urge attorneys and other PCs without a mental health background who are not covered by these state laws to also make mandated reporting issues a part of their process. PCs inform the parents, and the children, if interviewed, that if there is a suspicion of abuse or neglect, or concern that any of the parties involved may be dangerous to themselves or another, it will be reported to the proper agency. Although a report may result in the termination of a PC's services, it is just as likely that the PC's work will continue with the family. If the PC has explained the exception carefully and engages the parents in the process of reporting so it is not a surprise to the parents, most parents are able to work through the professional necessity of the report.

When interviewing children it is good practice to let the child know at the outset of the interview that the PC will review with the child any information to be shared with the parents. The child may not want some information shared, and the PC will keep that information confidential, unless it meets a reporting mandate, discussing with the child the information that the PC will share to help the parents focus on the child's needs and wishes and coparent more effectively (for a more detailed discussion of this, see Chapter 9). Before interviewing a child the PC should discuss the confidentiality process with the parents and gain their agreement to allow some material not to be shared with the parents. It is important to note that in many states, depending on the age of the child, in the absence of such an agreement laws and regulations support the parents' access to the information shared by the child. Most important in the parenting coordination process is that informed consent, including an explanation of the limits of confidentiality, is an ongoing process and not a moment in time. Although the first parenting coordination session or two are devoted at least in part to the explanation of the process (including role definition, areas of decision making, process of decision making, and limits of confidentiality), the explanations and clarifications continue throughout the PC's involvement as issues emerge.

ROLE CLARITY AND CONFLICTS

PCs need to avoid multiple relationships or conflicts that may appear to impair the their objectivity, competence, or effectiveness (see Standard 3.05, APA, 2010a; Guideline 1, APA, 2012; Guideline 4.02, APA, 2013). A *multiple relationship* exists when the practitioner is in a professional role with a person, such as serving as the PC, and simultaneously in another role with that person or someone closely associated or related to that person. A multiple relationship can also exist where there is a promise to enter into a future relationship with the person or someone closely associated with the person (APA, 2010a). For example, PCs should avoid personal or business relationships with the parties in the matter, or their relatives or significant others. This can become quite challenging if a PC has been working with the parents and then one of the parents begins a relationship with someone whom the PC has seen in psychotherapy or mediation, represented as an attorney, or evaluated as part of a custody evaluation. If such a situation occurs, the PC must take reasonable steps to resolve the multiple relationship with regard to confidentiality issues and potential harm (Standard 3.05b, APA, 2010a).

PCs must also be clear that they cannot serve in sequential roles with the same parties (Guideline IV, AFCC, 2006; Guideline 1, APA, 2012; Guideline 7, APA, 2010b). For example, a professional cannot move from being a couple's therapist to being a PC, even if the couple requests the role shift. The two roles are very different in terms of confidentiality requirements and role definition. It would be extremely difficult for the PC to maintain the boundaries of the hybrid PC role if the parties had experience viewing the PC as a therapist, which is a more intimate relationship regardless of the theoretical orientation of the therapist. The change in roles can potentially cause confusion and feelings that may cause harm to the client and the relationship. Likewise, if a professional was previously a consultant to one of the parties, he or she cannot switch roles to become the PC. A professional cannot move from an individual therapy, consultation, or legal counsel role to a PC role.

PCs also cannot become custody evaluator (i.e., someone who is evaluating the parenting capacity of the parents), either during their term as a PC or after it has concluded (Guideline IV, AFCC, 2006; Guideline 1, APA, 2012; Guideline 7, APA, 2010b). The differences between the two, even if both are court-ordered roles, may result in potential harm and confusion for the parties. There are differences of opinion, however, about whether an individual can first serve as a custody evaluator and then later become the parents' PC. Often, judges, attorneys, and the parents want the custody evaluator to become the PC, in part because the family and its issues and conflicts are so well known to the evaluator. However, the roles are very different, and one could argue that the results of the evaluation may create the impression of bias or partiality. Custody evaluators who take on the PC role, must do so with great caution, noting the differences between the roles.

There are also some differences in opinion among the AFCC (2006) and APA (2012) guidelines about an individual who first served as a mediator later becoming the PC for those same parents. The strongest argument against it involves the differences in confidentiality requirements. Mediation is a confidential role, and parenting coordination is not. PCs who were former mediators in the same dispute and who are required to testify in court would find it very difficult to suspend all their knowledge from mediation, compartmentalizing that information and process, and shielding it from testimony. On the other hand, if the parents agree that the mediator will help them resolve their dispute and come to a mutually agreeable solution, without the requirement that it is a confidential process, that neutral situation could potentially move into another alternative dispute-resolution process, such as parenting coordination.

Beyond these guidelines and cautions, the issues we have discussed so far must be considered in the context of the jurisdiction and region in which the PC practices. In rural communities it may be very difficult, or even unavoidable, to maintain role differentiation, and professionals may need to fill more than one sequential role or engage in more than one relationship. Professionals who live in a small town or rural area are probably not working in anyone's best interests if they isolate themselves or avoid commerce in the area. However, professionals in smaller towns need to ask themselves if the multiple relationships in which they may end up will cause harm or be exploitive (Guideline 3.05, APA, 2010a). If they are not deemed harmful and exploitative, and a professional believes the relationship will be necessary, he or she should provide accurate and repeated information about the role differences and be sure to avoid harming any clients. Younggren and Gottlieb (2004) advised that when practitioners consider entering a multiple relationship, they think prospectively about how a professional disciplinary body may retrospectively consider the relationship if a complaint is filed. Documentation of the decision-making process, including consultation with other professionals, will help practitioners manage risk.

Another challenge to PCs is maintaining role clarity. Clients may pull for a PC to act as a therapist, an evaluator, or a parenting coach, and the PC may find it easy to drift into that other role, as it is related to the role of the PC. A PC is not conducting family therapy, couples therapy, or individual therapy. If any of those functions appear to be necessary, the PC is obligated to refer the clients to a therapist to meet the apparent need. If the PC believes the client or any combination of family members needs psychotherapeutic services and the PC is fulfilling that role in some capacity, that is the sign that a referral is necessary. It is the PC's job to maintain the boundaries of his or her role and refer out for the services the parties require. Some of the red flags the PC should attend to include meeting with one party frequently, as opposed to the couple; attempting to assess parenting capacity in order to make decisions; providing ongoing therapeutic or legal guidance to one of the parties; and not billing for time spent with one or both parties.

CONFLICTS OF INTEREST

There are times when a professional may receive an appointment from the court to serve as a PC, without the court being aware that that individual cannot serve because of a conflict of interest due to personal, professional, legal, financial, or other interests or to relationships that could appear to impair their objectivity (Standard 3.06, APA, 2010a; Guideline 4.02, APA, 2012). In this case, the individual must decline the appointment, explaining to the court that it presents a conflict of interest (Guideline III, AFCC, 2006) and that as a professional he or she needs to avoid situations that can create bias in action or appearance (Guideline II, AFCC, 2006). It has been argued that allegations of bias (Barsky, 2011; Sullivan, 2004) are the most frequent complaints leveled against PCs. AFCC (2006) Guideline III states that a PC shall disclose potential conflicts of interest as soon as practical after he or she becomes aware of the conflict. Consider this example: A PC has been formally retained and has worked with a couple for 3 months when it comes to the PC's attention that one of the parents, the father, has been dating for 6 months a woman who was a party in a custody evaluation conducted by the PC 3 years prior. In this example, the PC has a conflict of interest because this previous relationship may compromise, or appear to compromise, his or her impartiality. The PC may not disclose the nature of the conflict, and even if the evaluation report is a matter of public record, because the PC will not want to disclose information that the girlfriend may consider private. The PC must inform the court that a conflict has emerged and suggest that a new PC be appointed.

PCs must not create conflict by providing other therapeutic, mediation, or legal services to parties who are related to or interested parties to the PC's clients. That would include family members and significant others. In addition, the PC cannot have any financial incentive or relationship that may, or even appear to, compromise impartiality. For example, a PC must not accept a stock tip from a client, buy a car from a client, or invest in a client's company.

Maintaining impartiality throughout the PC process can be difficult. PCs may be pulled in by the fame, celebrity, wealth, profession, or lifestyle of a client. One client may be more likable than the other, or offer fewer challenges to the PC. One of the clients may behave unreasonably or make greater demands on the PC. Payment delays may challenge the impartiality of the PC. To avoid bias, PCs need to be aware of their personal issues, triggers, and experiences that may lead to a compromise of their impartiality. PCs should always focus on maintaining impartiality. For example, a PC should keep the focus on the children and the impact of agreements and decisions on the children; carefully listen to both parents; and strive to ensure that all decisions are data driven and that, to an outside observer, the rationales for all decisions are clear and defensible.

RECORD KEEPING

As noted in APA's (2007) "Record Keeping Guidelines," records benefit both practitioners and clients in the documenting of the planning and implementing of services, facilitating practitioners' monitoring of their work, and providing a record when there has been a significant gap in service or when another professional provides services. In addition, appropriate record keeping benefits both the practitioner and client in the event of a legal or ethical proceeding. The need for documentation of services and the maintenance of records is a requirement within APA's Ethics Code (Standard 6.01, APA, 2010a). APA's (2013) specialty guidelines for forensic psychology go even further and clearly indicate that documentation of all data in forensic matters (of which parenting coordination is a specific example) needs to be of "enough detail and quality to allow for reasonable judicial scrutiny and adequate discovery by all parties" (p. 10). In the hybrid role of a PC, the importance of thorough documentation and appropriate maintenance of records is arguably even higher than in other areas of forensic practice. The importance of adequate record keeping is noted in both the AFCC PC guidelines (Guideline X, AFCC, 2006) as well as APA's PC guidelines (Guideline 6, APA, 2012). A number of states (e.g., Arizona, Colorado, North Carolina, Oklahoma) have included specific record-keeping requirements for PCs in their laws and regulations, and leading authors have recommended specific requirements (e.g., Sullivan, 2004; see also Chapters 4 and 5 of this volume). In spite of these standards and guidelines, the laws, and the information in the literature, a recent national survey of PCs (Hayes, Grady, & Brantley, 2012) made it clear that there is still uncertainty about the level of appropriate documentation and with whom the documentation should be shared. Of note is that over one third of the surveyed PCs reported there were no legal requirements to document sessions, and 16% believed they had no requirement to document decisions (Hayes et al., 2012).

Guideline 2 of APA's (2007) record-keeping guidelines provides a comprehensive review of issues related to the content of records, including considerations regarding the level of detail, that provides a good foundation for both psychologist and nonpsychologist PCs. Guideline VII of the AFCC (2006) guidelines notes that there should be a written agreement covering issues not addressed in the court order; fee payments, billing practices, and retainers are cited as specific examples. In Chapter 5 of this volume, Matthew J. Sullivan describes in detail issues to be covered in the court order (e.g., under what authority the PC operates, the scope of the PC's authority, procedures and fees, grievance procedures, terms of appointment, and termination/withdrawal) as well as a service agreement. Such an agreement—along with the order, the parenting plan, custody evaluations, and other pre-parenting coordination legal documents—need to be maintained in the record.

Each meeting with the parents, whether in person or on the phone, needs to be documented, including the date, time, duration, persons in attendance, and a summary of the content of the meeting. Records should be maintained of any e-mail communication (see Chapter 5, this volume, for a more detailed discussion of electronic communication within the parenting coordination process). Consistent with the specialty guidelines of forensic psychology (APA, 2007), the records need to be detailed enough to provide sufficient foundation for any decisions. All decisions and agreements resolving disputed issues should be dated and, as much as possible, written bilaterally with the parents (see Chapters 4 and 5 for additional details about writing agreements and a sample summary letter). Consistent with AFCC (2006) Guideline X, the PC should document whether a resolution was agreed on by the parties or whether it was the result of arbitration. Depending on the court order and the jurisdiction, summaries of meetings and agreements may be forwarded to both parents, their attorneys, and the court. It is important that agreements are written in clear language, and we recommend that letters to the parents include a request for them to "please review this letter for accuracy." Any disputes about the content of an agreement are better resolved in close proximity to the time of the agreement.

In addition to the resolutions that are agreed on, AFCC (2006) Guideline X also recommends that the record include notes from all conversations with parents, children, and other persons with whom the PC communicates regarding the case. Files of e-mails from the parties need to be secured in a safe manner. In addition, the record should include billing information and court dates. Consistent with the record-keeping guidelines (APA, 2007) and the AFCC (2006) guidelines (Guideline X), it is the PC's responsibility to create detailed, legible, professional, and comprehensive records of the parenting coordination process and information related to that process and the decisions made by the PC. The PC must maintain the record in a secure manner to protect it from unauthorized access, or damage and destruction. APA's (2007) record-keeping guidelines provide a detailed discussion of issues regarding security as well as the length of record retention and disposition of records.

ETHICS AND RISK MANAGEMENT

Working with high-conflict couples can be cumulatively stressful for the PC. Some basic guiding principles can be useful in helping PCs minimize risk and maximize self-care. Being clear about one's role and understanding the legal and ethical obligations is the first guiding principle. Similarly, in light of Ethics Code Standard 2.06b (APA, 2010a), psychologists—and, by extension, PCs—need to be aware of when personal problems are beginning to interfere with their professional duties and either seek consultation or limit, suspend, or terminate those duties. This suggests that PCs need to also take steps to prevent such problems from arising. The Ethics Code (Standard 2.03, APA, 2010a) reminds psychologists to undertake ongoing efforts to develop and maintain their competence. For all PCs, regardless of professional affiliation, those efforts include not only education and training but also self-care, including self-awareness and recognition of difficulties associated with this work and in themselves (Wise, Hersh, & Gibson, 2011; see also Chapter 5, this volume). Relying on guidelines and best practices (AFCC, 2006; APA, 2012, 2013) and making use of consultation (Guideline I, AFCC, 2006;

Guidelines 2a and 3, APA, 2012; Guidelines 2.01 and 2.02, APA, 2013) are essential to being a competent PC and for maintaining one's own health and welfare.

REFERENCES

American Psychological Association. (2002). Criteria for practice guideline development and evaluation. *American Psychologist, 57*, 1048–1051. doi:10.1037/0003-066X.57.12.1048

American Psychological Association. (2003). *Guidelines on multicultural education, training, research, practice, and organizational change for psychologists*. Retrieved from http://www.apa.org/pi/oema/resources/policy/provider-guidelines.aspx

American Psychological Association. (2007). Record keeping guidelines. *American Psychologist, 62*, 993–1004. doi:10.1037/0003-066X.62.9.993

American Psychological Association. (2010a). *Ethical principles of psychologists and code of conduct (2002; revised June 1, 2010)*. Retrieved from http://www.apa.org/ethics/code/principles.pdf

American Psychological Association. (2010b). Guidelines for child custody evaluations in family law proceedings. *American Psychologist, 65*, 863–867. doi:10.1037/a0021250

American Psychological Association. (2012). Guidelines for the practice of parenting coordination. *American Psychologist, 67*, 63–71. doi:10.1037/a0024646

American Psychological Association. (2013). Specialty guidelines for forensic psychology. *American Psychologist, 68*, 7–19. doi:10.1037/a0029889

Association of Family and Conciliation Courts, Task Force on Parenting Coordination. (2006). Guidelines for parenting coordination. *Family Court Review, 44*, 164–181. doi:10.1111/j.1744-1617.2006.00074.x

Barsky, A. E. (2011). Parenting coordination: The risks of a hybrid conflict resolution process. *Negotiation Journal, 27*, 7–27. doi:10.1111/j.1571-9979.2010.00290.x

Beck, C. J. A., & Frost, L. E. (2006). Defining a threshold for client competence to participate in divorce mediation. *Psychology, Public Policy, and Law, 12*, 1–35. doi:10.1037/1076-8971.12.1.1

Coates, C. A., Deutsch, R., Starnes, H., Sullivan, M. J., & Sydlik, B. L. (2004). Parenting coordination for high conflict families. *Family Court Review, 42*, 246–262. doi:10.1177/1531244504422006

Fidler, B. J., & Epstein, P. (2008). Parenting coordination in Canada: An overview of legal and practice issues. *Journal of Child Custody, 5*, 53–87. doi:10.1080/15379410802070393

Fieldstone, L., Lee, M. C., Baker, J. K., & McHale, J. P. (2012). Perspectives on parenting coordination: Views of parenting coordinators, attorneys, and judiciary members. *Family Court Review, 50*, 441–454. doi:10.1111/j.1744-1617.2012.01459.x

Hayes, S., Grady, M., & Brantley, H. T. (2012). E-mails, statutes, and personality disorders: A contextual examination of the processes, interventions, and perspectives of parenting coordinators. *Family Court Review, 50*, 429–440. doi:10.1111/j.1744-1617.2012.01458.x

Sullivan, M. J. (2004). Ethical, legal, and professional practice issues involved in acting as a psychologist parenting coordinator in child custody cases. *Family Court Review, 42*, 576–582. doi:10.1177/1531244504042000313

Wise, E. H., Hersh, M., & Gibson, C. M. (2011). Ethics and self-care: A developmental lifespan perspective. *The Register Report*, 20–29. Retrieved from http://www.e-psychologist.org/index.iml?mdl=exam/show_article.mdl&Material_ID=117

Younggren, J. N., & Gottlieb, M. C. (2004). Managing risk when contemplating multiple relationships. *Professional Psychology: Research and Practice, 35*, 255–260. doi:10.1037/0735-7028.35.3.255

7

STRATEGIES FOR WORKING WITH DIFFICULT CLIENTS

MATTHEW J. SULLIVAN

In this chapter, I focus on special topics that may arise in providing parenting coordination services to high-conflict parents. Psychologically vulnerable clients provide unique challenges to the parenting coordination process. Standard methods of providing parenting coordination may require an adjustment to typical practice. Included within this area are the challenges of working with parents who have personality vulnerabilities (e.g., histrionic, narcissistic, borderline, and antisocial personality disorders). Later in the chapter, I present a case scenario to demonstrate how to keep the parenting coordination process from getting derailed.

The challenges of working in high-conflict, shared-custody arrangements stem from the mutual interaction of three levels of impasse in the separation and divorce transition: (a) individual, (b) interpersonal, and (c) contextual (Johnston & Campbell, 1988; Johnston, Roseby, & Kuehnle, 2009). When this array of negative parental, coparental, and surrounding

http://dx.doi.org/10.1037/14390-008
Parenting Coordination in Postseparation Disputes: A Comprehensive Guide for Practitioners, S. A. Higuchi and S. J. Lally (Editors)

system factors affects children, the parent's maladaptive behaviors reverberate through the family system to create a perfect storm of shared-custody dysfunction.

Within the individual level of impasse, parenting coordination cases are predominated by parents who suffer from significant personality vulnerabilities. In the *Diagnostic and Statistical Manual of Mental Disorders* (fifth edition; American Psychiatric Association, 2013) paradigm, parenting coordination cases are populated by parents who have personality pathology. The narcissistic, histrionic, borderline, and antisocial typologies are characterized as "conflict engagers." Guided by the principle "If there is a problem in my situation, it's someone else's responsibility to fix it," the interpersonal perceptual distortions and maladaptive coping strategies of these clients manifest in problematic patterns of interactions with the other parent, professionals involved, and, unfortunately, their children. When in the parenting coordination role, the major challenge of the work stems from both these interpersonal difficulties playing out with the parents and with the parenting coordinator (PC) in the case management role.

Despite each parent's assertions that he or she is the healthy individual in the coparent dyad, it is a rare high-conflict case where only one parent manifests significant personality vulnerability, though each parent may have quite a different character style and contributions to the conflict. In fact, clinical experience suggests that narcissistic/dependent and histrionic/compulsive coparent pairings are common in the high-conflict population.

The next level of systemic impasse is one involving interpersonal conflict that was often present throughout the intimate relationship and led to the dissolution of that partnership and contributes to the clients' inability to establish a functional coparenting relationship. Johnston et al. (2009) characterized these problematic separations as often traumatic, ambivalent, and with a high historical incidence of violent interaction. The entrenched negative engagement that culminated in these conflicted separations continues to organize the negatively polarized perceptions, beliefs, and behaviors of the other parent after separation.

Finally, at the contextual level of impasse, the conflicted parents have typically sought the alliance of extended family, members of their community, and legal and mental health professionals, creating a surrounding context of tribal warfare in their situation. Further exacerbating, entrenching, and polarizing their conflict is the fact that these parents have often been immersed in the legal adversarial court system since the onset of their separation. These "frequent flyers" of the family courts, who often have contested hearings several times a year, hone their litigation skills, which are adaptive in the legal–adversarial process of the court but are antithetical to functional coparenting. Table 7.1 lists the characteristics of strategies parents use that

TABLE 7.1
Characteristics Associated With Successful Litigants and Successful Parent Clients

Successful Litigants	Successful Parent Clients
Use relationship rules that are adversarial.	Use relationship rules that are cooperative.
Use legal representation for advocacy purposes.	Work directly and collaboratively with the other parent.
Frame self-interest as the child's interest.	Let the child's interest take precedence over self-interest.
Use strategies that undermine and sabotage the other parent's functioning.	Use strategies that support and enhance the other parent's functioning.
Demonstrate distrust that leads to minimal and selective sharing with the other parent.	Demonstrate trust that leads to open and honest sharing with the other parent.
Let chaos and obfuscation drive the litigation process.	Let structure and clear communication drive the coparenting process.
Use information to obtain an advantage with contested issues.	Use information to constructively solve coparenting problems.
Develop continued dependence on litigation as the process to address problems.	Develop collaborative strategies (negotiation, give-and-take) to address problems.
Blame the other, don't take responsibility for problems.	Admit one's contribution to problems, take responsibility.
Deplete financial and emotional resources on litigation.	Preserve financial and emotional resources for family needs.

are adaptive in litigation but create a tragic legacy that PCs inherit when they begin to work with these clients postadjudication.

After months, if not years, of litigation "training" in this context, these parents volunteer or are ordered into a parenting coordination process, with their financial and emotional resources depleted and their children often manifesting a variety of adjustment issues, stemming largely from exposure to the effects of their toxic conflict.

To be effective with these high-conflict parents, management of these clients requires the ability to construct and maintain clear and firm professional–client boundaries and to emphasize the need for each parent to take responsibility and to be accountable for his or her behavior in the process. The PC must be prepared and empowered by the court to impose and enforce consequences for problematic behavior and, ultimately, if this cannot be accomplished, must be vigilant to professional and personal risk that can emerge in this work.

When a PC inherits the typical case from the court system, he or she must orient the parents to a new, more functional model of engagement with each other. The PC must set the rules of engagement: the relationship structure between each parent and that between the PC and between the parents.

Setting this structure up immediately (through very detailed procedures) is both challenging and essential to management of the case. Maintaining the structure is even more challenging. In the following sections, I describe the establishment and maintenance of boundaries in parenting coordination work.

BOUNDARIES AND PARENTING COORDINATION WORK

The coparenting relationship will almost always require a parallel model of coparenting, with the enhancement being the communication linkage provided by the PC (Sullivan, 2008, 2013). A completely parallel model used in more severe cases is when the parents no longer work directly with each other but now work through the PC. In this instance the PC works with each parent individually and serves as a bridge of communication between each parent. This middle position or linkage function in the high-conflict coparenting relationship requires a well-articulated set of structures and boundaries to manage the coparenting relationship.

As I noted in Chapter 5 of this volume, PCs get into trouble in cases when they fail to immediately establish the rules of the relationship. These rules define expectations of client behavior in the PC process. The PC establishes the boundaries that will almost certainly be challenged sooner or later in his or her work with clients. Having these rules explicit, clear, and behaviorally specific is critical. This is accomplished by providing comprehensive policies and procedures for client conduct in the parenting coordination process. Ideally, these are spelled out in the "Order of Appointment of Parenting Coordinator" (see Appendix 7.1 for an example; located at http://pubs.apa.org/books/supp/higuchi), which I believe should be a standardized template order in the jurisdiction, not individually crafted and customized for each case. In Chapter 5, I discussed how PCs can comprehensively detail their policies and procedures in the appointment order, or in an informed consent/parenting coordination service agreement, if the PC has been appointed by private consent. The underlying structure for parenting coordination work must be in place before the PC begins work on a case, and this is best accomplished by working only with a court order or service agreement (if working with a private consent agreement). As discussed in Chapter 5, the appointment order should cover such areas as the PC's source and scope of authority, definitions of the rules of the parenting coordination procedures, payment of fees, and procedures to follow in the event of objections to or complaints about the PC.

Once the explicit rules of the relationship are set down, the work of maintaining these boundaries is the core "training" of parents that occurs in parenting coordination work. Although some tolerance of problematic behavior is expected, the PC must address violations of the policies and procedures, of expectations of functional coparenting, and of the parenting plan. If the rules in these three areas cannot be maintained, the PC process will certainly fail.

The behavioral theory and treatment that inform a PC about coparent training is enormously useful. First, expectations of conduct need to be behaviorally specific. What, precisely, is lateness to a meeting with the PC? How is lateness defined for a parent delivering a child to the other parent's home for a transition? What constitutes disrespect to one's coparent in e-mail communication? Second, can a violation of the rule/behavioral expectation be verified? If there is an allegation that the other parent violated a provision in the parenting plan and the only evidence involves a "he said, she said" allegation, or if a child is expected to be a witness to the violation, enforcement of the rule is probably not possible.

Third, coparent training is most effective when an immediate consequence is delivered. Consequences can include providing verbal negative feedback to a parent, documenting a violation in a letter to the parents, providing a letter describing the violation to the court, and direct sanctions (e.g., reallocating the fees for time the PC spent handling a particular issue), if this is permitted in the appointment order, or temporarily mandating that parent assume the full burden of transporting the child(ren). It is important not to forget providing positive consequences, such as verbal and written praise for good conduct.

The PC's continuous monitoring of cases and ready accessibility make immediate response to rule violations possible. A PC can address within minutes or hours an alleged violation of respectful, businesslike, and child-focused communication; lateness to a transition; or verification that a child has unilaterally been signed up for an extracurricular activity. The PC should investigate to determine whether a violation has occurred and, if so, intervene to address the situation. This is not possible through the courts, where such violations require the filing of contempt motions, which can literally take months to be heard. Finally, we know from behavioral theory that, for a consequence of a rule violation to be effective the magnitude and severity are not as important as a consistent, predicable consequence. Consequences that "fit the crime," that are not particularly punitive but reinforce the intolerance of problematic behavior are most effective. See Table 7.2 for a list of possible "sanctions" that PC's can have in their arsenal of tools to facilitate smooth work with parents.

Ideally, consequences for rule violations will have been discussed and agreed on before an offense occurs. It is easier to get up-front agreement for consequences, because parents often feel the other parent will be the one to violate rules. Once agreed on, these consequences should be documented in summaries of parenting coordination work, so it depersonalizes the PC's action when he or he is "forced" to provide a consequence to honor the parent's agreement.

TABLE 7.2
Parenting Coordinator Tools to Shape Client Behavior

Tool	Examples
Warnings with increasing potency	• Delivered just to one parent verbally • Delivered verbally to the parent with the other parent present • Delivered in writing to the parent as part of the case file • Put in a formal report to the court. Positive feedback is as potent as negative.
Sanctions	• Payment of the fees for the PC's time to address the issue, when the time was spent only on dealing with that issue • Driving responsibility: usually allocated equally, this can be temporarily allocated to one parent as a consequence for lateness • Contributing to a charity of the other parent's choice
Natural consequences	• Setting time frames for parents to respond to requests (48 hours is typical with an e-mail sent marked with "RR" [response requested]) can be paired with the up-front understanding that nonresponse allows the requesting parent to proceed with unilateral action (e.g., setting a health care appointment, signing up for parent participation on a field trip)

Note. PC = parenting coordinator.

PARALLEL PARENTING

Parallel parenting is a process whereby the PC disengages high-conflict parents as much as possible, while still supporting the critical functions of coparenting: child-focused information exchange and day-to-day decision making. A parallel parenting model consists of four areas of intervention or components:

1. a highly detailed parenting plan,
2. the appropriate communication channel between parents,
3. regular parent meetings to address issues that arise as parents implement their parenting plan, and
4. management of the parents' engagement with others who are involved with the family.

Coparenting conflict breeds in the areas where rules do not exist and where rules can have different interpretations. Many parenting plans that PCs inherit have both of these problems.

An initial task of PC work, after first setting up a detailed parenting plan, is to establish, monitor, and maintain a functional communication link between parents. To accomplish this, the PC manages the communication channel between the parents, and often between the parents and other professionals and nonprofessionals who may be involved with the child. The control and management of information between parents allows the PC to titrate the parents' engagement along a continuum. The continuum ranges from no direct contact (all communication goes through the PC) to direct but monitored contact through e-mail (all e-mail communication is copied to the PC). When setting up the appropriate communication channel for parents, the goal is to minimize the amount of conflictual communication that characterizes difficult clients, structure the nature of that communication, and monitor parent communication so that the essential functions of child-focused information exchange and decision-making occur, without unnecessary interaction that creates opportunities for conflict to escalate. As I described in Chapter 5, moving coparent engagement into cyberspace (e.g., e-mail communication) is extremely effective in creating functional disengagement in the communication between high-conflict parents.

The third component of conflict management is having regular joint parent meetings to address issues that arise as parents implement their parenting plan. These highly structured meetings provide the PC the opportunity to educate and train parents in functional engagement around child issues they need to address. Regular meetings, initially with higher frequency (twice a month) and moving to less frequency (sometimes twice a year), create a framework in which to train parents in addressing issues in a proactive, problem-solving manner. In these cases, the adage "An ounce of prevention is worth a pound of cure" is apt. The preferred goal of these meetings is to resolve, by the parents' agreement, child-related issues through more constructive dialogue, consultation from the PC, negotiation, and compromise. When efforts to resolve issues through agreement fail, the PC is usually empowered and expected to make a recommendation or decision to resolve the disputed issue.

Decisions that the PC makes in these cases ideally have a consistent focus on the best interests of the child and create an expectation on the parents' part of how the PC will decide future issues, should arbitration by the PC be necessary. This consistency and predictability of responses by the PC (accompanied by an educational component of the decision) to child-related issues is an essential conflict management tool. It also functions in shaping more attuned approaches to handling these issues in the future. When successful, the PC becomes the symbolic "super-parent," and his or her direct involvement in helping resolve conflicted issues becomes less important as both parents compare their positions about issues with what they anticipate the PC's position will be and, often, adjust their initial position to one they know will be supported by the PC.

A fourth component of case management is accomplished by broadening the PC's coordination function to include involvement with professionals and nonprofessionals who are involved with the child(ren). Without outreach by the PC, health professionals' (e.g., therapists, pediatricians) and education professionals' (e.g., teachers, principals, tutors) support of children is often compromised as they get drawn into the parents' conflict. For example, a child's therapist may become aligned with one parent, unwittingly promoting that parent's agenda in a custody war that results in continued conflict with the other parent. PC involvement with children's therapists and parents' therapists in high-conflict shared custody situations is critical to support effective mental health intervention. Without such proactive parenting coordination work there is high likelihood that therapy interventions actually reinforce the polarized and dysfunctional high-conflict dynamics.

Greenberg and Sullivan (2012) described models and structures that support collaborative work between PCs and children's therapists, as well as how parenting coordination functions when there are multiple members of the collaborative team. In that article, the authors discussed a how a PC-led treatment team approach is particularly important when the progress in mental health interventions requires some level of decision making to implement the parenting plan. In this model, the PC coordinates the effective collaboration among the treatment team members, maintaining clear role boundaries between professionals. This team collaboration may be needed to manage the negative impact of interparental conflict on any treatment modality, to provide mechanisms for setting and reviewing progress toward treatment goals for the family system, and to address predictable tensions arising between treating professionals who are working in high-conflict shared-custody situations.

In the following case scenario, I describe some typical challenges to PCs in their work with high-conflict parents. Strategies to address these challenges are provided to keep cases on track despite clients' efforts to derail the process.

CASE SCENARIO: THE "B" CASE

In the "B" case, a comprehensive child custody evaluation resulted in a court-stipulated parenting plan that provided for a step-up of the mother's time share from two nonovernight visits per week to one overnight (Saturday) on alternate weekends and then to an equal time-share schedule (2-2-5-5: Monday–Wednesday morning Parent A, Wednesday afternoon until Friday morning Parent B, with parents alternating weekends from Friday afternoon to Monday morning) custody arrangement whereby the mother would have her time share on Mondays and Tuesdays, the father on Wednesday and

Thursdays, and then parents would then alternate weekends. In the child custody report, some problematic parenting issues were identified in the mother and some rejection by the child of the mother were observed. However, no alienation[1] was noted. The case was high in conflict, and the father expressed concerns about Johnny, their 10-year-old son, having increased time with his mother. Individual parent coaching for the mother was ordered by the court, and therapy for Johnny was ordered to continue. A PC was appointed to implement the phase-in plan and coordinate the recommended interventions.

PCs are often appointed in cases where there is a phased or step-up time-share plan, with recommendations provided regarding the time frames for increases in a parent's time (i.e., after 2 months, the first increase will occur, then after another 2 months, the second increase will occur) contingent upon a review of specified factors (e.g., children's adjustment, the parent's compliance with and progress from court-ordered treatment). The PC's role in these cases is to support and coordinate the therapist's work with family members, making sure that necessary information sharing between involved professionals about goals and objectives occurs. In addition, the information and feedback derived from these team contacts also help the PC when he or she is reviewing the appropriateness of the scheduled modifications of the time share. Similarly, coparenting can be supported and the PC can then use the information derived from their intensive involvement to make a determination of whether the increase should occur when the time frames are approaching.

Parent Tactic 1: Direct Confrontation

In the "B" case, the initial increment—adding a Saturday overnight with the mother every other weekend, to create an alternating weekend period from Saturday morning to Sunday evening—was recommended by the court to occur 2 months after the PC was appointed. After working with the parents, reviewing the child's adjustment, and getting feedback from the child therapist and parent coach, the PC approved this increase. Within minutes of communicating this decision to the parents, the PC received the following e-mail response from the father:

> I completely disagree with you to increase Mother's time to an overnight and your approach to this problem. You have completely ignored my son's distress. You wonder why I don't trust you or have faith in you! You never consider my wonderful child who is suffering and you don't keep your word. You also said Mother can be harsh with Johnny, yet off he

[1] *Alienation* is a dynamic in high-conflict, shared-custody situations whereby one parent engages in a campaign of denigration and hate toward the target parent that damages the relationship the child has with the target parent.

> goes for an overnight! You've betrayed his trust in you as well. I demand you reconsider this decision immediately and plan to call my attorney to object to your decision.

A common response from a parent who disagrees with the PC's actions is direct confrontation. This father is devaluing, criticizing, and threatening legal action in an attempt to have the PC question and potentially reconsider his decision. These boundary pushes can be intense, intimidating, and at times professionally threatening. PCs must do whatever is necessary to hold firm to the recommendation or decision they have made. Assuming they have made a well-reasoned, child-focused determination, if PCs are influenced by the questioning of their judgment and authority to back down from their determination, it is likely that the process will be undermined and ineffective.

Parent Tactic 2: Violation of the PC's Orders

Not long after Johnny began to spend additional time with his mother, the father, still unhappy with the PC's support of the scheduled increase, took Johnny to the doctor's office for his annual medical checkup. He did this without the knowledge and consent of the mother (or the PC). Their parenting plan had a provision, consistent with shared legal custody, that neither parent was permitted to unilaterally take a child to a routine health care appointment without the knowledge and consent of the other parent.

When the mother discovered this violation, which occurred when, during their next scheduled parenting time, Johnny reported having seen the doctor, she contacted the PC to report this violation. She stated that this type of unilateral action was nothing new and was indicative of the father's ongoing devaluation of her parental role. She added that she hoped that the PC would take some action that would support the court's orders about health care.

The PC contacted the father, who readily admitted having taken his son to the doctor's appointment without telling the mother. He stated that Johnny had not wanted the mother to attend because he was concerned it would be embarrassing if she were in the examining room when he disrobed. When confronted about this being a violation of the order, the father stated, unapologetically, that there was no reason for the mother's attendance at the checkup.

The PC wrote the following in a letter to both parents addressing this issue:

> I am taking the following actions based on my court-appointed role in this case. I am documenting this violation of the court order in this letter, and I will reallocate my fees for addressing this issue 100% to the father. The father's actions are not acceptable coparenting behavior, and I will take whatever actions are necessary in the future to protect the intent of your parenting plan.

The PC's actions reflect the earlier discussion of a behaviorally guided intervention. The PC immediately investigated and verified the problem behavior and then applied an appropriate consequence and provided a rationale for that consequence. This intervention is an example of the importance of enforcing the coparenting rules as established in the custody orders.

Parent Tactic 3: Attempts to "Split" the Involved Professionals

A common strategy parenting coordination clients use to support their position in a dispute with a coparent is to attempt to align professionals and nonprofessionals (e.g., extended family, clergy, coaches). If the PC takes a position or makes a decision that is unfavorable to that client, the client may use the support of those individuals to reinforce the client's opposition to the PC's actions. This splitting tactic is best addressed in a proactive and preventative manner before the splitting occurs, particularly if there are other mental health professionals involved in the case.

The PC must think of professionals who are involved with the family as part of the collaborative team. In this framework, attorneys, judges, therapists, educational professionals, nannies, and significant others are either assets or liabilities to the goals of the parenting coordination process. The PC therefore must work proactively to assess each of these individuals' positions with regard to the family system dynamics, exploiting the involvement of those that promote a child-focused, nonaligned perspective and minimizing the damage of individuals involved with the family system who maintain the parents' high-conflict dynamics. In the "B" case, the PC had obtained the necessary releases of confidentiality at the onset of the case to allow a free exchange of information about each professional's work with family members. This opening up of the treatment information allowed the therapists for the child and parents to work with the PC, and the PC was able to obtain useful information to guide his interventions. This structured team approach allowed the PC to support and protect the therapists by monitoring compliance with the treatment plan. The team approach also allowed therapists to provide information within the scope of their role to aid in the PC's work to implement the court orders.

In the "B" case, the PC was working from the onset of his involvement with the child therapist, who was supporting the child's adjustment to increasing the amount of time spent with his mother. It was the PC's job to make the determination of time share (the implementation of the parenting plan) and the child therapist's role to provide treatment and not be drawn into the time-share issues. Similarly, the PC's role was to protect the therapist from efforts on a parent's part to pull the therapist out of her therapeutic role. The father was contacting the child's therapist to put increasing pressure on her to stop the implementation of the step-up plan. Both the therapist and the PC were in agreement that Johnny's adjustment to the increase was not putting him at psychological risk and that the father was opposing the increase for other, non–child-focused reasons.

The PC and therapist were in frequent contact by e-mail and had regular phone conferences to discuss the case status. After a joint meeting with the parents, the PC noted the father's reports of Johnny's distress and anticipated that the father would be contacting the therapist. The PC had the following e-mail dialogue on hand to support the therapist in handling the father's pressure and to prevent splitting the therapist and PC. The latter would undermine the goal of increasing the child's time share with the mother.

PC: I am still of the opinion that it is important to hold the status of overnights and work through the issues. The issues are (1) supporting the mother in handling Johnny sensitively; (2) challenging Johnny's manipulative tendencies and encouraging him to be clear about his issues and more mature in his behaviors; and (3) supporting the father, who is furious with my decision to increase the mother's parenting time, susceptible to and encouraging Johnny's negative feelings about his mother, and will work to split the team. Let's stay in close collaboration and, I hope, things will settle down.

Child therapist: For your information, the father contacted me again today, saying that Johnny is going into "deeper crisis" after saying he was suicidal last week, and he is threatening to "file a motion with the court"—not specifying what that means, if I do not respond to his last inquiry (which I have already done). I doubt that my response will settle the father down, and I anticipate that he will continue to contact me to report that Johnny's crisis is deepening and demand I do something.

PC: The father, as you know, can be quite forceful and intimidating, but you seem to have a good, focused message for him. Feel free to refer him to me if you feel caught with his questioning.

Parent Tactic 4: Forum Shopping

This strategy is an escalation of the splitting tactics parenting coordination clients can use to forge alignments that promote their destructive agendas. When efforts to align members of the professional team fail, parents may seek other forums in which to advance their agenda and undermine the PC's authority in the case. Five examples of challenging PC authority outside the relationship that a parent has with the PC are (a) making formal legal objections to the PC's recommendations and orders, (b) requesting a child custody evaluation, (c) making a motion to appoint minor's counsel (i.e., legal representation for the children), (d) hiring a new attorney, and (e) making a report of suspected child abuse. When these client actions are contrary to the PC's appropriate efforts to protect the best interests (or at least reduce the detriment) of a child in these high-conflict situations, they are particularly challenging for the PC.

In each of these examples, parents attempt to use new professionals and new processes in order to have another forum in which to promote their perspectives and agendas with the hope of undermining or eliminating the authority of the PC. If their efforts to review, object to, and undermine the PC's work in successive forums are successful, progress on the case goals can be stalled or completely derailed. The PC must be vigilant when a client moves issues within the PC's scope of authority to other forums and should address them forcefully and competently.

In the "B" case, when the father was unable to split the therapist–PC team collaboration, he made a motion with the court to appoint minor's counsel for Johnny. His declaration in support of his motion stated that Johnny's voice was not being heard in the PC process and that having an attorney for him would be a necessary protection for him in this case. The PC wrote a letter to the court (copied to the parents and their counsel) rebutting this motion, calling out the previous efforts of the father to undermine the PC process and appealing to the court to deny the father's motion. The court heard the father's motion, denied it, and ordered the father to pay both parents' attorney's fees, admonishing him for attempting to undermine the PC's appropriate work to implement the court-ordered parenting plan. The court's support of the PC when the client attempted to use the court to undermine the process was critical to the PC's ongoing work in this case.

Parent Tactic 5: Professional Threats Against the PC

Disgruntled clients have a variety of ways to attempt to remove a PC in their case. The most common tactic is a failure to pay the court-ordered fees. The question then arises, can a PC continue to work on a case when one coparent is not paying their fees? Perhaps describing this situation another way helps answer this question: Is it permissible for a court-appointed neutral professional to also have his or her client be a debtor to the professional? I think not, and continuing to work on a case when one or both clients owe fees creates a role conflict. It also violates the fee contract that, as discussed earlier, should have been established at the outset of parenting coordination. These two issues require a PC to do one of two things: (a) take preventative action to set up the fee arrangement so a situation in which clients owe fees (through retainer or deposit arrangement) never arises or (b) suspend work if the fee contract is not impeccably adhered to (if payment is due in 30 days, then work is suspended immediately if payment is not received in 30 days).

In the "B" case, the father took action to remove the PC from the case. He initiated a grievance against the conduct of the PC, alleging bias in the PC's work. This client action was particularly problematic because it not only was a direct assault on the authority and role of a PC in that case, but it also could have damaged the PC's professional reputation. Again, preventative measures were effective in addressing the father's grievances. The PC had a several-step grievance procedure as part of his appointment order. The protective value of having a grievance procedure in the contract for services is that it controls and channels the processing of a grievance. In this case, the series of required steps in the grievance process proceeded first informally to the PC, then to the court, and only then to other forums (e.g., licensing boards or private professional organizations such as the American Psychological Association [APA] or American Bar Association). The judge in the "B" case reviewed the grievance, supported the work of the PC, and admonished the father for bringing the grievance to the court. The judge's review of the grievance supported the ongoing work of the PC and provided important findings about the PC's conduct in the case if later the father chose to file subsequent complaints to the licensing board or the PC's professional organization.

This case example brings up a controversial question in PC work: When a grievance or complaint is filed with the court or other reviewing agency, can a PC continue to work on that case? First, a PC's ability to continue to function impartially may be impaired, in which case he or she must withdraw from his or her role in the case. If the PC determines he or she can continue to act impartially, the PC must consider whether his or her new role in an adversarial proceeding with the client (e.g., in a licensing board complaint process) creates a dual and incompatible role.

In the "B" case, the angry and oppositional stance of the father escalated when the PC determined that the second scheduled step-up in the mother's time share should proceed as ordered. The PC received a letter, addressed to APA initiating a complaint. The e-mail that accompanied this attachment stated the following:

> I have filed an ethics complaint to the American Psychological Association that cites your gross failure to follow the court directives, failure to act impartially, and how you abuse your legal authority and act in ways that are very destructive to our coparenting relationship and Johnny's welfare. Because there is a conflict of interest with my filing the ethics complaint against you with the APA, I request that you resign your appointment immediately and replace us with a parenting coordinator who can act in a fair and balanced way that is respectful toward both parties.

The PC determined that, despite his ability to continue to act impartially in his role, defending the APA complaint placed him in an adversarial role that created multiple, conflicting roles that necessitated a withdrawal from the case. The PC informed the clients of the decision to withdraw and made appropriate referrals for other professionals to potentially assume the role.

SUMMARY OF PARENTING COORDINATION CASE MANAGEMENT STRATEGIES

1. Ideally, make as few decisions as possible. Whenever PCs make decisions to resolve disputed issues, their relationship takes a hit with clients who are not supported by the decision. Given parenting coordination clients' psychological vulnerabilities, the likelihood that the relationship is irreparably damaged by unfavorable decisions is high.
2. Maintain impeccable procedures. Even if the outcome of parenting coordination work does not inspire confidence in a parenting coordination client, the procedures must be performed in such a manner as to inspire confidence. Impeccable parenting coordination procedures are the foundation of effective work with high-conflict coparents.
3. Help clients save face when you provide critical feedback and/or adverse decisions. Parenting coordination clients may have significant narcissistic vulnerability and, when emotionally injured, may engage in retaliatory behaviors that make them adversaries. Creating a corrective emotional experience for these clients that communicates some tolerance and benign treatment while maintaining firm expectations of rule following is the art of parenting coordination work.
4. Prevent splitting, or address it immediately. The "B" case illustrates the importance of keeping the professionals working on the case working as a collaborative team and aligned as much as possible with the PC's position in the case.
5. Consult with trusted professionals. Parenting coordination work is incredibly challenging, and practicing it without ready access to both legal and psychological consultation decreases a PC's effectiveness and increases professional risk. Seeking consultation to obtain input into your thinking and actions, to help shore up uncertainty and confidence, and as a protection from professional risk is essential.

6. Know when to withdraw from a case. I have never withdrawn from a case and regretted taking that action. The combination of the difficulty of parenting coordination work and the tenacity and dedication that most PCs bring to their work creates a higher likelihood that PCs will continue to work on a case when their effectiveness is diminishing and their professional risk is rapidly rising. The fact that clients will be "rewarded" by one's withdrawal from a case because of their malicious actions to rid themselves of appropriate PC involvement is not a good reason to continue working on a case. Making a decision to withdraw is often prudent, particularly if it is supported by a peer consultation.

REFERENCES

American Psychiatric Association. (2013). *Diagnostic and statistical manual of mental disorders* (5th ed.). Washington, DC: Author.

Greenberg, L., & Sullivan, M. J. (2012). Parenting coordinator and therapist collaboration in high conflict shared custody cases. *Journal of Child Custody*, 9, 85–107. doi:10.1080/15379418.2012.652571

Johnston, J. R., & Campbell, L. (1988). *Impasses of divorce: The dynamics and resolution of family conflict*. New York, NY: Free Press.

Johnston, J. R., Roseby, V., & Kuehnle, K. (2009). *In the name of the child: A developmental approach to understanding and helping children of conflict and violent divorce* (2nd ed.). New York, NY: Springer.

Sullivan, M. J. (2008). Coparenting and the parenting coordination process. *Journal of Child Custody*, 5, 4–24. doi:10.1080/15379410802070351

Sullivan, M. J. (2013). Coparenting: A lifelong partnership. *Family Advocate*, 36(1). Available at http://apps.americanbar.org/abastore/index.cfm?fm=Product.AddToCart&pid=51311003601PDF

8

SETTING UP A PARENTING COORDINATION PROJECT IN THE COURTS: THE DISTRICT OF COLUMBIA PROGRAM

STEPHEN J. LALLY, SHIRLEY ANN HIGUCHI, AND JENNIFER JOYNER-HALL

In this chapter, we describe the development of a parenting coordination program within the District of Columbia court system (hereafter the *DC Program*). The DC Program is unique in that it involved the collaboration of a number of interested organizations, used advanced graduate students to deliver the services, and was later adopted by the court as the first permanent parenting coordination office: the Office of the Parenting Coordinator (OPC). We describe the origin and development of the program, review its initial years, and discuss its transition from a grant-supported project to the court-funded OPC. In addition, we discuss the development of similar programs in other states and countries and review the lessons learned from the project.

http://dx.doi.org/10.1037/14390-009
Parenting Coordination in Postseparation Disputes: A Comprehensive Guide for Practitioners, S. A. Higuchi and S. J. Lally (Editors)

ORIGIN OF THE DC PROGRAM

The DC Program's origins date back to 2002, when discussions took place between the first two authors of this chapter about potential collaboration among psychologists, attorneys, and the DC court. At that time, the first author (Lally) was the department head of an American Psychological Association (APA)-accredited clinical psychology program and president of the District of Columbia Psychological Association (DCPA). The second author (Higuchi), in addition to being the assistant executive director of legal and regulatory affairs at the APA Practice Directorate, was president-elect of the DC Bar. Attorneys in the Family Law Section of the DC Bar brought to Higuchi's attention the facts that there was a large number of divorce and custody cases pending in the DC Superior Court, that most of the litigants were indigent, and that there was a need to bring parenting coordination services to these economically disadvantaged families. At that time, the attorneys had successfully used DC's Special Master status to appoint parenting coordinators (PCs) to assist parents who were locked in conflict and who could afford parenting coordination services. Higuchi began to explore a method of bringing such services to DC's economically disadvantaged parents.

In September 2003, Higuchi convened a meeting with representatives of the Family Law Section and the Pro Bono Section of the DC Bar, APA, DCPA, DC Superior Court, and Argosy University to develop a plan to bring parenting coordination services to the low-income litigants in DC's Family Court. It was agreed at this initial planning meeting to use advanced psychology graduate students, under supervision, to provide parenting coordination services. The participants recognized that these students would need intensive supervision and that such supervision would ensure that the PCs would consistently follow a parenting coordination model of intervention. This model of intensive supervision parallels models used for training law students and junior attorneys who are paired with senior attorneys. Given the use of graduate students, the group decided that the program would focus on situations with moderate conflict and that cases with severe conflict or particularly complicated situations would be excluded (e.g., ongoing domestic violence; history of sexual abuse; active substance abuse; or untreated serious, persistent mental illness). At this initial meeting, four goals were established: (a) provide parenting coordination to individuals who typically could not afford such services, (b) pilot a model of interdisciplinary collaboration that could be transferred to other settings, (c) develop a model of training that could be used by either graduate students or licensed professionals, and (d) collect outcome data on the effectiveness of parenting coordination.

At follow-up meetings in fall 2003 and spring 2004 with an oversight committee the details of the program were worked out. It was decided that students would all be advanced (4th year and above) clinical psychology graduate students at Argosy University. APA's Committee for the Advancement of Professional Psychology awarded a grant to DCPA to administer the program, and Argosy University funded the stipends for the supervisors and provided ancillary assistance (e.g., pagers, copying). Family law attorneys with the DC Bar provided consultation and didactic seminars, and the DC Superior Court provided the facilities and designated the judges for the program. An initial 2-day training for the doctoral student PCs was held in August 2004 with an experienced PC, a family law attorney, a Superior Court judge, and the first two authors of this chapter. This initial training was followed by a presentation to all of the family court judges at the Superior Court about parenting coordination, the program, and its goals. The presentation was well received, and there was broad support for the program (see Bailey, 2004). There was also an advisory committee made up of attorneys, psychologists, and a family law judge. Committee members provided both training and individual consultation as well as providing, as a committee, formal case conferences. In addition to the committee, Higuchi, in her role at the Practice Directorate of APA, contracted with a nationally recognized PC who provided regular and as-needed consultation to the program's clinical administrator/supervisor.

INITIAL YEARS OF THE PILOT PROGRAM

The first referrals were received in December 2004, and the first cases were started in January 2005. In fall 2005, after a change in leadership at DCPA, the state association withdrew from the program, and the administration of the program was transferred from DCPA to APA's Practice Directorate. The Practice Directorate and Argosy University provided additional financial commitments in 2005 and 2006. Through 2008, 10 advanced clinical psychology students were trained in the pilot program. They all had completed at least 3 years of coursework and 2 years of formal supervised practicum before serving as a doctoral student PC and, as is frequently found in professional schools, most had significant relevant clinical experience before entering graduate school. For example, of the first three doctoral student PCs, one had received her law degree and worked as both an attorney and certified mediator prior to graduate school, another had prior experience working with young children in a therapeutic setting, and the third had worked in a forensic facility. Their knowledge and skill from graduate school provided a solid foundation for working as a PC, but didactic seminars were held throughout the year to provide additional training in such areas as mediation, specific legal issues (e.g., writing parenting plans), and the PC model used by the program. The students' practicum was typically 10 months in length;

however, some elected to extend their training. Parenting coordination cases that extended beyond the length of the practicum were either transferred to a new doctoral student PC or handled by the supervisor.

As noted above, the typical model of supervision in psychology had to be modified for the DC Program. From the beginning, the participants recognized that parenting coordination would require more intensive supervision than the typical model of 1 hour a week of supervision in which the student and supervisor discuss cases. What evolved was a model that more closely parallels the training model in law, whereby more seasoned attorneys mentor new attorneys, who serve as "second chairs." For the DC Program, in addition to weekly individual and group supervision, the supervisors were present during all hearings. They were also present during the initial meetings with the parents; meetings that the children attended; and, on a rotating basis, other meetings with the parents. As the doctoral student PCs acquired more experience, the supervisor would adopt a less active role; however, the supervisor still remained intensely involved in the case. The supervisor also adopted a more active role when crises arose as well as when there was a transition of a case from one doctoral student PC to another. For some cases, the supervisor assigned two doctoral student PCs, and they functioned as a team to meet the multiple needs of the family and address high levels of conflict.

During the pilot period, services were provided to 42 parents involving 21 families (Child Trends, 2010). The parents' ages ranged from 22 to 66, with the mean being 41. Most (84% of those who provided racial/ethnic information) were African American. However, these figures do not fully capture the diversity of the families seen by the program. Parenting coordination traditionally has been delivered to relatively affluent families in which there are a mother and father who, after a period of living together as a married couple, are divorced and now share joint custody of their children. For the DC Program, many of the parents had never married, and some had never lived together. In at least two instances, the court had awarded visitation to a largely absent father after he had been brought to court for nonpayment of child support. Extended families were very involved in many of the cases. In one case, because of the death of a father, a paternal grandmother and a mother were the primary custodians. In another case, the two parties were an uncle and an adoptive mother. These extended family members were important caregivers and attachment figures for the children. Often, the doctoral student PCs used these large extended family networks as a resource (e.g., having various family members transport a child between two households so as to reduce the child's exposure to conflict between the parents), and the PCs frequently included the extended family when making decisions.

The unique challenges in providing parenting coordination services to low-income families are reviewed at length in Chapter 10 of this volume. For the DC Program, these challenges shaped the work in a number of different ways. For example, when parenting coordination is delivered in middle-class or affluent settings, a PC typically is appointed after an extensive custody evaluation has already been conducted. In these cases, there is frequently a well-articulated parenting plan in place, the children's educational and emotional needs have been thoroughly evaluated, therapeutic interventions are in place, and the parents have well developed formal (e.g., therapists) and informal (e.g., friends and family) support systems. Although financial issues may be a source of conflict in affluent and middle-class families, they tend to have a basic sense of economic security and, unlike the families served by the DC Program, they are not typically worried about adequate food, safe housing, reliable transportation, or unemployment. In the DC Program, with its economically disadvantaged families, none of the families involved in the pilot project had participated in a formal custody evaluation prior to the custody decision, and most did not have parenting plans. In the absence of such evaluations and plans, the supervisor and the doctoral student PCs conducted an evaluation to assess the nature and dynamics of the conflicts and difficulties with the families. This evaluation and its formulation helped guide the work with the family (e.g., assessing whether the parties can engage in coparenting or needed a parallel parenting plan because of the level of conflict). It is important to note that these evaluations were not evaluations of custody. In cases where there was no parenting plan, the supervisor and doctoral student PCs worked with the parties and assisted in drafting one.

The doctoral student PCs' work followed many of the methods traditionally used by PCs, including mediating parents' disputes, educating the parties on parenting skills and children's developmental needs, and training the parents in conflict resolution. Because in the District of Columbia the Special Master status grants the PC quasi-judicial authority and immunity, the supervisor of the doctoral student PCs would sometimes make binding decisions when the parties were unable to come to an agreement. However, unlike PCs in more affluent settings, the doctoral student PCs at times served rather like case managers, helping the families identify resources in the community. For example, in the case where a child was doing poorly in school, the PC helped the parents secure an assessment for special education services. Because of various factors, including work schedules, commuting times, and child care issues, PCs had to be flexible with scheduling visitation and parenting coordination sessions; for example, at times they scheduled telephone conference calls when it was not possible to have a face-to-face meeting. At times, families had difficulties securing affordable child care for their meetings with the PC, and so the PC would assist in helping parents find alternatives. The following vignette illustrates some of the work done in the doctoral student PC in the program.

A Case From the Parenting Coordination Program

One case from the initial years of the program involved a situation in which the court had awarded joint custody to the parents. Even though the mother had moved to a different state, the court had ordered a parenting plan that had the 2-year-old child traveling between each parent every 2 weeks. Additionally complicating the situation was the mother's intense reluctance to interact with her former husband. Although there was denial of any history of domestic violence, she perceived him as neglectful. At the onset of the case there was little communication between the mother and father, and what communication did exist between the parents was primarily hostile. The mother was fearful to the point of being nearly catatonic in the presence of the father, and the father would ruminate to an almost obsessive level about details of child care (e.g., whether their daughter should be toilet trained, why she needed a blanket). There were two sets of grandparents, who were interested and involved, and a potential resource.

During the initial assessment conducted by the supervisor and doctoral student PC, it was clear that the child was attached to both of her parents. Because of the mother's response to the father, the supervisor and student PC recommended that she get counseling to help her address the emotions associated with the relationship. But given the level of conflict between the parents and the mother's level of fear, the parents were not ready for coparenting. The doctoral student PC worked to promote more effective parallel parenting (Association of Family and Conciliation Courts [AFCC], Task Force on Parenting Coordination, 2003). The PC limited direct communication between the parents and had them use e-mail instead. E-mails were sent first to the PC, who would, if needed, rewrite them. The PC also gave feedback to the author of the e-mail, helping the parent learn to write in a less hostile fashion. The goal of this intervention was to eventually reduce the reliance on the PC as an intermediary and help the parents to begin to communicate directly with one another about their daughter's best interests. These PC-monitored e-mails were used to inform the other parent of what was happening in each household so as to ensure some level of consistency in the daughter's life (e.g., whether she tried a new food, had a new favorite toy). Because the grandparents were very involved with the family and were still able to communicate with each other effectively, they were set up as the designated emergency channel.

In this case, the supervisor and doctoral student PC also focused on parent education. Initially the mother, in her fearful manner, said she did not care or want to know what happened during the 2 weeks her child was with the father. The PC focused on assisting both parties to understand the daughter's normal developmental needs for attention and consistency. In response to the PC's suggestion, and in line with the little girl's need for consistency, the mother made a tape recording of her reading a story that could be played during the 2 weeks when the child was with the father. Pictures of both parents were placed in both households, as were duplicate toys. The doctoral student PC also helped the father shift from his obsessive focus on whether his daughter had passed some developmental milestone and better understand his daughter's needs (e.g., that a blanket can serve as a transitional object).

In sum, the doctoral student PC, working closely with the supervisor and within the constraints of a developmentally problematic parenting plan (i.e., shifting a 2-year-old between two houses in different states), helped the parents to focus on their daughter's interests, educated them about her needs, and taught them skills in adaptive communication.

Outcome Data

One of the goals of the DC Program was to provide outcome data to investigate the general efficacy of parenting coordination as well as the specific effectiveness of the PC project. To help facilitate that goal, Higuchi helped secure a grant from the Annie E. Casey Foundation. With support from this grant, APA's Practice Directorate retained Child Trends, a highly respected nonprofit research center focusing on improving outcomes for children. This center evaluated the DC Program's data and recommended ways to replicate it in other jurisdictions. The report (Child Trends, 2010) found positive trends in the program's impact on families and the court. An analysis of court activities revealed several significant associations between the receipt of parenting coordination services and decreased use of court resources. The results are reviewed in detail in Chapter 13 of this volume as well as in other publications (Child Trends, 2010; Lally & Higuchi, 2008). These data were used by the pilot project and members of the court to successfully advocate for the DC Program to be adopted by the court.

TRANSITION TO A PERMANENT OFFICE OF THE COURT

In 2008, the DC Program was officially adopted by the Superior Court of the District of Columbia. In 2009, the court began funding the OPC, and the supervisor for the program became a full-time court employee. Since the court adopted the DC Program, several changes in the model have been initiated. Although the court program still adheres to the initial mission of the PC project, the program has had to make adaptations to accommodate the court's current needs and limitations. The program's demand, staffing issues, and training are areas in which the initial pilot program and current operations differ.

Changes in the Demands of the Program

At first, the pilot program received referrals only from a select number of Domestic Relations Branch (DRB) judges, to keep the caseload manageable. Under the current court administration, OPC continues to accept referrals from DRB judges, but now all DRB judges are eligible to refer parties. Over the years, OPC has actively established a rapport with all calendar DRB judges, and therefore there has been an influx of referrals. OPC offers an annual training to DRB judges about the referral process that assists in determining appropriate cases. More collaboration is done with a referring judge to assist in determining the appropriateness of a case. As a result of working together, referrals that meet the necessary criteria are more frequently referred and accepted.

Services of the office are also in high demand among the nonjudicial community. Either from working together on previous cases or by word of mouth, guardians ad litem and families are now able to directly request the presiding judge to refer them to OPC should they meet the eligibility criteria. If the judge finds the case appropriate and agrees, a referral will be granted. Given the popularity of the program and the opportunity for successful coparenting, OPC now maintains a substantial waiting list for services.

Staffing

The current DC Program operates with only one licensed clinical psychologist. The pilot program that was initially presented to the court articulated a model that would include two licensed psychologists: one who would be more responsible for the administration of the program and another whose primary responsibility would be supervising advanced doctoral-level students. Given funding issues, the court has been able to fund only one psychologist for the office. As a result of these staffing constraints, the training of advanced doctoral students is no longer a primary goal of OPC. OPC's priority is focused on creating a stable structure for the program to ensure its existence in the years to come. With more emphasis on data collection and other outcome measures, the program hopes to provide data demonstrating the need for the DC Program to justify its expansion and the hiring of additional staff.

Training

Training still remains an objective of OPC. Despite the shift toward focusing on structural issues, OPC has continued to provide educational opportunities to advanced doctoral students. Each spring, OPC actively seeks out advanced doctoral students for a year-long externship. These doctoral students must have sufficient clinical experience and an interest in developing a particular skill set in alternative dispute resolution pertaining to child custody matters. Instead of collaborating with only one university, the current model involves selecting one or two students each year from several local psychology doctoral programs.

OPC has also started collaborating with the DC Court's Child Guidance Clinic. The clinic has an APA-accredited internship program that trains doctoral-level interns in providing mental health services for court-ordered youth. This forensically focused internship, in collaboration with OPC, offers a rotation for doctoral students who have expressed an interest in PC work. Although these students are only with OPC for 4 months, they work closely with the externs and clinical director on cases that need additional support. The interns are also helpful with running short-term coparenting groups.

Future Goals for the Office of the Parenting Coordinator

Once OPC achieves stability and adequate personnel, the staff hope to accomplish three main goals while continuing to provide quality parenting coordination services: (a) increasing collaboration with other court offices, (b) developing a training program model that provides continuous opportunities to psychology students and other alternative dispute resolution professionals interested in learning advanced skills in parenting coordination, and (c) providing parenting coordination services in Spanish.

OPC believes collaborating with the court's Supervised Visitation Center would be beneficial for families who have achieved unsupervised visits but lack the ability to coparent in a healthy manner. In working with this population, the OPC believes that it will reduce repeat appearances in court and will provide families with the skills necessary to work together. Given that these families are not provided with opportunities to learn how to come together to make joint decisions, working with OPC could afford them that opportunity. OPC also seeks to collaborate with the Multi-Door for Alternative Dispute Resolution Program to help increase its scope. Some families are referred to both programs, and collaborating with the Multi-Door Program would eliminate duplication of services and may minimize the amount of time families spend on waiting lists (both at OPC and the Multi-Door Program). Usually by the time families are referred to OPC, they present as overwhelmed, with a significant history of coparenting issues, and have often lost hope that their coparenting abilities can improve.

The Multi-Door Program also provides an excellent example of training for professionals who are interested in mediation. OPC would like to offer a similar program, in which professionals (e.g., psychologists, lawyers, mediators, social workers) who are interested in learning parenting coordination could attend trainings and gain supervised training experience with actual

OPC clients. There is a clear need for pro bono PCs within the DC Superior Court. By actively training more professionals, the pool of qualified PCs could be expanded to more clearly meet the existing need.

Last, OPC staff find it essential to be able to provide parenting coordination services in Spanish. At this time, OPC accepts only clients who are fluent in English or American Sign Language. Being able to provide such services in Spanish would be a great contribution to the community, given the influx of Spanish-speaking families engaged in litigation for contested custody issues.

OTHER COURT PROJECTS AND INITIATIVES

Shirley Ann Higuchi has been instrumental in the presentation of the development of the DC Program and its evolution to OPC at APA's State Leadership Conference (Barrett, Lally, & Hass, 2005; Josey-Herring, McKinney, & Harner, 2008; Parker & Lally, 2006), APA's Annual Convention (Barrett, 2007; Bartnoff, 2005; Berman, 2005; Delaney 2005; Deutsch, 2006, 2007; Hass, 2007; Higuchi, Hass, Deutsch, Koocher, & Sullivan, 2008; Lally, 2006, 2007; Sullivan, 2006, 2007), and the AFCC's annual convention (Higuchi, Lally, Hass, & Nessman, 2008), as well as in a variety of publications (Bailey, 2004, 2005; Lally & Higuchi, 2008; Nordal, 2010). In addition, Higuchi has organized a series of preconvention continuing education workshops in which the work of the DC Program and the experienced PCs associated with it have informed advanced training in parenting coordination (Higuchi et al., 2009; Higuchi, Deutsch, Kelly, & Sullivan, 2010). This dissemination of information has influenced other jurisdictions, and OPC has served as a template or model for other courts. In the following sections we describe some of these efforts.

The San Diego County Project

Spurred by the success of the DC Program, professionals in the San Diego court system investigated ways to develop their own parenting coordination program. Lawyers, psychologists, and judges consulted with Higuchi and APA's Practice Directorate, and then they convened to strategize on setting up a program. In 2012, During the AFCC "New Frontier Conference: Exploring the Challenges and Possibilities of the Changing Landscape for the Children and the Courts," held in Santa Monica, California, the presiding judge of the San Diego court announced that his court would commit to the establishment of its own PC court program. In announcing this program he emphasized how the San Diego court will serve low-income, high-conflict families by using qualified doctoral and postdoctoral psychology students under the supervision of a licensed clinical psychologist. The purpose of the program, which is modeled after the DC Program, is to provide the court with a sophisticated case management tool for those cases that do not seem to lend themselves to litigation or other means of dispute resolution. The doctoral (PsyD) clinical psychology program at the California School of Professional Psychology (CSPP) at Alliant International University in San Diego took the lead and agreed to be a major stakeholder in the project. In 2012, under the leadership of Dr. Neil Ribner, professor and director of the PsyD program, with the support of the campus provost and the CSPP's dean and assistance of APA's Practice Directorate and Higuchi, the San Diego Parenting Coordination Project was launched. The project collaborates closely with the presiding judge of the family court. In addition, an advisory board was created to oversee the project. The board consists of a family court judge, two family law attorneys, two licensed psychologists, a member of the San Diego domestic violence council, the director of the CSPP clinical PsyD program, and the clinical supervisor. The CSPP dean was also invited to participate on the board because the plan was to take the parenting coordination project to the other CSPP campuses in California after it was well established in San Diego.

Other Jurisdictions Interested in Establishing a Parenting Coordination Program

In addition to San Diego County, the Maryland Psychological Association contacted the APA Practice Directorate to request consultative services to assist in establishing a parenting coordination program. This request was fueled in part by the new rules governing parenting coordination. These rules were unanimously approved by the Maryland Court of Appeals (e.g., Maryland Rule 9-205.2, n.d.). Maryland Rule 9-205.2 (n.d.), effective July 1, 2011, defines *parenting coordination* as "a process in which the parties work with a parenting coordinator to reduce the effects of conflict on the parties' child" and defines a *parenting coordinator* as "an impartial provider of parenting coordination services" (p. 1; see Chapter 2, this volume, for a more detailed review of the Maryland Rule). At the time of this writing, the development of a court-based parenting coordination program in Maryland is still in the discussion stages.

An International Need

The success of the DC Program spurred interest not only from domestic U.S. jurisdictions but also from the Japanese government.[1] In December 2010, representatives of the Japanese government, in collaboration with Georgetown

[1]We thank Ieshia Haynie for her research and contributions to this section.

University's Law School, visited the DC Superior Court's OPC to explore whether a similar PC program could be established in the Tokyo court system. Current Japanese legal institutions are working to better resolve the complicated issues surrounding visitation, custody, and divorce. Although Japanese society's views toward family and society have changed in a more progressive direction in recent decades, the law has not evolved accordingly. This lack of evolution is especially clear in the methods used to determine custody and visitation as well as the *kyōgi rikon*, or divorce-by-mutual-consent system. Many activists and policymakers, both domestic and international, would like to see a legal paradigm shift in the Japanese divorce system toward a view that is more similar to that of the United States. Alternative divorce resolution methods, including parenting coordination, offer a potential avenue to guide such a shift.

LESSONS LEARNED

The DC Program largely succeeded in its goals of providing parenting coordination services to economically disadvantaged parents, developing a model for training PCs, creating a template for cooperation by various stakeholders, and collecting outcome data regarding the effectiveness of parenting coordination. In retrospect, some of the lessons learned might have been anticipated, but many were apparent only after the project was put into place.

- *Importance of collaboration between stakeholders*. It is clear that the collaboration among the various stakeholders—national and state psychological associations, the local bar association, private attorneys, a local university, and the judges of the court—was a significant asset of the DC Program. The stakeholders were able to make unique contributions and generally worked together in a cohesive fashion to meet short- and long-term needs. This collaborative project also offered unique benefits to all of the stakeholders. However, one of the challenges of this project occurred when there was a change in the leadership of the local state psychological association and the new leadership decided to withdraw support for the project. Because the initial grant had been placed with the association and the association was responsible for supervising the administrative aspects of the project, this withdrawal of support created a number of problems. A lesson learned is that it is important to secure broad support within all stakeholders and not to place the responsibility for any structural aspect of a program on entities where long-term support within an organization cannot be ensured.

- *Prioritizing goals*. In a project with multiple goals, it is difficult to prioritize all of the goals. For this project, the desire to provide services and the goal of collecting outcome data were sometimes in competition. For example, the doctoral student PCs and their supervisors would sometimes put off completing all of the outcome measures and give priority to the immediate clinical issues that were being presented. This decision was appropriate for their role, but it meant that some of the data were not collected, which weakened the analysis of the project. Ultimately, the outcome data were needed to make the argument for the court's funding of the project. Project staff attempted to address the need for these data by having someone other than the PCs collect the initial and follow-up data. However, this effort was hampered by problems associated with the withdrawal of one of the stakeholders, discussed in the preceding bulleted item. For future projects, we recommend that the data collection be totally separated from the provision of services and that this activity be located in a stable position that is not vulnerable to shifts within specific stakeholders.
- *Decisions around collecting outcome data*. Because so little data had been collected on parenting coordination, the project took the tactic of broadly assessing a number of potential indicators of change. In addition to collecting information about the frequency and type of court hearings, parents filled out measures of conflict (the Acrimony Scale; Emery, 1982; Emery, Matthews, & Wyer, 1991; Shaw & Emery, 1987) and cooperation (the Parenting Alliance Measure; Abidin & Konold, 1999), as well as measures of their children's adjustment (Child Behavior Checklist; Achenbach & Edelbrock, 1983). Additionally judges, attorneys, guardians ad litem, and parents were surveyed about their satisfaction in both a quantitative and qualitative manner. One dilemma relates to balancing the desire for comprehensive assessment with the need not to overburden participants. In the DC Program, there initially was an effort to also get schoolteachers and child-care providers to assess the children's adjustment, but that plan was dropped because of the perception that it would overburden project staff and parents. A second issue is the nature of the assessment tools. Well-validated measures (e.g., the Parenting Alliance Measure, Child Behavior Checklist) provide reliable information to help guide the field, but they may be less compelling to funders and the court. It was clear that, for those audiences, the qualitative

statements by judges and attorneys carried at least equal weight. Future projects will need to be sensitive to balancing measures both in terms of burden on the participants and potential impact on the receiving audience.

- *Education and training for judges.* The DC Program, facilitated with the assistance of a senior judge in the family court, worked hard to provide education and training to the judges in the court to help them understand the program and make appropriate referrals. This effort was not something that could be done on a single occasion but required a number of luncheon meetings by Higuchi as well as informal discussions with referring judges. Although there was an effort to restrict the cases to those of moderate severity, it was clear from remarks by referring judges as well as external consultants that the project had many complex and difficult cases that were more than moderate in their severity. The referral of these more severe cases stemmed in part from judges' positive regard for the program and a desire to get help with their difficult cases. On occasion, cases were turned down, and the case was used as an opportunity to further educate the judges about the project's criteria. This educational aspect of the project has continued with the creation of OPC, and the current director has been successful in facilitating appropriate referrals to OPC. The lesson learned is that the training and education process for judges needs to be ongoing.
- *Use of graduate students.* The project provided evidence that advanced graduate students can function effectively as PCs. However, the use of graduate students, even with these moderate cases, requires intensive supervision. As noted above, the model of supervision for a PC is more akin to that for a second chair in legal practice. In addition, although advanced graduate students bring a significant amount of knowledge and skill, there is a need for ongoing intensive didactic training to supplement the standard curriculum that is the foundation of clinical psychology training. Conversely, the use of graduate students not only provided a means of ensuring greater consistency in the manner services delivered (compared with pro bono private practitioners, who are not under supervision), but also the students were able to provide some unique contributions. They used their research skills and immediate access to a graduate school's resources to provide the latest information about child development or evidence-based interventions.

Overall, the DC Program helped articulate a unique means of training for this emerging area of practice. It is notable that the American School of Professional Psychology at Argosy University in Washington, DC, was awarded the Innovations in Education award in 2008 by the National Council of Schools and Programs in Professional Psychology for their contributions to this project.

- *Consultation and advisement.* Even though the supervisors for this project were experienced broadly in forensic psychology and specifically in parenting coordination, it was invaluable to have both an advisory committee and ready access to a nationally recognized PC. The former provided a useful forum in which to review difficult cases, provide feedback, and support for the supervisor's decisions and was a source of extensive knowledge about local laws as well as the inner workings of the court system. The latter provided assistance with what were often complicated cases and provided guidance on developing innovative interventions to meet the unique challenges of economic and ethnic diversity.
- *Diverse communities.* The DC Program required modification of traditional PC interventions to meet the needs of diverse families (see Chapter 10 of this volume). It is important that in any replications of this project, models developed from private practice for affluent families are not rigidly applied to parents from communities with diverse and nontraditional backgrounds. As noted above, the input of an experienced advisor in parenting coordination can help a project director examine when procedures or processes need to be modified.
- *Grants.* This project significantly benefited from a grant received by the Annie E. Casey Foundation that was secured through the efforts of Higuchi and APA's Practice Directorate. Although grant writing was not proposed as one of the goals of the project, in retrospect it should have been noted as an important function. We recommend that any future replication of the DC Program consider from the very beginning the need to secure grants to fund both services and the collection of outcome data.
- *Publish and present.* Last, only recently has there been a significant increase in published information about parenting coordination models and effectiveness. It is important as this field grows that practitioners communicate with colleagues about successes and failures, because only with this information will

the field advance. From the beginning, this project was active in disseminating information about its methods and results in various professional forums. We strongly recommend that future projects replicate this broad effort to share their experiences with the larger parenting coordination community.

This review of lessons learned during the creation of the DC Program provides a guide for other jurisdictions seeking to replicate it. Many of these lessons (e.g., clarifying the structure. deciding on priorities) need to be anticipated and addressed in the early planning stages. Others (e.g., communicating with judges, publicizing results, applying for grants) need to be periodically revisited throughout the life of the project. Although the path to develop the pilot project and have that project incorporated as a permanent office within the court was neither smooth nor direct, the experiences of the DC Program demonstrate that such a journey can indeed be achieved and provides a road map for how to bring the potential benefits of parenting coordination to underserved families.

REFERENCES

Abidin, R. R., & Konold, T. (1999). *Parenting Alliance Measure: Professional manual*. Odessa, FL: Psychological Assessment Resources.

Achenbach, T. M., & Edelbrock, C. S. (1983). *Manual for the Child Behavior Checklist and Revised Child Behavior Profile*. Burlington, VT: University of Vermont, Department of Psychiatry.

Association of Family and Conciliation Courts, Parenting Coordination Task Force. (2003). Parenting coordination: Implementation issues. *Family Court Review, 41*, 533–564. doi:10.1111/j.174-1617.2003.tb00914.x

Bailey, D. S. (2004). Reconceptualizing custody: APA's Practice Directorate is co-piloting a pioneering program to ease litigious divorce's impact on children. *Monitor on Psychology, 35*(8), 44–45.

Bailey, D. S. (2005). A niche that puts children first: Psychologists in many states are becoming parent coordinators to help divorcing parents focus on their children's needs. *Monitor on Psychology, 36*(1), 46–48.

Barrett, R. F. (2007, August). Provision of pro bono parenting coordination services: Collaborative pilot project. In S. A. Higuchi (Chair), *Provision of pro bono parent coordination services*. Symposium conducted at the 115th Annual Convention of the American Psychological Association, San Francisco, CA.

Barrett, R. F., Lally, S. J., & Hass, G. (2005, March). In S. A. Higuchi (Chair), *New practice opportunities: Launching a parent coordinator program in your state*. Symposium conducted at the American Psychological Association Practice Organiza- State Leadership Conference, Washington, DC.

Bartnoff, J. (2005, August). Value of parent coordinators from a judge's perspective. In G. P. Koocher & S. A. Higuchi (Chairs), *New marketing opportunities—Innovations in child custody: The parent coordinator.* Symposium conducted at the 113th Annual Convention of the American Psychological Association, Washington, DC.

Berman, P. C. (2005, August). What psychologists bring to the role of parent coordinator. In G. P. Koocher & S. A. Higuchi (Chairs), *New marketing opportunities—Innovations in child custody: The parent coordinator.* Symposium conducted at the 113th Annual Convention of the American Psychological Association, Washington, DC.

Child Trends. (2010). *The Parenting Coordination (PC) Project Implementation and Outcomes Study report.* Retrieved from http://www.apapracticecentral.org/update/2010/04-29/pc-report.pdf

Delaney, L. A. (2005, August). Value of a parent coordinator from a lawyer's perspective. In G. P. Koocher & S. A. Higuchi (Chairs), *New marketing opportunities—Innovations in child custody: The parent coordinator.* Symposium conducted at the 113th Annual Convention of the American Psychological Association, Washington, DC.

Deutsch, R. M. (2006, August). Provision of parent coordination services in Massachusetts. In G. P. Koocher & S. A. Higuchi (Chairs), *Parent coordination.* Symposium conducted at the 114th Annual Convention of the American Psychological Association, New Orleans, LA.

Deutsch, R. M. (2007, August). Practice of parent coordination. In G. P. Koocher & S. A. Higuchi (Chairs), *Practicing as a parent coordinator.* Symposium conducted at the 115th Annual Convention of the American Psychological Association, San Francisco, CA.

Emery, R. E. (1982). Interparental conflict and the children of discord and divorce. *Psychological Bulletin,* 92, 310–330. doi:10.1037/0033-2909.92.2.310

Emery, R. E., Matthews, S. G., & Wyer, M. M. (1991). Child custody mediation and litigation: Further evidence on the differing views of mothers and fathers. *Journal of Consulting and Clinical Psychology,* 59, 410–418. doi:10.1037/0022-006X.59.3.410

Hass, G. A. (2007, August). Diversity and the practice of parent coordination. In G. P. Koocher & S. A. Higuchi (Chairs), *Practicing as a parent coordinator.* Symposium conducted at the 115th Annual Convention of the American Psychological Association, San Francisco, CA.

Higuchi, S. A., Carter, D. K., Deutsch, R. M., Sullivan, M. J., Eisen, R., Fidler, B. J., & Kelly, J. B. (2009, August). *Parenting coordination: Practice, research, and the interface between psychology and law.* Workshop conducted at the 117th Annual Convention of the American Psychological Association, Toronto, Ontario, Canada.

Higuchi, S. A., Deutsch, R. M., Kelly, J. B., & Sullivan, M. J. (2010, August). *Advanced topics in parenting coordination.* Workshop presented at the 118th Annual Convention of the American Psychological Association, San Diego, CA.

Higuchi, S. A., Hass, G. A., Deutsch, R. M., Koocher, G. P., & Sullivan, M. J. (Chairs). (2008, August). *Partnering with the legal community to provide parent coordination services as a market opportunity*. Symposium conducted at the 116th Annual Convention of the American Psychological Association, Boston, MA.

Higuchi, S. A., Lally, S. J., Hass, G. A., & Nessman, A. (Chairs). (2008, May). *Expanding the role of parenting coordination in the courts*. Symposium conducted at the 45th annual conference of the Association of Family and Conciliation Courts, Vancouver, British Columbia, Canada.

Josey-Herring, A., McKinney, M., & Harner, S. (2008, March). In S. A. Higuchi (Chair), *Integrating psychology with the law: Working with judges and lawyers to establish an innovative parenting coordination program in your jurisdiction*. Symposium conducted at the American Psychological Association Practice Organization State Leadership Conference, Washington, DC.

Lally, S. J. (2006, August). Provision of pro bono parent coordination services. In G. P. Koocher & S. A. Higuchi (Chairs), *Parent coordination*. Symposium conducted at the 114th Annual Convention of the American Psychological Association, New Orleans, LA.

Lally, S. J. (2007, August) Provision of pro bono parenting coordination services: Initial outcome data. In S. A. Higuchi (Chair), *Provision of pro bono parent coordination services*. Symposium at the 115th Annual Convention of the American Psychological Association, San Francisco, CA.

Lally, S. J., & Higuchi, S. A. (2008). The American Psychological Association Parenting Coordination Project: The development of the project and an initial review of the first 2 years. *Journal of Child Custody, 5*, 101–121. doi:10.1080/15379410802070435

Maryland Rule 9-205.2. (n.d.). Retrieved from http://www.courts.state.md.us/family/pdfs/mdrule9-205-2.pdf

Nordal, K. (2010). An emerging practice area. *Monitor on Psychology, 41*(7), 62.

Parker, M., & Lally, S. J. (2006, March). In S. A. Higuchi (Chair), *Professional opportunities for your membership: Establishing a parent coordinator project in your state*. Symposium conducted at the American Psychological Association Practice Organization State Leadership Conference, Washington, DC.

Shaw, D. S., & Emery, R. E. (1987). Parental conflict and other correlates of the adjustment of school-age children whose parents have separated. *Journal of Abnormal Child Psychology, 15*, 269–281. doi:10.1007/BF00916354

Sullivan, M. J. (2006, August). Parent coordination in California. In G. P. Koocher & S. A. Higuchi (Chairs), *Parent coordination*. Symposium conducted at the 114th Annual Convention of the American Psychological Association, New Orleans, LA.

Sullivan, M. J. (2007, August). Ethical considerations in the practice of parent coordination. In G. P. Koocher & S. A. Higuchi (Chairs), *Practicing as a parent coordinator*. Symposium conducted at the 115th Annual Convention of the ican Psychological Association, San Francisco, CA.

III

SPECIAL ISSUES AND POPULATIONS

9

INCLUDING CHILDREN IN THE PARENTING COORDINATION PROCESS: A SPECIALIZED ROLE

JOAN B. KELLY

The core roles and functions of the parenting coordinator (PC) have been described in earlier chapters of this book and elsewhere (American Psychological Association [APA], 2012; Association of Family and Conciliation Courts, Task Force on Parenting Coordination, 2006; Carter, 2011; Deutsch, Coates, & Fieldstone, 2008; Kelly, 1994, 2002, 2008; Kirkland & Sullivan, 2008). One additional specialized role—the practice of including children in the parenting coordination process when relevant and appropriate—provides significant benefit to children and parents, and enhances the PC's effectiveness. Listening to children's voices helps parents resolve their child-related disputes and reduces child-focused conflict.

In this chapter, I first describe the goals, rationale, and criteria for including children; the risks and benefits of listening to children; and the experience and knowledge base needed by the PC. In the remainder of the chapter, I describe a semistructured nontherapeutic model for interviewing children

http://dx.doi.org/10.1037/14390-010
Parenting Coordination in Postseparation Disputes: A Comprehensive Guide for Practitioners, S. A. Higuchi and S. J. Lally (Editors)

that enhances a PC's consistency and thoroughness as well as child responsiveness. Child and adolescent participation in the parenting coordination process is not considered to be psychotherapy, although being heard about important matters may sometimes have a therapeutic effect for children of all ages. Although in this chapter I focus specifically on including children in the parenting coordination process, the structured interview is effective in child custody mediations, child custody evaluations, guardian ad litem interviews, and judicial interviews, with appropriate adaptations compatible with the particular forum in which they take place.

INCLUDING CHILDREN IN THE PARENTING COORDINATION PROCESS

Children's input in the parenting coordination process is important, and the PC's goal is to ensure that their unique needs and individual desires are recognized and taken into careful consideration. Despite what some people may assume, children are indeed capable of meaningfully participating in the parenting coordination process, and my own experience has shown that they usually are grateful to have their voices heard.

Goals and Rationale for Listening to Children in the Parenting Coordination Process

The overall goal for including children's voices in the parenting coordination process is to expand the PC's knowledge of each child's particular needs and wishes as provided directly by the child. This information supplements and complements information that is filtered through the often polarized, and sometimes distorted, views and opinions of the parents. The PC uses this specific information to help parents reach appropriate agreements or to make decisions when parental negotiations do not succeed. Another goal of including children's voices is to help parents understand that children's views and needs are not mirror images of their own and that their children are separate, unique individuals. Appropriately differentiating child and parent as distinct individuals and establishing the need for parent–child boundaries are important tasks in high-conflict families (Johnston, Kuehnle, & Roseby, 2009; Kelly, 2003). Listening to the voices of children brings each child into focus for both the PC and parents in a powerful and unique way.

Children's interviews, when appropriately conducted, provide the PC with a more integrated and reliable view of the family and each child's particular experience within the family. The input sought from children is intended to be directly relevant to specific parental disputes and helps shape parents' agreements and PC decisions (if authorized). In adversarial proceedings, parents' needs and opinions are often cloaked and presented by lawyers and parents as children's "best interests" (Kelly, 1994, 1997). By obtaining children's input and providing sensitive feedback to parents, PCs can move beyond the simplicity of best interests clichés and more accurately describe children's needs and desires. Because the PC usually has a long-term contractual relationship with parents, he or she has the ability to establish a productive and trusted working relationship with children and can schedule sessions with them as disputes arise for which their input would be valuable. Listening to children's views and ideas, combined with careful feedback to parents, often enhances the PC's credibility with parents. In some instances, the process begins to empower children to raise questions and concerns at home that are important to them, and even sometimes to ask for an appointment with the PC when a big issue arises about which they want to comment.

Are Children Able to Participate Meaningfully?

Contrary to popular belief, theory, and inadequate research of past decades, children are not passive participants in their families but major agents and players. Across a wide age range, youngsters are reliable observers of their experiences within the family, their relationships to each parent, and their living arrangements and environments both before and after the parents' separation. They are capable of understanding and speaking to their experience—if they are provided with developmentally appropriate scaffolding by parents, teachers, and mental health professionals (Smith, Taylor, & Tapp, 2003).

Empirical studies (Dunn, Davies, O'Connor, & Sturgess, 2001; Kelly & Kisthardt, 2009; Smart, 2002; Smart & Neale, 2000; Smith & Gollop, 2001) have demonstrated that a large majority of school-age children and adolescents are not informed about the parental separation in advance or included in any discussions of the implications the separation has for their lives. They do not typically have opportunities to ask questions or make suggestions. Interim and final parenting plans are most often imposed on them without any consideration of their views. However, research indicates that youngsters in separated and divorced families want their voices to be heard and their needs and opinions considered in divorce processes. They understand the difference between providing input and making a decision. Most children and adolescents prefer that their parents and other decision makers make decisions after listening to and considering children's views and ideas (Birnbaum & Bala, 2010a; Birnbaum, Bala, & Cyr, 2011; Boshier, 2006; Cashmore & Parkinson, 2008; Gollop, Smith, & Taylor, 2000; Kelly, 2002; Parkinson & Cashmore, 2008; Smart, 2002; Smart & Neale, 2000; Smith et al., 2003; Taylor, 2006; Taylor, Tapp, & Henaghan, 2007). In all divorce-related forums studied, including judicial interviews, children and adolescents expressed positive evaluations of the opportunity to be heard (Birnbaum & Bala, 2010a; Kelly, 2002; Parkinson, Cashmore, & Single, 2007; Smart & Neale, 2000; Taylor, 2006; Williams, 2008) and thought that it led to better decisions and outcomes. Adolescents were more likely to see their parenting plans or living arrangements as fair when they had opportunities for input, compared with adolescents who were not consulted (Cashmore & Parkinson, 2008). Even when judicial decisions did not reflect the child's expressed views and desires, most children reported that the process of being heard was important and valuable (Birnbaum & Bala, 2010a).

There is no comparable empirical research on the experience of children and adolescents being included in the parenting coordination process. In my decades of experience, first conducting research interviews of children to understand their reactions to their parents' divorce, then later in custody mediation and parenting coordination processes, not one child or adolescent refused to come for an interview. Some came reluctantly, but once present and offered a supportive ear in a structured interview context, the vast majority of children were lively, informative, happy to be heard, and grateful to have their centrality acknowledged in the postseparation family. Furthermore, they were eager to have most, if not all, of their ideas and opinions conveyed to their parents in a sensitive feedback process. Some expressed a desire to their parents to return to the PC so that additional ideas and concerns could be discussed (Kelly, 2002).

Criteria for Including or Excluding Children in the Parenting Coordination Process

There are specific reasons why the PC should or should not include children in the parenting coordination process, including the need to have written, formal authorization to include them. Other factors to consider are the children's age and developmental capabilities, the nature of the parents' disputes, and the PC's own background and experience in working with children.

Including Children

PCs are advised to include children in the process only if there is explicit written authorization in a stipulation, court order, or private consent agreement to speak with the child. The format for listening to children, either in separate interviews, conjointly with siblings, and even occasionally with parents, should not be at the parents' discretion. If a PC believes that children's input is valuable in this often contentious process, then he or she should ensure that appropriately protective and directive language is included in the contract for the PC's services. PCs might consider declining a case if a parent opposes any PC contact with children. More often, after an explanation of the importance of including children's voices, these parents mute their opposition and agree to enabling language in the stipulation, order, or consent agreement.

The question of which children can or should be included in the parenting coordination process depends on the child's age, developmental capabilities, the content of parental disputes, and mental health professionals' knowledge and experience in talking with children. Assuming child-related knowledge and experience, many PCs include children from age 6 and up. It is helpful to see preschool and kindergarten age children at least once to get a sense of the younger children, observing their play, language, and cognitive capacities. They may occasionally be included in interviews with an older sibling, if appropriate, to observe their relationships with older siblings. Talking with very young children requires an understanding of their limited language, memories, cognitive capacities, and immature sense of time and the need to frame questions and comments in a manner that can be understood.

In determining when or how often to listen to children, most PCs believe that children are to be consulted periodically, as necessary, rather than on a regular basis, and only when the content of the parental dispute is directly relevant to the child and important for the child's well-being. Children do not need to be consulted about minor schedule changes or other disputes that do not directly affect their activities, relationships, or well-being. On the other hand, in a parental dispute about whether a 7-year-old should attend a 2-week sleepover camp, the child's views and feelings about a lengthy separation from both parents will be important in working with the parents to reach an agreement.

Excluding Children

Some PCs may lack knowledge of child development and be inexperienced in working with children and thus decide it is inappropriate for them to interview children (Kelly, 2002; Warshak, 2003). Certainly such caution is warranted, although I believe that the relevant knowledge and skills can be acquired with diligence, attendance at specialized seminars that offer training in interviewing children in the context of divorce processes, and ongoing consultation. In particular, mental health professionals can learn to conduct these brief interviews in a sensitive and productive manner, as can some experienced family lawyers. Some PCs, instead of conducting the interview themselves, establish a collaborative relationship with an experienced colleague who interviews a child or children as the need arises and provides written and verbal information to the PC, similar to the role of the child specialist in collaborative divorce processes. This adds a layer of complexity to the parenting coordination process, and more cost. If such an arrangement were developed, it would be essential to include its details in the stipulation, court order, or private consent agreement.

A PC may decide not to include children previously traumatized by parental violence, emotional abuse, or the mental illness of a parent and who may be reluctant to meet with a PC for the purposes of sharing their opinions and views. The PC will assess the value of directly obtaining the child's input and the costs and benefits to the child. Although some of these children want to be heard, they are more likely to need ongoing psychotherapy in which the therapist and PC communicate as necessary about the child's needs.

As indicated above, very young children (under age 5) are generally not included because their information is unlikely to be sufficiently reliable or specific to be useful. Sometimes there are very informative surprises. A 7-year-old who had been stridently refusing contact with her father for 9 months was interviewed with her 4-year-old brother following a carefully planned weekend visit with the father. She immediately reported to the PC, "We had a terrible time! . . . It was just awful! . . . He doesn't pay any attention to our needs . . . just his own needs! He is so selfish!" The 4-year-old piped up, "I had a *really* good time . . . I *love* my daddy . . . I *miss* my daddy!" In response, the sister angrily insisted to her brother, "No you didn't! . . . you had a *terrible* time!" This most revealing and helpful interview also spoke to the high vulnerability of the younger boy's future relationship with his father, given the (unwarranted) highly negative attitudes of mother and sister toward his father.

PCs also may decide not to speak with children when parents demonstrate the ability to reach an agreement on their child disputes with the PC's assistance. Other children have had a stressful succession of inquisitive professionals in the form of custody and child abuse evaluators, child legal representatives, and therapists in highly contested and protracted adversarial proceedings. They are wary, and weary, of being on the spot again. In such cases, the PC may choose not to become yet another "helping" professional, in particular if the child currently has a positive working relationship with a therapist with whom the PC may consult as necessary (and when authorized to do so in the parenting coordination stipulation, court order, or private consent agreement). As an example, I once asked the therapist of a 12-year-old to learn what she could about the girl's wishes for her summer activities about which her parents had widely divergent and disputed ideas of her best interests. The therapist later discussed this with the child and provided me with the child's preferences and additional helpful comments about why the preferred activities would help this youngster's problems with the emotional constriction and anxiety relating to ongoing intense parent conflict.

Risks and Benefits for Children in Participating in the Parenting Coordination Process

Involving children in the parenting coordination process has both risks and benefits. Most risks are minimal; the biggest potential threat is a poorly conducted interview that may yield incomplete or inaccurate information as well as make the child feel ill at ease. Potential benefits are that the child feels validated and listened to and that the PC can find out, directly from the child, how various aspects of postseparation life have been going.

Potential Risks

The potential risks for children and adolescents who participate in the parenting coordination process are relatively small due to the ongoing nature of the PC's relationship with the family. Through successive meetings, e-mails, and phone conversations, PCs accumulate knowledge about parental anger and negative behaviors as well as children's vulnerabilities. In this respect, the work of the PC is substantially different from that of the custody evaluator, who generally meets with the child a few times in a compressed time frame in order to make recommendations about the ultimate question of custody or access. In this latter setting, children are more likely to experience parental pressure and manipulation because the stakes are quite high for everyone. Children's opinions and wishes can also be unduly influenced by worries about a parent's well-being, an unhealthy identification with a parent, or fear of a punitive response from a parent if they say the "wrong thing." Some younger children have unstable opinions and wishes, and others may want some result that is not in their best interests. All of these potential risks are substantially diminished in the parenting coordination process, for two reasons. First, a PC does not have the authority to change custody arrangements or substantially alter the parenting plan; second, a PC becomes aware of coercive parental influences on children's views through communications with parents and other professionals.

More worrisome risks for children in being interviewed in the parenting coordination process are the quality and tone of the interview. Poor interview techniques yield poor, incomplete, or erroneous information, including a failure to match the child's age with developmentally appropriate language and questions, and the use of confirmatory strategies to get answers that the PC wants or thinks are correct. In addition, an interview style and approach that is too therapeutic, vague, lacking structure, or unfocused is not likely to be useful. Sometimes child interviewers structure their questions and comments to confirm their biases, or are dismissive of children's views, wishes, and opinions, because they do not fit the PC's beliefs about what children need. Just as with custody evaluators or judges, PCs may come to the process with their own psychological baggage, a reliance on outdated research or untested theory, or a vulnerability to being aligned with or persuaded by a parent or lawyer to do their bidding. Open and structured interviews reduce the likelihood of confirmatory biases, as does consultation.

Potential Benefits

There are additional specific benefits for children, parents, and parent–child relationships in listening to children's voices. It is helpful to develop a "conflict history" of each child's experience in a high-conflict family before the separation and at the current time (I provide more details on this in the next section) that becomes the basis for subsequent strategic work with parents on behalf of the child. The PC can validate the child's experience and make simple, empathic statements about how painful and difficult this experience can be for children and teenagers. Children are asked if they have comments or advice they want the PC to give to their parents about the conflict. The following are typical comments: "Tell them I hate it when they fight . . . I want them to stop it" and "Tell my dad that when he says mean things about my mom, it makes me sad . . . and kinda angry . . . I don't like it." In this early session, the PC begins the process of forming an alliance with the child and becoming an advocate for the child's needs, being careful not to demonize the parents in any way. The PC tells the child that he or she will be working with the child's parents to encourage them to stop fighting or arguing in front of the child and the child's siblings and to help the parents learn to leave their children out of their conflict. The PC asks for permission to talk with children's parents about how upsetting the conflict is (assuming that it is experienced by the child in that way). Children's information provides the basis for future work with parents on behalf of the child.

A second direct benefit for children is the exploration of the child's current situation to find out how things are working for the child in general and in the child's postseparation life and living situations (I provide more details about specific inquiries in the next section). Children are then asked whether there are things they would like to see improved or changed, or things that would make their lives easier and happier. The child begins to perceive that the PC is a helping ally, and one can often observe a sense of relief, as if the PC is lifting some heavy burdens from the child's shoulders.

As the PC works with parents, settling disputes, structuring their communications to avoid conflict, encouraging emotional disengagement, and helping them focus more clearly on their children, some parents begin to settle down into less acrimonious patterns of interaction. When the child's voice is a part of the process, the goal of restructuring the coparental relationship into a more civil businesslike partnership with parallel parenting is more easily reached (Hetherington & Kelly, 2002; Kamp Dush, Kotila, & Schoppe-Sullivan, 2011; Kelly, 2007; Maccoby & Mnookin, 1992).

Knowledge and Skills Necessary for Including Children

To interview children effectively in any divorce process, a mastery of interviewing skills with youngsters is essential. Although the base knowledge underlying good skills is beyond the scope of this chapter, several points are important. These are child-friendly interviews, not adversarial interrogations; they should feel supportive to the child. Judicious use of empathy, as opposed to sympathy, is helpful in appropriate instances. Skilled interviewers will note heightened anxiety or withdrawal if the child feels pushed too hard and change course accordingly. Most important, all those who interview children in divorce processes will be more effective if they like children, find them interesting, and are comfortable and relaxed in their presence.

Developmentally appropriate communications are characterized by clarity in word choice; simple and short sentences, rather than complex ones with multiple topics; and simple, brief questions that are asked one at a time. Research indicates that children use words and numbers before they understand their meaning, sometimes repeat others' sentences without understanding their meaning, and readily respond to questions with incomplete or inaccurate knowledge of their meaning (Poole & Lamb, 1998; Saywitz, 1995). This indicates the need to check in with children to make sure they understood your words, comments, and questions and that you accurately understood what they have said. Most adult language directed at children is characterized by short utterances, in particular, commands and questions, for example, "Do your homework," "How was school?" and "Don't hit your sister!" Children are not typically engaged in interactive conversations in which they are given the opportunity to provide a narrative description (Ceci, 1994; Poole & Lamb, 1998). Although their work was written for the context of child sexual abuse investigations, Poole and Lamb (1998) and Saywitz (1995) provided helpful research, developmental issues in interviewing children, examples of egregious interviewing, and positive guidance for interviewers (see also Ceci & Bruck, 1995; Garbarino & Stott, 1990). When interviewers use open-ended questions, as demonstrated in later sections of this chapter, children's narratives are richer and more accurate. It is important to note as well that younger children have an immature knowledge of time and temporal concepts. In discussing children's living arrangements after separation, PCs will need to be careful in describing and inquiring about typical patterns of parenting plans (i.e., when children are at each residence), using concrete language and visual aids as necessary to ensure understanding.

Familiarity with the research literature on children's age-related responses to separation (Wallerstein & Kelly, 1980), and factors that increase risk or promote resilience in children following separation and divorce will provide PCs with an understanding of the types of situations children and adolescents are most likely to experience (Fabricius, Sokol, Diaz, & Braver, 2012; Hetherington & Kelly, 2002; Johnston et al., 2009; Kelly, 2012; Lamb, 2012; Pruett, Cowan, Cowan, & Diamond, 2012; Sandler et al., 2012). For example, knowledge of the types of parent conflict that are most destructive, and of which protective parental behaviors have been found to diminish the negative impacts of high conflict, will provide guidance for PCs in asking high-quality questions of both parents and child and in increasing understanding (Birnbaum & Bala, 2010b; Buchanan, Maccoby, & Dornbusch, 1991; Grych, 2005; Kelly, 2003, 2007, 2012). Similarly, keeping current on research on elements of effective parenting after separation, and typical problems in parent–child relationships following separation, will help guide PCs (Amato & Fowler, 2002; Fabricius et al., 2012; Kelly, 2012; Lamb, 2010; Pruett et al., 2012). It is not necessary to be a child development expert, but PCs should be familiar with the attachment formation process; age-related language, thinking, and social skills; developmental differences in expression of anger; development of objectivity and abstract thinking; and normative parent–child relationships and peer relationships at different ages (see Siegler, DeLoache, & Eisenberg, 2010; Thompson, 2006).

THE STRUCTURED INTERVIEW MODEL FOR INTERVIEWING CHILDREN

In the following sections, I explain the value of interviewing children during parenting coordination and describe a model that helps PCs prepare for the interview, conduct the interview, and provide feedback to parents.

Purpose and Nature of the Interview

The purpose of interviewing children during parenting coordination is to get an honest sense of how they feel about their parents' conflict and what they want. It is important to note that the interview does not comprise a form of psychotherapy; instead, the point is to find out about the child's needs, experiences, and wishes as they pertain to the parents' divorce and conflict.

The Purpose of Child Interviews

There are typically two types of meetings with children. The first is an initial "getting to know the child" session early in the case for the purpose of beginning to establish a relationship with the child; educating him or her about the role of the PC; and learning about the child's experiences with the parents' separation and divorce, and in particular, parental conflict. Additional later sessions are scheduled as needed for learning about specific ideas, needs, and concerns relevant to particular parental disputes. These boundaries help the PC enjoy a working relationship with the child that does not blur or merge inadvertently into psychotherapy. In most instances, child input is routinely sought when parents are disputing such things as extracurricular activities, summer camps, joint parental attendance at school and recreational events, parent–child relationship problems and communication, and problematic transitions between households.

The primary goal of the structured child interview I describe in this section is to gather focused information that is relevant to particular parental disputes and the child's family living situations and that will typically be used, in whole or part, to help the parents reach agreements. It is a child-focused protocol in which the child largely determines the vocabulary, content, and pace and the interviewer directs the flow of the interview by raising specific issues. Skillful PCs find 1-hour sessions are generally sufficient and appropriate for the child's capacity for attention and focus. Another session might be scheduled if more information is needed or there are multiple topics to explore.

Child Interviews Are Not Therapy

As indicated earlier, there is general agreement that child interviews, whether for mediation, custody evaluation, legal representation, or parenting coordination, are not psychotherapy or counseling (see the APA's, 2012, parenting coordination guidelines). The parents have not provided their consent for therapy, the child is not an identified client, and the PC does not make formal diagnoses or bill insurance for sessions. This role change is a critical issue for all PCs who are mental health professionals to understand and master. In the course of a given session, PCs may hear about child or adolescent difficulties in the postseparation family or in social and educational functioning but does not take on the competing—and unethical—dual role of therapist to help children. If significant problems are apparent, a recommendation for therapy (e.g., a specialized drug treatment program) would be appropriate, accompanied by a rationale describing the child's need. In some jurisdictions, the PC would have the authority to make a decision or arbitrate this issue if the parents were not able to agree.

Effective Interviewer Style

The most effective way of learning about children's experiences, needs, and wishes in a high-conflict postseparation family is to have an open, honest dialogue with the child about issues the PC must address on behalf of the child that arise from parent conflict. A friendly, responsive but professional demeanor, offering support as needed while staying focused on the issues, is most effective. The PC's posture should be relaxed, calm, and alert, with good eye contact. Some inexperienced child interviewers are prone to overdo praise or gush with forced emotion, which is inappropriate and seen as fake by many children. Others will be tense, moving abruptly through topics, not stopping to explore important comments, out of anxiety or an effort to quickly complete the interview.

Assuming the PC has established a relationship earlier with the child, the PC would begin a typical session by getting an update on how things are going in the child's life. This might include questions about behavior or problem raised by one or both parents recently, such as not completing homework ("What do you think is the problem? Possible solutions?"). The PC then moves directly to addressing and settling the current dispute(s).

This approach is demonstrated in the following (modified and condensed) interview with an 8-year-old girl named Mary.[1] Mary was interviewed after information had been gathered by phone from each parent.

> *PC:* Your mom and dad are having a dispute[2] about who should be at your piano recital. . . . They can't agree on this, and I'd like to find out what you think. [pause] Are you aware that they have some conflict about this?

Many children are aware not only of the content of the dispute but also of one parent's, if not both parents', positions.

The PC then reviews the dispute:

> *PC:* Your dad just found out about your recital next week and wants to attend . . . he thinks it's important that he be there. Your mom doesn't think he should be allowed to come to the recital. (Pause) Do you know why?
>
> *Mary:* Sort of . . .
>
> *PC:* Can you tell me? (Or, "Your mom said that since she pays for your lessons, it is 'her activity' with you, not your dad's.")[3] It's important for me to find out what you think about this so I can help your parents settle this.

[1]This and all subsequent names are pseudonyms, and case examples have been modified to protect confidentiality.

[2]The choice of words will depend on the child's age and sophistication; other word possible word choices include *disagreement, having some conflict, argument*. In my own work as a PC, I avoid strong words like *fighting*, unless the child uses them first.

[3]Ownership of a child's activity, either because of payments in support of the activity or because the event falls on a parent's scheduled time, is a common dispute. A PC would do well to tell parents that the PC regards children's activities as belonging to the child, rather than a parent, and that it honors and generally pleases children to have both attend their activities if they can behave in a civil manner.

The PC then gets the particulars of where the recital is taking place, whether Mary likes studying piano, what pieces Mary will be playing, and learns through this dialogue that Mary is proud of her accomplishments. Although the PC had asked for these details from the parents, she establishes common ground by repeating the questions with Mary.

> *PC:* Would you like your dad to be present . . . to hear you?
>
> *Mary (shyly and quietly):* I *really* want him to be there . . . to see me play.

The PC reassures Mary that most children who are proud of their work want both parents to see and appreciate it. The PC asks about the postrecital reception and whether Mary has any concerns or worries about both parents being present in the same room.

> *Mary (hesitantly):* Maybe you can tell them how to behave, too.

Mary is reassured by the PC's intention to develop some rules for her parents, and the PC asks Mary what ideas she has.

> *Mary:* They don't have to sit together . . . maybe on opposite sides of the room.
>
> *PC:* Would you like them both to come to the reception afterwards, or just one of them?

Mary affirms that it would be nice to have them both there, and the PC tells her what she will say to the parents about being in the same space in a polite way, but not talking to each other except to say hello. She asks Mary if that sounds OK. Mary is very pleased.

The Structured Child Interview

This interview model has six phases: (I) Beginning the Interview, (II) Establishing Rapport, (III) Obtaining Focused and Specific Information, (IV) Integrating the Child's Narrative, (V) Reviewing the Interview With the Child, and (VI) Feedback to Parents. If a child is to be interviewed only once, as is typical in custody mediation and judicial interviews, all six phases would normally be included. In the parenting coordination process, once the PC has seen children, subsequent sessions will typically cycle through the last four phases. In the following sections, I briefly describe each of the six phases.

The Child Interview Site

The office setting should be child friendly, with several comfortable chairs near or around a low table (not a large desk), and space to sit on the floor with pillows. No special equipment is required. The most important consideration is to limit distractions that will interrupt the child's focus in the interview. Structured games (e.g., checkers, Chutes and Ladders), intricate building materials, Legos, and complex puzzles are counterproductive because they allow the child to avoid talking. Instead, stick doll figures, animal hand puppets, small cars and trucks, and drawing materials are sufficient, but not critical, for productive sessions. In my own work as a PC, I do not ask children to draw a family or any other drawing assignment, because being absorbed in an elaborate drawing project is a distraction and can take a good bit of time. If a child chooses to draw, ask him or her to wait before starting another "so that I can ask some important things about your mom and dad" (or whatever topic is current). Although dollhouses may be valuable for custody evaluations or research, they are not necessary and can be a distraction; also, dollhouse play is not a reliable source of information. It is helpful to have "tension relievers" (e.g., diamond-shaped magnets).

Preparing Parents to Talk With Children

Prior to a first child interview session, the PC should explain again to parents the reasons for listening to children and the length of the sessions (typically 1 hour) and should describe the relaxed atmosphere and the focus on understanding the child's experiences, views, and needs. Parents should be reassured that if a child does not want to talk, that is all right, and that most do talk quite readily. Parents and child benefit if the PC rehearses parents on major points to convey to their children about coming for an interview with the PC. These points, phrased as though they are being communicated from parent to child, include the following:

- We are working with a professional, called a *parenting coordinator*, to help us reduce our conflicts and make decisions when we have arguments.
- We want you to have the chance to talk to the parenting coordinator we are working with.
- The parenting coordinator is interested in your ideas and opinions about how things have been going since the separation, and what we can to make things better.
- You don't need to take sides—you can say what you want.
- You will not be making decisions; we will, or the parenting coordinator will help us.

The PC should mention that it is sometimes tempting for parents to coach children prior to the child interview about how they want a dispute or issue to be settled; the PC should ask parents to refrain from such behavior, describing the stress it places on children.

Phase I: Beginning the Interview

At the first meeting, the PC greets the child, invites him or her to the office, settles on what name the child prefers, and thanks the child for coming: "I've been meeting with your parents, so I've heard them talk about you. It's nice to meet you myself." The PC then explores the child's understanding of why he or she has come to talk with the PC, what the child was told by parents, and corrects any distortions or misunderstandings. The PC first describes his or her role and work with parents, emphasizing in particular the twin goals of (a) helping parents agree when they argue about something that affects the child and (b) helping parents reduce their conflict. Then the PC explains the purpose of consulting with the child:

> Your ideas are important . . . it will help me when your parents have a disagreement or dispute to know what you think would work for you. . . . You won't decide things but you will have a chance for input.

The PC discusses whether the sessions are confidential (a big word that probably needs to be explained) and that at the end of each session the PC will review the things the child has said and ask what he or she especially wants the parents to hear. As always, and in particular with younger children, the PC will check in to see whether the child understands. Throughout all interviews, it is important to take detailed notes, including direct quotes, and explain why ("I want to make sure that I get it right and that I remember things well").

Phase II: Establishing Rapport

The purpose of establishing rapport is to help the child feel comfortable and safe, to reduce anxiety about the interview and interviewer. It takes only a few minutes of the hour but is well worth it. Benign, general questions are asked first, including such things as what grade the child is in, favorite and least favorite subjects in school, the child's views of his or her teacher, favorite activities and hobbies, whether there are pets and where they are now living, and views of siblings and friends. The PC should avoid inquiring about whether the child understands what the truth is but instead should ask the child to let the PC know if he or she does not understand any questions that are asked. The PC should make sure that questions are really questions, not answers. "You like school, right?" is a closed-choice question with the interviewer's preferred answer. A better phrasing is, "How is school for you since your mom and dad stopped living together . . . since they separated?" because this allows the child to answer on his or her own terms. The PC should not rush but instead give the child a chance to process syntax and the cognitive demands of the questions.

Phase III: Obtaining Focused and Specific Information

This third phase is the core of the structured interview: the targeted information gathering phase. It follows rapport building with a simple statement of wanting now to learn more about what things have been like for the child since the parents' separation or divorce. This focus in Phase III is also appropriate for custody mediators who talk to children, and it can be readily adapted for custody evaluations, child legal guardian interviews, and judicial interviews.

First is a quick review of the separation itself—how the child found out that his or her parents were going to separate.[4] Typical questions include: Who told the child, was he or she surprised, does the child know why, what did the child think about the separation, was it upsetting, and how is it now? Next is a review of the child's current living arrangements, asking the child his or her schedule for both weekends and midweek:[5] "What days during the school week are you with your mom?" "When or what days do you see your dad? Do you sleep overnights there during the school week?" "What happens on weekends: Where do you live, and sleep?" The PC already has this information, but the questions provide an entry into the topic of how the living arrangements are working for the child, things that aren't good, things that are OK. "Who takes you to school in the morning; how does that work?"[6] The PC continues by inquiring how the child gets from house to house: "Who takes you? Does that work OK for you?" "Is there ever conflict between your parents at that time? If so, what happens?" Additional questions might include the following:

- Can you take some of your favorite stuff between houses?
- Does your room feel like a home at both Mom's and Dad's house?
- Do you share a bedroom with anyone?
- Are there some things that you'd like me to suggest to your parents that would make it easier?

The last part of this opening focus on the separation and living arrangements is to ask the child to describe daily routines in each home (e.g., meals, homework, household chores, TV time, fun activities, bedtime routines). This

[4]With younger children, the concrete phrases "not live together anymore" or "live in two separate homes" would be more appropriate until the PC can determine that the child knows the meaning of the words *separation* and/or *divorce*.

[5]Younger children understand the concrete concepts embedded in the phrases "during the week, when you are in school," and weekends, "when you don't have school," before they have the ability to conceptualize and describe schedules in more abstract temporal terms.

[6]I tend to avoid the word *feel*, instead asking "how things are working," "how is that for you?", and "what's not working?"

inquiry helps the PC understand the child's adaptation to and satisfaction with new living arrangements. PCs do not need to visit children's homes.

The Child's Experience With Conflict

For children who have lived in high-conflict family situations, inquiries about their experiences with parent conflict before separation and at the current time are particularly relevant for future educational interventions with parents. The child's responses will also guide interventions in future sessions, in particular, in teaching the child how to respond protectively when parents make demeaning comments about the other parent (e.g., "It hurts my feelings when you say mean things about Mom/Dad . . . it makes me sad/mad").

Much of this inquiry about conflict experiences will take place in the initial getting-to-know-you session with continued updates as appropriate in future sessions. Questions can address the frequency and intensity[7] of conflict before the separation and at present, whether the child has seen or heard violence (i.e., hitting, shoving) between the parents and, if so, whether the child was scared and what, if anything, the child did when one or both parents yelled at or hit each other. Examples of specific questions include the following:

- Did you try to stop them from fighting? What was that like. . . . Did it work?
- Does Mom or Dad ask you to give messages to the other parent? If so, are they angry ones? How does their conflict make you feel?
- Are there any problems when your mom or dad calls you at your other parent's home?
- When you have a back-to-school night or soccer match, do you like to have both parents attend, or only one?

The PC may make empathic statements regarding how painful and frightening these experiences can be for children, if appropriate. Children should be asked if they have advice they want the PC to give their parents. It is typical to hear something along these lines: "Tell them I hate it when they fight or say mean things about my other parent" and "Tell them to stop it!" Although it may appear that questions regarding conflict and a child's responses would take a long time, it is usually possible to accomplish this smoothly and efficiently and proceed onward.

[7]One would not use these technical terms with children younger than 10 or 11, instead starting with "how often," which also can be difficult for younger children to quantify, and following up with "Did it happen a lot? Or just a little bit?" This may help the PC develop some understanding of the child's prior experience.

Children's Relationships With Both Parents

It is essential for the PC to understand the nature and quality of children's relationships with both parents from the child's vantage point, to complement, contrast, and extend the parent's perspective. To build a body of information that will provide guidance for the PC's future work with parents, questions rooted in reliable social science research about parenting effectiveness, closeness in parent–child relationships, and child adjustment following separation and divorce are the focus of this inquiry (for reviews, see Clarke-Stewart & Brentano, 2006; Fabricius et al., 2012; Hetherington & Kelly, 2002; Kelly, 2007, 2012; Kelly & Emery, 2003; Lamb & Lewis, 2013; Pruett et al., 2012; Sandler et. al., 2012; Sandler, Miles, Cookston, & Braver, 2008). One important dimension of parenting addressed by research is relationship quality, which is assessed via such variables as parental warmth, emotional support, acceptance, and encouragement; positive communication, including listening to the child; conflict; and negativity. A second dimension is effective discipline, including explaining and enforcing age-appropriate rules and expectations, enforcing rule compliance, and avoiding harsh and disproportionate punishment. These components characterize authoritative parenting, the most effective parenting style associated with positive child outcomes, in contrast to coercive, authoritarian parenting.

Starting with the general question "How are things between you and your mom (or dad)?", the PC's inquiry should focus on feelings of closeness, whether the child feels supported, how each parent expresses anger and affection, and help with activities and school projects. What things does the child like to do with each parent? How easy is it to talk with Mom/Dad? Does the parent listen to the child about important things? If parent and child have a conflict, how does it get worked out? Are there different rules in each home and, if so, how does that work? Other specific questions may include the following:

- How does Mom (Dad) discipline you when you break a rule or don't do what they ask?
- Do you think Mom (Dad) is fair?
- Are your brothers and sisters treated the same?

As with each set of questions, it is important to check in as necessary to make sure you have understood the child's family reality accurately. After initiating open-ended questions, the PC should follow up with additional specific questions as appropriate to develop a greater understanding of the child's experience.

The Child's Ideas and Perspectives on the Current Parental Disputes

In this segment of Phase III, the PC should explain to the child that his or her mom and dad have a disagreement and have not been able to agree about the particular dispute for which the child is being asked for input. In the parenting coordination process, many disputes arise about children's extracurricular activities, or summer programs and schedules. Whether focused on activities, or the time-share issue in a custody dispute, the PC should provide a simple description of the dispute. The following questions between a PC and an 11-year-old child named Lisa illustrate this process.

> *PC:* I've been talking to your dad and your mom, and they have different ideas about what you should do this summer. They haven't been able to agree yet, and I am helping them to decide. Are you aware of this? (Many children know about the dispute.) It's important for me to hear what you think, and what you would like.

If children are not aware of the dispute, the PC acquaints them with its major points:

> *PC:* Your mom feels strongly that you should take a sailing program for 2 weeks, and then Girl Scout camp later in the summer after your vacations with your parents. Your dad feels strongly that you should sign up for an additional Spanish class to get better at speaking it, and also get tutoring in math. That's quite a difference, isn't it?

In the example case of Lisa, the PC tells her that she has reviewed her grades and scores and talked to her teacher. The PC asks Lisa what she would like to happen, and Lisa gives a clear response:

> *Lisa:* I don't want more Spanish and math . . . I work hard in school, I get As, and I just want to hang out this summer and do fun things. I told Mom that I wanted to go to sailing camp with one of my friends . . . it will be fun!

> *PC:* Why do you think your dad wants you to have more school?

> *Lisa:* I've told him already I don't want to do that . . . he always pressures me about school. I wish he'd stop it.

> *PC:* From what I've learned, you are doing well in school. Your ideas for summer make sense and sound like something new and fun. I want to share your comments about this with your parents; is that OK?

Lisa gives the PC permission to do so, the PC thanks her for her input, and says that if her parents don't agree after the PC's feedback, the PC will make the decision. The PC inquires as to whether Lisa has anything else to bring up, responds to any further issues, and thanks her for coming. In a custody evaluation or child custody mediation, this direct and open approach would be similar:

> *PC:* Your mom and dad have not been able to agree about how much time and what days you will spend with your mom and with your

> dad, and they have different ideas about whether you should spend an overnight at your dad's house during the school week.

The evaluator or mediator would then explore these issues further with the child.

The related questions of suggestibility and the credibility of children's comments, wishes, and perspective are important ones and beyond the scope of this chapter (see Bruck, Ceci, & Hembrooke, 1998; Ceci & Bruck, 1995; Kuehnle, 1996; Poole & Lamb, 1998; Saywitz, 1995). In the parenting coordination process, the PC has multiple opportunities over time to assess these issues with children and parents. In general, once the PC has ensured that the child has understood the questions, she or he should listen for whether the child or adolescent sounds rehearsed or stilted, uses very adult language, persistently repeats certain phrases and statements, directly echoes a parent's position, or is unable to produce memories and descriptions that provide support for his or her wishes or perspectives. If the PC suspects that the child's wishes sound very much like one of the parent's strongly held positions, it is effective to ask a child how much of what the child said is his or her idea, why it is important to the child, and whether the child's mom or dad wants him or her to share the same idea. For example, when a preadolescent tells you how much he or she hates a parent, and argues vigorously against any contact with that parent, but is unable to provide a coherent and detailed underlying story that explains this rigid and strident position, it is reasonable to be wary. The PC should look for characterizations of parents that are framed as all good or bad with no nuance or shades of gray, which suggest a strong and potentially unhealthy alignment with one parent (unless the PC knows the parent to be destructive, harsh, critical, and lacking in expressions of support, and the child is realistically estranged; Fidler, Bala, & Saini, 2013; Kelly & Johnston, 2001). Is the child capable of independent thinking on the disputed issues commensurate with his or her age? PCs and other professionals experienced in interviewing children develop the ability to discriminate what is really the child's voice, presented in age-appropriate language choice and syntax, rather than the pressured voice of a parent with an agenda.

Phase IV: Eliciting and Integrating the Child's Narrative

An effective child interview elicits a narrative that tells the PC about the child's life at the current time and his or her reaction to continuing family situations and parental disputes set in motion by the separation. The various topics and sample questions proposed in the previous section are not intended to be a rigid menu for interviewers to follow. The interview structure should focus on issues that research and practice have identified as being important to children of separation and divorce. Each child presents him- or herself differently and has both similar but distinct issues and conflicts compared with other youngsters. Although the child interview is structured, it also is flexible. It starts with certain points of inquiry but explores in more depth as appropriate, expands in some areas noted to be relevant to the child, ignores other irrelevant topics, and stops when the PC has a good understanding of the child's situations and views.

Most children, starting at age 8, are ready to provide such pertinent information and appreciate being included. A calm PC style; a supportive structure; and age-appropriate language, phrasing, and questions will reward PC efforts with clear, often poignant responses that create a more fully integrated story about the child in the family context of ongoing parental disputes, as well as parental support, and the larger world in which the child engages. Age 8 should not be a rigid dividing line for excluding younger children, because they too can provide thoughtful perspectives or comments. The decision to include children younger than 8 years will most likely be related to the PC's experience and comfort with younger children. Although the child's experience with parental anger is powerful and often damaging, it is important to remember that it is not the totality of the child's life experience.

Phase V: Reviewing the Interview With the Child for Feedback to Parents

Children and adolescents generally have important things to say in interviews that merit feedback to parents in the hopes of reaching a constructive resolution of a particular dispute that meets the child's needs, or for motivating positive behavioral change. In voluntary settings, such as a private sector custody mediation interview, specific feedback is usually given with the permission of the child. In the parenting coordination process, it is not mandatory that the PC share the child's observations and wishes with parents, but providing such feedback to help resolve disputes is essentially the rationale for including children. It would be disrespectful to children to interview them without providing appropriate feedback to the parents, unless the child has strong opinions to the contrary. If a child consistently refuses to allow the PC to share any of his or her thoughts with parents or to help the PC make recommendations and decisions, it would be appropriate not to include the child as the process continues.

At the end of the interview, the PC reviews the child's major statements or views with the child, using direct quotes when possible, and asks which comments the child would like the PC to share with parents. Sometimes children and adolescents express their ideas, reactions, and feelings quite strongly. With particularly sensitive or derogatory comments about a parent, it is useful to model how the PC will phrase it (e.g., reframing to delete swearing, softening a child's harsh statements while retaining meaning), to obtain the child's approval or make the message palatable to a parent. The following are some examples:

- Can I tell them you said it hurts your feelings and makes you sad when they say mean things about each other?
- Can I say how much you love each of them but get very upset when they act like that's not OK? That you want to be close and be with each of them, and don't want them to be mad at you for feeling that way?
- I'm not going to say that you called your parents #$@#, but will it be OK if I say that you were pretty angry about their fight the other day over attending your school play? And you'd really like them to be more mature?

It is surprising how often children and adolescents say, "You can tell them everything!" This often expresses how frustrated and upset they are about the negative parental behaviors of one or both parents and from being excluded from important dialogues about their lives. Providing feedback is possible, of course, only if the PC takes detailed notes throughout the interview, which is essential as well for interviews and phone contacts with parents and other professionals. If the parenting coordination is guided by a stipulation and court order for PC services, the PC may file a motion in court to withhold child notes demanded by an angry parent if the PC believes it will be harmful to the child and the parent–child relationship. Over my 15 years of PC practice, I have never had a parent demand the child's records, and only once was I subpoenaed to appear in court, which required the notes. In this instance, detailed notes from interviews with this child and parents were very important in leading the judge to approve my decision.

Phase VI: Providing Feedback to Parents

Providing feedback from child interviews to parents requires preparation and sensitivity to both children and parents. Before providing feedback, the PC should review the child's comments and take time to formulate a presentation of information that may not be welcomed by one or both parents. It is best if each child is discussed separately, providing general observations first about the child's participation—how extensive, willing, anxious, thoughtful the child was and whether he or she wanted to share some or all information shared with parents:

PC: John was very willing to talk with me and was comfortable in saying what was important to him. When we went over the interview at the end, he told me the things that were important for me to share with you. He was serious, thoughtful, and very impressive.

Use "affect" words to describe some of the situations in which children find difficult to engage the parents' emotional attention, such as, "John is worried about . . . struggling with your angry behaviors toward each other . . . fears that you won't love him if he says how he feels . . . missing his dad very much and wants to find a way to see him more." Use specific quotes from the child when possible, because the sometimes unwelcome news is heard more readily when presented in the child's voice and choice of words. It also deflects parent feelings of PC favoritism or lack of impartiality to hear children's voices directly through the PC.

After providing feedback for each child, the PC should ask for the parents' reactions to the input, and discuss. Sometimes a parent will start to cry, others may ask more questions, and some may angrily disagree with what you said:

> *PC:* Susan was worried that you would be angry but still felt that I should tell you these things. It takes children a lot of courage to say important things about their parents' behaviors. I told her I would talk with you about her worry.

The next step is to raise questions about how each parent will use the information provided, either to help settle the dispute that was the focus of the child interview or in talking with their child directly. If a child's input does not support a strong parent opinion, it is important that the PC acknowledge this up front and then provide the feedback:

> *PC:* In talking with Sam, I learned quite a bit about how he feels about the possibility of a sleepover camp. Dad, I know that you really wanted him to attend a 2-week sleepover camp because you thought he needed to be "toughened up."

In this case, the PC had learned from the mother something that the father acknowledged: that Sam had not experienced any lengthy separations from either parent before and had very little experience sleeping over at friends' homes. Sam had told the PC that he really didn't want to go because he thought he would be very homesick. The PC explained to Sam that most 7-year-olds would have trouble with a 2-week separation:

> *PC (to parents):* Sam told me he was willing to try out the day camp that was suggested by Mom that has one overnight stay each week. He thought he'd be OK with that, and he'd like to do it with his friend, David. He also told me that "Maybe next year I'll be ready for a longer sleepover camp!"

After discussing normal developmental issues further, and the possible longer term fallout from an extended separation when a child is not ready, Sam's father agreed to the 2-week day camp. Such direct feedback is seen by parents as the greatest help in resolving parental disputes and relieves the PC of making a decision.

Sensitive child input can serve as a wake-up call to parents to begin changing their hostile behaviors and attitudes toward ex-partners. Hearing the child's words and how strongly the child wants his or her parents to stop hurtful behaviors is sobering to all but the most angry and hardened parents. Some parents have told me in later sessions that they thought constantly about what the child had said, and it motivated them to work on changing behaviors. In one post-feedback session, a tearful mother apologized to her children's father for her anger and for fighting to limit his time with the children. She then invited him to join her in reducing their anger toward each other and become the supportive and thoughtful parents they were before their separation 4 years earlier.

CONCLUSION

In this chapter, I have provided a conceptual framework and supporting research suggesting that including children is a valuable addition to the parenting coordination process. The rationale and goals for including children in the parenting coordination process were described, as were suggestions to help PCs prepare for interviewing children. I also described a structured interview format that I have found to be valuable for consistently eliciting helpful and rich information from children. A child interview, sensitively undertaken, enables the PC (or custody mediator, child custody evaluator, or judge) to develop a rich understanding of children's needs, perspectives, and wishes on topics relevant to each family's disputes. The input provided by children often helps parents reach beneficial agreements and, when parents are unable to agree, gives the PC the information needed for arriving at sound decisions that may directly affect children's future well-being.

REFERENCES

Amato, P. R., & Fowler, F. (2002). Parenting practices, child adjustment, and family diversity. *Journal of Marriage and Family, 64*, 703–716. doi:10.1111/j.1741-3737.2002.00703.x

American Psychological Association. (2012). Guidelines for the practice of parenting coordination. *American Psychologist, 67*, 63–71. doi:10.1037/a0024646

Association of Family and Conciliation Courts, Task Force on Parenting Coordination. (2006). Guidelines for parenting coordination. *Family Court Review, 44*, 164–181. doi:10.1111/j.1744-1617.2006.00074.x

Birnbaum, R., & Bala, N. (2010a). Judicial interviews with children in custody and access cases: Comparing experiences in Ontario and Ohio. *International Journal of Law, Policy and the Family, 24*, 300–337. doi:10.1093/lawfam/ebq011

Birnbaum, R., & Bala, N. (2010b). Toward the differentiation of high-conflict families: An analysis of social science research and Canadian case law. *Family Court Review, 48*, 403–416. doi:10.1111/j.1744-1617.2010.01319.x

Birnbaum, R., Bala, N., & Cyr, F. (2011). Children's experiences with family justice professionals in Ontario and Ohio. *International Journal of Law, Policy and the Family, 25*, 398–422. doi:10.1093/lawfam/ebr014

Boshier, P. (2006). Involving children in decision making: Lessons from New Zealand. *Australian Journal of Family Law, 20*, 145–153.

Bruck, M., Ceci, S. J., & Hembrooke, H. (1998). Reliability and credibility of young children's reports. *American Psychologist, 53*, 136–151. doi:10.1037/0003-066X.53.2.136

Buchanan, C. M., Maccoby, E., & Dornbusch, S. (1991). Caught between parents: Adolescents' experience in divorced homes. *Child Development, 62*, 1008–1029. doi:10.2307/1131149

Carter, D. K. (2011). *Parenting coordination: A guide for family law professionals*. New York, NY: Springer.

Cashmore, J., & Parkinson, P. (2008). Children's and parents' perceptions on children's participation in decision making after parental separation and divorce. *Family Court Review, 46*, 91–104. doi:10.1111/j.1744-1617.2007.00185.x

Ceci, S. (1994). Cognitive and social factors in children's testimony. In B. Sales & G. VandenBos (Eds.), *The psychology of litigation and legislation* (pp. 11–54). Washington, DC: American Psychological Association. doi:10.1037/11103-001

Ceci, S., & Bruck, M. (1995). *Jeopardy in the courtroom: A scientific analysis of children's testimony*. Washington, DC: American Psychological Association. doi:10.1037/10180-000

Clarke-Stewart, A., & Brentano, C. (2006). *Divorce: Causes and consequences*. New Haven, CT: Yale University Press.

Deutsch, R. M., Coates, C. A., & Fieldstone, L. (2008). Parenting coordination: An emerging role to assist high conflict families. In L. Fieldstone & C. A. Coates (Eds.), *Innovations in interventions with high conflict families* (pp. 187–221). Madison, WI: Association of Family and Conciliation Courts.

Dunn, J., Davies, L., O'Connor, T., & Sturgess, W. (2001). Family lives and friendships: The perspectives of children in step-, single-parent, and nonstop families. *Journal of Family Psychology, 15*, 272–287. doi:10.1037/0893-3200.15.2.272

Fabricius, W. V., Sokol, K. R., Diaz, P., & Braver, S. L. (2012). Parenting time, parent conflict, parent–child relationships and children's physical health.

In K. Kuehnle & L. Drozd (Eds.), *Parenting plan evaluations: Applied research for the family court* (pp. 188–213). New York, NY: Oxford University Press.

Fidler, B. J., Bala, N., & Saini, M. (2013). *Children who resist post-separation parental contact: A differential approach for legal and mental health professionals*. New York, NY: Oxford University Press.

Garbarino, J., & Stott, F. (1990). *What children can tell us: Eliciting, interpreting & evaluating information from children*. San Francisco, CA: Jossey-Bass.

Gollop, M., Smith, A. B., & Taylor, N. J. (2000). Children's involvement in custody and access arrangements. *Child and Family Law Quarterly, 12*, 396–399.

Grych, J. H. (2005). Interparental conflict as a risk factor for child maladjustment: Implications for the development of prevention programs. *Family Court Review, 43*, 97–108.

Hetherington, E. M., & Kelly, J. (2002). *For better or for worse*. New York, NY: W. W. Norton.

Johnston, J. R., Kuehnle, K., & Roseby, V. (2009). *In the name of the child* (2nd ed.). New York, NY: Springer.

Kamp Dush, C. M., Kotila, L. E., & Schoppe-Sullivan, S. J. (2011). Predictors of supportive coparenting after relationship dissolution among at-risk parents. *Journal of Family Psychology, 25*, 356–365. doi:10.1037/a0023652

Kelly, J. B. (1994). The determination of child custody. *The Future of Children, 4*, 121–142.

Kelly, J. B. (1997). The best interests of the child: A concept in search of meaning. *Family Court Review, 35*, 377–387. doi:10.1111/j.174-1617.1997.tb00480.x

Kelly, J. B. (2002). Psychological and legal interventions for parents and children in custody and access disputes: Current research and practice. *Virginia Journal of Social Policy & the Law, 10*, 129–163.

Kelly, J. B. (2003). Parents with enduring child disputes: Multiple pathways to enduring disputes. *Journal of Family Studies, 9*, 37–50. doi:10.5172/jfs.9.1.37

Kelly, J. B. (2007). Children's living arrangements following separation and divorce: Insights from empirical and clinical research. *Family Process, 46*, 35–52. doi:10.1111/j.1545-5300.2006.00190.x

Kelly, J. B. (2008). Preparing for the parenting coordination role: Training needs for mental health and legal professionals. *Journal of Child Custody, 5*, 140–159. doi:10.1080/15379410802070476

Kelly, J. B. (2012). Risk and protective factors associated with child and adolescent adjustment following separation and divorce: Social science applications. In K. Kuehnle & L. Drozd (Eds.), *Parenting plan evaluations: Applied research for the family court* (pp. 49–84). New York, NY: Oxford University Press.

Kelly, J. B., & Emery, R. E. (2003). Children's adjustment following divorce: Risk and resilience perspectives. *Family Relations, 52*, 352–362. doi:10.1111/j.1741-3729.2003.00352.x

Kelly, J. B., & Johnston, J. R. (2001). The alienated child: A reformulation of parental alienation syndrome. *Family Court Review, 39*, 249–266. doi:10.1111/j.174-1617.2001.tb00609.x

Kelly, J. B., & Kisthardt, M. K. (2009). Helping parents tell their children about separation and divorce: Social science frameworks and the lawyer's counseling responsibility. *Journal of the American Academy of Matrimonial Lawyers, 22*, 1401–1420.

Kirkland, K., & Sullivan, M. (2008). Parenting coordination (PC) practice: A survey of experienced professionals. *Family Court Review, 46*, 622–636. doi:10.1111/j.1744-1617.2008.00228.x

Kuehnle, K. (1996). *Assessing allegations of child sexual abuse*. Sarasota, FL: Professional Resource Press.

Lamb, M. E. (2010). (Ed.). *The role of the father in child development* (5th ed.). New York, NY: Wiley.

Lamb, M. E. (2012). Mothers, fathers, families and circumstances: Factors affecting children's adjustment. *Applied Developmental Science, 16*, 98–111. doi:10.1080/10888691.2012.667344

Lamb, M. E., & Lewis, C. (2013). Father–child relationships. In C. S. Tamis-LeMonda & N. Cabrera (Eds.), *Developmental science: An advanced textbook* (2nd ed., pp. 469–517). New York, NY: Psychology Press.

Maccoby, E., & Mnookin, R. (1992). *Dividing the child*. Cambridge, MA: Harvard University Press.

Parkinson, P., & Cashmore, J. (2008). *The voice of a child in family law disputes*. Oxford, UK: Oxford University Press. doi:10.1093/acprof:oso/9780199237791.001.0001

Parkinson, P., Cashmore, J., & Single, J. (2007). Parents' and children's views on talking to judges in parenting disputes in Australia. *International Journal of Law, Policy and the Family, 21*, 84–107. doi:10.1093/lawfam/ebl022

Poole, D. A., & Lamb, M. E. (1998). *Investigative interviews of children. A guide for helping professionals*. Washington, DC: American Psychological Association. doi:10.1037/10301-000

Pruett, M. K., Cowan, P., Cowan, C., & Diamond, J. (2012). Supporting father involvement in the context of separation and divorce. In K. Kuehnle & L. Drozd (Eds.), *Parenting plan evaluations: Applied research for the family court* (pp. 123–151). New York, NY: Oxford University Press.

Sandler, I., Miles, J., Cookston, J., & Braver, S. (2008). Effects of father and mother parenting on children's mental health in high and low conflict divorces. *Family Court Review, 46*, 282–296. doi:10.1111/j.1744-1617.2008.00201.x

Sandler, I., Wolchik, S., Winslow, E., Mahrer, N., Moran, J., & Weinstock, D. (2012). Quality of maternal and paternal parenting following separation and divorce. In K. Kuehnle & L. Drozd (Eds.), *Parenting plan evaluations: Applied research for the family court* (pp. 85–122). New York, NY: Oxford University Press.

Saywitz, K. J. (1995). Improving children's testimony: The question, the answer, and the environment. In M. Zaragoza, J. Graham, G. Hall, R. Hirschman, &

Y. Ben-Porath (Eds.), *Memory and testimony in the child witness* (pp. 113–140). Thousand Oaks, CA: Sage.

Siegler, R. S., DeLoache, J. S., & Eisenberg, N. (2010). *How children develop* (3rd ed.). New York, NY: Worth.

Smart, C. (2002). From children's shoes to children's voices. *Family Court Review, 40*, 307–319. doi:10.1111/j.174-1617.2002.tb00842.x

Smart, C., & Neale, B. (2000). "It's my life too"—Children's perspectives on post-divorce parenting. *Family Law, 30*, 163–169.

Smith, A. B., & Gollop, M. M. (2001). What children think separating parents should know. *New Zealand Journal of Psychology, 30*, 23–31.

Smith, A. B., Taylor, N. J., & Tapp, P. (2003). Rethinking children's involvement in decision-making after parental separation. *Childhood, 10*, 201–216. doi:10.1177/0907568203010002006

Taylor, N. J. (2006). What do we know about involving children and young people in family law decision making? A research update. *Australian Journal of Family Law, 20*, 154–178.

Taylor, N. J., Tapp, P., & Henaghan, M. (2007). Respecting children's participation in family law proceedings. *International Journal of Children's Rights, 15*, 61–82. doi:10.1163/092755607X185555

Thompson, R. A. (2006). The development of the person: Social understanding, relationships, conscience, self. In N. Eisenberg, W. Damon, & R. M. Lerner (Eds.), *Handbook of child psychology: Vol. 3. Social, emotional, and personality development* (6th ed., pp. 24–98). New York, NY: Wiley.

Wallerstein, J., & Kelly, J. B. (1980). *Surviving the breakup: How children and parents cope with divorce*. New York, NY: Basic Books.

Warshak, R. (2003). Payoffs and pitfalls of listening to children. *Family Relations, 52*, 373–384.

Williams, S. S. (2008). *Through the eyes of young people: Meaningful child participation in family court processes*. Victoria, British Columbia, Canada: International Institute for Child Rights and Development.

10

PARENTING COORDINATION AND DIVERSITY ISSUES

GISELLE A. HASS

In this chapter, I address the issues that arise when providing parenting coordination services to diverse populations and individuals with nontraditional parenting arrangements, as well as to economically challenged parents. Given the diverse racial, ethnic, socioeconomic, and sexual orientation populations in the United States and Canada, parenting coordination clients will be increasingly likely to come from a variety of groups (American Psychological Association [APA], 2003). My discussion addresses some of the unique challenges and opportunities parenting coordinators (PCs) face when integrating these issues into their work and how to obtain the knowledge and skills to work effectively with multicultural populations. It is important to emphasize that families from nontraditional populations are immensely varied and do not fit any stereotype. The review I provide in this chapter is less than

The author wishes to acknowledge Dr. Karen Daum for having participated in the research and discussion of these issues, which are described in her clinical research project (Daum, 2007) completed as part of her doctoral degree requirements at Argosy University, Washington, DC.

http://dx.doi.org/10.1037/14390-011
Parenting Coordination in Postseparation Disputes: A Comprehensive Guide for Practitioners, S. A. Higuchi and S. J. Lally (Editors)

exhaustive and is intended to provide an awareness of issues PCs should consider, but PCs need to evaluate each case on its own merits. Of note is that diversities often overlap and intersect in ways that generate unique families with unique challenges and strengths.

APA's position, delineated in the *Ethical Principles of Psychologists and Code of Conduct* (2010), is the aspiration that psychologists

> strive to benefit those with whom they work and take care to do no harm (Principle A), recognize that fairness and justice entitle all persons to access to and benefit from the contributions of psychology and to equal quality in the processes, procedures and services (Principle D), and respect the dignity and worth of all people. (Principle E; APA, 2010)

APA's (2012b) parenting coordination guidelines also highlight the importance of awareness of family diversity in parenting coordination practice by explicitly recognizing the importance of tailoring the services to each family's unique cultural, racial, ethnic, ability, gender, religious, and income circumstances. Given the increased diversity in North American society, it has become necessary to learn how to take into consideration all the various characteristics of the families one serves in parenting coordination interventions. There is an abundant literature demonstrating that turning a blind attitude toward clients' diversity leads to inequitable outcomes (Brewer & Brown, 1998; Wolsko, Park, Judd, & Wittenbrink, 2000).

Aside from the ethical mandates, it makes good clinical sense to integrate diversity factors into parenting coordination work as part of a holistic approach to understand the complexity of human beings. In Urie Bronfenbrenner's (1977) seminal article, he stated that "the understanding of human development demands . . . . examination of multi-person systems of interaction not limited to a single setting and must take into account aspects of the environment beyond the immediate situation containing the subject" (pp. 513–514). This ecological model posits that individuals, and the processes taking place within and between them, must be viewed as interdependent and must be analyzed in systems terms. Given that parenting coordination work is by nature a multiperson system, taking into consideration each family's contextual circumstances is crucial to effective parenting coordination practice.

A generalization of Bronfenbrenner's (1977) conceptualization to parenting coordination work is the notion that the sources of conflict in divorce and coparenting within and between the parties are interactive and often reciprocal. Parents' developmental and cultural experiences influence their attitudes and behaviors as well as their ability to negotiate disagreements and relationship dissolution. The characteristics of high conflict may manifest over a variety of custody-related issues, such as financial support, custody arrangements, access to the children, and values and methods of child rearing

(Johnston, 1994). These are issues often influenced by the social context of the parents, including variations in socioeconomic status; cultural, racial, and ethnic values; religious norms; gender; and physical/cognitive ability. One parent's attitude and behavior, in turn, influences the attitude and behavior of the other parent both as an individual and a coparent and directly affects the parents' relationship with the children and the intensity of the conflict. For greater effectiveness in this complex role, PCs need to understand the unique identities and particular circumstances of their clients' lives and tailor their interventions accordingly. Insufficient knowledge or mismanagement regarding the complexity of the clients' lives can

- discourage parents from participating in the process,
- discourage parents from seeing parenting coordination as a resource to solve their coparenting problems,
- discourage parents from following through with parenting coordination guidance and with the parenting coordination process,
- keep parents from being honest and engaged in the process, and/or
- determine the success or lack of success of the process.

PCs who work with parents from diverse populations need to gain the skills and knowledge to work effectively with individuals of different backgrounds because the models of intervention that have been developed for parenting coordination work are not universally applicable. PCs will benefit from following the guidance of Lederach (1995) regarding cross-cultural problem solving, which suggests a combination of prescriptive and elicitive approaches. In the *prescriptive approach*, information is transferred and the professional is an expert, model, and facilitator, and the goal is to teach new strategies for facing conflict. In the *elicitive approach*, the professional is a catalyst and facilitator of the process of discovery and creation, guiding the participants in the creation of their own conflict-resolution models.

Although the literature makes clear that diversity issues matter in parenting coordination work, PCs often do not truly understand exactly how, where, and when they are supposed to address them. Considerations of client diversity always apply, but whether they make a difference in particular case must be determined together with the clients by taking into consideration their own experience and perceptions. Parents from diverse populations are just as vulnerable to stress as parents from more traditional groups. At times, their challenges may combine to produce extenuating circumstances that drain their energies, patience, time, money, and desire to cooperate when it feels as if everything in their lives is depriving and going wrong. Frequently they are also plagued by unnecessary stress generated by social discrimination and, at times, a racial/ethnic minority status. Because of this, any hypothesis regarding the impact of a client's particular ethnic/cultural, socioeconomic, sexual orientation, religious, or physical/cognitive ability background needs to be assessed before labels of psychopathology or lack of cooperation are applied, for example, in cases of impasse. A PC's integration of diversity issues proceeds by considering how these factors explain some or all of the problems, coping strategies, attitudes, and behaviors that bear on parenting coordination work. These data should be weighed among competing hypotheses and integrated into a meaningful understanding of the case, strategy, and interventions. Giving the parents the benefit of the doubt often allows the PC to explore a competing hypothesis that may lead to the resolution and removal of external obstacles and barriers to more productive paths of action.

Issues of diversity will increase the complexity and sophistication of a parenting coordination case and often demand the use of creative approaches to or accommodations of traditional parenting coordination practice in regard to priorities, usual procedures, attitude, case strategy, the depth and extent of interventions, and the need for creativity and resourcefulness in the interventions.

ASSESSMENT

The PC's first step when working with a particular client is to determine what, if any, diversity issues are involved in the case and then assess their relevance and impact. Diversity, unlike other relevant issues in the parenting coordination process, is largely determined by the client. The concept of the "client's identities and context" (Hays, 2008) is a good way to think about clients' multiple identifications that provide a background to the way they feel about themselves. The PC must be aware of these potential areas of identity and ask questions. For this to happen, the PC must let go of any preconceived notions. For example, a person's name and last name may not be related at all to his or her ethnicity; that a couple was married in a particular religion does not automatically imply that they follow the tenets of that religion; and although a physical disability may be visible, its impact may vary—it could be of great, some, or no relevance to the particular presenting issues.

A number of observations can be made when meeting parents for the initial interviews. The clients' language fluency and accent, physical appearance, preferred spatial distance in interpersonal encounters, eye contact, mannerisms, clothes, and other such visible characteristics can serve as basis for hypotheses—not assumptions—that can be further explored. In this way, a constellation of different characteristics would begin to enrich the PC's understanding of the parents and the world they inhabit. Although it is usually considered taboo to ask personal questions about an individual's personal background (e.g., religion), it is important that the PC explore these matters, because otherwise his or her personal assumptions may prevail (Hays, 2008). Asking parents to describe themselves in their own words is always a good first step to give them the freedom to disclose what they believe is important to their identity and perspective. In an open-ended interview format, parents should be able to narrate spontaneously their background and idiosyncratic values. After this, the PC may pose follow-up questions or invitations to greater disclosure. For instance, if the issue of religion was not previously disclosed or disclosed in only a general manner, a question might be, "What are your religious beliefs?" (Berg-Cross & Zoppetti, 1991), or "Do you have a religious or spiritual practice now?" (Hays, 2008, p. 72). Hays (2008) provided in her book a list of questions designed to explore issues of diversity, for instance, "Would you tell me about your cultural heritage or background?" (p. 72) and "What is the nature of your disability?" (p. 70).

To establish an adequate base knowledge and rapport, it is important that the PC go beyond initial observations and explore how the environment interacts with a particular client's unique characteristics. Background knowledge of the community in which the PC is practicing and the way that the different local environment responds to various racial, ethnic, or religious identities is essential. For instance, the courts in certain jurisdictions may or may not be respectful of the rights of gay parents, or schools in certain cities may be indifferent to the celebrations of certain ethnic or religious holidays. This information about the community may help provide clients with a sense of understanding and consideration for their specific needs. Furthermore, it is important that the PC gain an understanding of whether these specific cultural characteristics influence the balance of status, power, and equality between the parents and whether they would interfere with the PC's goals for the family. As Elkin (1987) noted, these goals can include having a continuation of the family's concept, lessening the feelings of rejection and abandonment among the children, providing the needed stability and continuity of contacts for the children, equalizing power and authority between the parents, and decreasing the likelihood of an overburdened parent.

Finally, it is also important to consider how the clients will see the PC and how this perception is useful or detrimental to the process. As instruments of change, PCs introduce their own experience either as part of the dominant culture and/or as part of the authority figures who interact with clients. Developing an unbiased and culturally aware attitude involves identification of the personal background, values, and attitudes that PCs have toward diverse groups and an acknowledgment that they themselves are also part of the multicultural tapestry (APA, 2003). PCs who have increased contact with groups that have customs and traditions that differ from the PC's own under low-prejudice conditions and with the focus on personal communication (Brewer & Brown, 1998) have an advantage in that these experiences help them understand both their own and other frames of reference. Chin (1994) advised that, in clinical situations, one acknowledge the similarities and differences between one's own cultural background and that of the client, and acknowledge a lack of familiarity regarding some aspects of the client's background, while at the same time professing an openness to learn and be helpful. A PC who does this will thus be in a better position to explore how a client's diverse characteristics might influence the particular goals of the parenting coordination process.

In the following sections, I review variations for parenting coordination practice with diverse parents; including those from various racial, cultural, and ethnic backgrounds; those of low socioeconomic status; lesbian/gay/bisexual/transgendered (LGBT) parents; parents who are members of religious minorities; nontraditional families; and parents with physical or cognitive disabilities.

CULTURAL, RACIAL, AND ETHNIC DIVERSITY

Of significant importance is the role that ethnicity and culture may play in the parties' conflict. An individual's *ethnicity* refers to the subscription to the heritage mores and practices including race, family country of origin, culture, and religion. One might subscribe to multiple ethnicities concurrently and emphasize one over the other at different points in time (APA, 2003).

According to APA's (2003) multicultural guidelines, an individual's *race* is determined by phenotypic characteristics such as skin color, hair type, and other physical features. Society has generalized assumptions and misconceptions regarding what are believed to be the physical characteristics of each specific race. For the purposes of parenting coordination work, race may contribute little or much to the conflict between the parents. For example, it is likely the color of the person's skin is irrelevant to the parenting coordination process when the parents do not consider it relevant to the issues of contention. When a parent's race is being used by the other parent to denigrate him or her, the PC needs to put a stop to this form of abuse and turn this into a nonissue.

Yet, race can be dramatically relevant in cases of mixed-race relationships or when there are children of a mixed or different race than one or both parents. For example, Nyree,[1] an African American, and James, a Caucasian, had a 5-year-old girl named Maya. Maya spent every other weekend and Wednesday evenings with her father. An issue of contention for Nyree, as

[1]This and all subsequent names are pseudonyms, and the example cases are composites to protect confidentiality.

much as for Maya, was James's inability to care for and braid Maya's afro-textured hair in the way that Nyree did and their African American culture expected. Maya started to refuse going to school on Mondays because her hair was matted and unkempt, and the parents were emotional and inflexible around this issue. It would be an error for a PC in such a case to believe that this issue was of less importance than others, because it was something at the core of the child's racial identity. Thus, the PC presented to the parents a report reviewing psychological literature regarding girls' hair and issues of health, identity, appearance, and self-esteem, and asked them to discuss it. Once the parents understood that the issue was beyond aesthetics and that it deeply influenced Maya's feeling about her body appearance and social impact, James said he was willing to find a hairdresser to clean and condition Maya's braids on Sunday evenings, and Nyree agreed to go to school earlier on Thursdays to check and correct the tension of Maya's braids. This solution provided a bridge of understanding for mother, father, and child that made them feel respected and understood.

In some custody cases, one or both parties may be from communities or countries where divorce is extremely rare and custody is almost always given to only one of the parents. One of the changes with living in the United States is that acculturation may bring a greater sense of empowerment for many men and women regarding their personal rights and roles as parents outside the boundaries they had in their native communities or cultural groups. The PC needs to deal with these dual identities and the implications regarding the social role a parent may have in his or her family and cultural community. For instance, it is important that the PC explore with a female client what her ethnic identity and her community would expect from her regarding her new role as a single mother. Because female and male roles differ significantly in Indian, Arab, Latino, and some Asian communities, for example, it is important that the PC have knowledge of the nuances of these varying roles in order to provide the parents with the best chances of obtaining community support and personal satisfaction in their new social status.

Related to this issue of acculturation are changes that may occur within a person's sense of identity after a relationship dissolves. Parents may revert to traditions or customs from earlier times in their lives, and the common ground they developed as a couple is abandoned. For instance, religious practices may be abandoned by the parent who initially gave up his or her religious practice, or cultural holidays that were never celebrated all of a sudden become important for a parent. Although it is true that on many occasions these issues emerged only as another symbol of the postseparation conflict, at other times they indeed represent a parent's struggle to recover his or her former self and desire to be more grounded to traditional values that will help that parent heal from the dissolution of the relationship.

In one case example, Shah asked the PC to help her and her ex-partner negotiate visits with the children to the home of her male cousin, who lived 180 miles away, necessitating a full weekend be taken from the children's time with their father twice a month. The father asserted that the last time they visited her cousin was 2 years earlier and that she never had much interest in getting close to him. The PC uncovered that Shah held patriarchal values and wanted to get close to a male family member who would replace the structure and guidance that her husband used to provide. Once the PC understood the real origin of such request, the PC was in a better position to dispel quick labels that may have characterized Shah as selfish or manipulative and help the parents negotiate a solution that would meet her need for a male authority figure in Shah's life.

Among the issues that may have a significant impact in the dynamics of high-conflict parents and that PCs may evaluate are the following: individualist or collectivist values that affect family structure, relationships, and conflict resolution; child-rearing practices; parental attitudes regarding education, the children's role, and parent–child relationships; the dynamics of separation and grieving; cultural values and norms regarding divorce and being single; cultural assumptions about conflict and its resolution; and language and communication. For instance, parenting styles vary among cultural groups. European American/White families may focus on encouraging their children to develop self-sufficiency and self-determination (McGill & Pearce, 2005), whereas other cultures may foster in their children a sense of interdependence and even concealing their competence, such as in Japanese culture (Shibusawa, 2005). Although it is useful to be aware of these broad characterizations of parenting style associated with different cultural groups, it is important to assess the degree to which these characterizations hold true for the specific parents with whom the PC is working. When parents of different cultural groups, or even from different educational and socioeconomic groups within the same culture, clash regarding their parenting practices, the impact on children can be very destructive. In these cases, PCs may need to dedicate some time to discuss and negotiate with the parents the basic values they want to transmit to their children and explain some of the research foundations of good parenting practices.

Immigration

Providing parenting coordination services when one or both parties are foreign born may present certain challenges. Issues related to immigration status may inhibit parents from seeking outside assistance because they fear discrimination, deportation, being perceived as not deserving the social and community services they seek, or being perceived as more likely to partake in illegal behavior. Research has shown that these perceptions may actually inhibit those individuals from seeking or accepting outside support or services when needed, including calling the police during violent disputes (Ammar, Orloff, Dutton, & Hass, 2005).

The evaluation of a person's degree of acculturation is important for PCs because it represents the degree of interaction between the person and the racial/ethnic majority group (Aponte & Barnes, 1995), and thus it reveals the parents' perspective regarding their values and assumptions about child-rearing practices, conflict resolution, and other concepts important in the PC work. The International Organization for Migration (2004) defined *acculturation* as "the progressive adoption of elements of a foreign culture (ideas, words, values, norms, behavior, institutions) by persons, groups or classes of a given culture" (p. 5). According to Berry and Kim (1988), the acculturation process includes five phases: (a) pre-contact, (b) contact, (c) conflict, (d) crisis, and (e) final adaptation. Bemak, Chung, and Pedersen (2003) noted that each phase of acculturation focus on two fundamental questions: "(1) How much of one's cultural identity is valued and retained? and (2) To what extent are positive relations with the dominant culture sought" (p. 30). An immigrant parent in an acculturation phase such as Berry and Kim's conflict stage, in which one resists the values of the dominant group, may clash with a coparent or children who are at another phase of acculturation to the host culture, such as final adaptation. Different acculturation levels between parents, even when both of them are immigrants, may lead to intense disputes, misunderstandings, and disagreement. The PC may find that the parents disagree in terms of decisions that have cultural meaning, such as raising the children to be bilingual; the age in which children are allowed to date; or, when a child has a mental health disorder, whether to pursue therapy, a natural healer, or both. Immigrant parents often have high standards for their children regarding strong assimilation and pressure that their children fulfill the parents' dreams. The degree of assimilation to the societal values of the host culture is also important for parents from diverse cultural groups and interracial parents. PCs need to be vigilant to ensure that disagreements regarding cultural values and standards do not become an unhealthy battle with the children.

In some cases, parental agreement to have the child obtain a passport, obtain citizenship in a different country, or travel outside the United States takes a different meaning when there is a real fear that the child will be kidnapped by the foreign-born parent. PCs need to be aware that some countries do not abide by the 1980 Hague Convention on the Civil Aspects of International Child Abduction. Depending on the contractual agreement and jurisdiction, decisions in this area may fall outside the scope of the PC's agreement and competence. In these cases a PC would best seek consultation from other professionals.

Language

APA's (2007) "Guidelines for Providers of Psychological Services to Ethnic, Linguistic, and Culturally Diverse Populations" state the following:

> Problems may arise when the linguistic skills of the psychologist do not match the language of the client. In such a case, psychologists refer the client to a mental health professional who is competent to interact in the language of the client. If this is not possible, psychologists offer the client a translator with cultural knowledge and an appropriate professional background. When no translator is available, then a trained paraprofessional from the client's culture is used as a translator/culture broker. (Guideline 6a, paragraph 28)

Even when the client seems to speak English fairly well, it is the PC's responsibility to make sure that the particular nuances of language during discussions, educational sessions, and binding recommendations are fully understood by both parents equally. When giving clients documents that have been translated from English into another language, the PC needs to make sure that the language is simple and devoid of too much legalese yet stays faithful to the original English document. It is also a good idea to place the translated document directly next to the original English one so the client can see both versions, because often language knowledge does not overlap. It is also recommended that the PC allow the client to take translated documents home so they can consult with someone before signing.

In addition to the PC's responsibility of making sure that a client understands and is an active participant in the parenting coordination process uninhibited by language barriers, psychological issues may also arise, such as the influence of language in cognitions and emotions. Guttfreund (1990) noted that emotions are more easily experienced in some languages than others. Information related to how language use may decrease the intensity of an argument may be helpful both for the PC and for other professionals working with the family, or for when the parents communicate among these professionals.

SOCIOECONOMIC STATUS

Custody decisions used to be largely influenced by the gender and economic status of the parent. Even today, many custody litigants may use the difference in economic resources or social status of one parent over the other to support the argument that one parent would best provide for the child. Luckily, most U.S. courts seem to have become sophisticated in conceptualizing the best-interest standard with the help of psychology literature.

Thus, using theories of attachment and child development, the ideal environment has become recognized as one that would aim to preserve and promote a healthy relationship with the child's caregivers, ensuring that the child's needs are responded and attended to appropriately (Willemsen & Willemson, 2000).

Low socioeconomic status is a multidimensional concept that includes not only a lack of financial means but also diminished assets critical for human development, such as health and education (Alkire, 2007). Yoshikawa, Aber, and Beardslee (2012) provided the following three categories: (a) *absolute poverty* relates to the presence and disparities in food, shelter, and other basic material needs; (b) *relative poverty* relates to income inequality at the lower range of income values; and (c) *subjective poverty* relates to the subjective perception of need. Gershoff, Aber, Raver, and Lennon (2007) found that low income correlated with lower parental investment of time and money in their children's learning, and perceived material deprivation more strongly predicted stress in the parenting role, harsh or unresponsive parenting, and variations in children's social and emotional development.

Moreover, the way a parent, family, and child experience the world is immensely different depending on their income, resources, and social class. The amount and quality of resources a family possesses tend to make a significant contribution to their dynamics, practices, and values. In particular, when working with low-income groups, it is important that the PC consider not only the effects of poverty and economic hardship but also the historical and current sociocultural factors that influence the family experiences. Low-income and indigent families in the parenting coordination process often present unique challenges, including a lack of legal advice, limited financial resources, direct and indirect hardships on the children, compromised parenting skills, high stress levels, and lower use of or access to community services. Each of these issues is explored in detail in the following sections.

Lack of Legal Advice

For indigent and low-income families in custody disputes, legal representation is often a luxury they cannot afford. Many courts have programs designed to provide self-help services, clinics, or other forms of legal advice to pro se litigants. The utilization of these services is at times encumbered by the educational limitations of the litigants, their limited free time to attend such meetings, or their lack of knowledge of these services. These same factors play a role in low-income high-conflict families' ability to pursue or take full advantage of mechanisms for alternative dispute resolution.

If the parents are not able to afford counsel, court orders may be issued with less focus on the specific needs of the children and based instead on the parents' priorities. In other cases, legal representation may represent a significant burden parents cannot afford once the custody has been determined. In either case, PCs often find themselves working directly with high-conflict families without the support of their legal advocates. Thus, the PC may inherit custody orders that were incomplete, or inadequate to meet the specific needs of the children, or the PC may have to make requests or render decisions that need to take into consideration the legal rights of the family members. Although knowledge of court-related matters, including legal and judiciary concepts and procedures, is essential for the role of PC (APA, 2012b; see also Chapter 2, this volume), psychologists and some PCs are not attorneys, cannot offer legal advice, and may have limitations in their ability to understand the far-reaching legal consequences of certain common parenting coordination practices. In spite of this, PCs are still responsible for protecting the rights of unrepresented litigants while being mindful of maintaining a fair and just process. There may be occasions on which the PC may require a consultation with an attorney or a court representative in order to more clearly sort out some issues.

In one case, a PC was appointed with the purpose of assisting a couple coordinate the shared time their 7-year-old son who had a moderate intellectual disability and his need for specialized services. Because the parents were too busy with the legal battle, their child was not diagnosed until he started school, at age 7. Because of this, the child was not receiving the type of services he needed for his disability. The PC's goal was to coordinate with service providers, school personnel, and medical insurance providers to procure services for the child. However, the parents were slow to produce the medical records needed, refused to sign several forms, and claimed that they did not have time to go to meetings. The PC seemed at risk of assuming responsibilities outside her role and without full parental involvement and, more important, the parents' lack of cooperation bordered on reportable medical neglect. Often, a PC can confer with the parents' attorneys to request help or to pressure and educate uncooperative parents about the potential legal consequences of their behavior, but these parents did not have legal representation. Therefore, the PC asked the court to appoint an educational advocate to work in coordination with her to educate the parents and manage the child's needs.

Limited Financial Resources

Divorce tends to reduce the standard of living for custodial parents and children and, to a lesser extent, for the nonresidential parent (Duncan & Hoffman, 1985). Reduced economic resources may lead to significant changes that may be disruptive or stressful to both parents and children (Kelly & Emery, 2003). This situation, coupled with the common dispute over child support and financing of the children's extracurricular activities, becomes an area where uncooperative parents with limited resources often play out their conflict.

Sometimes, the reduction in financial resources may affect the safety and adequacy of living accommodations, from not having enough to eat, to having limited heating during winter, to having to share a room with a sibling. Some families need to move their residence to locations they can better afford, move in with extended family, or go where they have greater social resources. Sometimes children need to change schools, and child care arrangements may need to be modified. Leisure activities and hobbies, including vacations, that may have been personally meaningful and stress relieving for parents and children, may have to be curtailed after relationship dissolution. Personal spending money for parents and children may also be affected by the new economic status. These types of changes not only are stressful for parents and children but also may become a battleground of conflict and resentment among the parties.

The role of the PC is to understand the impact of these changes on the family's quality of life and parenting. In many cases, the financial constraints could be partially alleviated by referring clients to agencies that help them obtain subsidies and services such as free school lunches, subsidized housing, free transportation, or medical or counseling services that offer fees on a sliding scale. In some cases, PCs need to do substantive legwork to help parents make decisions that will save them money, such as deciding on summer camps very early in the year to lock in lower rates, and to apply for scholarships. In other cases, PCs can suggest how parenting arrangements can be slightly modified to save money in aftercare, facilitate transportation, find free time that a parent can invest in a second job or training, and overall, steer coparents to cooperate in these issues for the benefit of the children.

A valuable modification to standard practice is to apply a rule of caregiving distribution based on parents' capacities rather than trying to divide it equally. For example, the parent who is able to help with homework would provide this help for the child every school day. If the child is in the care of the other parent, then the parent could provide homework help by phone, Skype, or web-based chat. In return, the parent who is able to read a fairy tale in a different language for the child will conduct this activity by phone, Skype, or through tape recordings on the nights the child is with the other parent. The parent who owns a car could have greater involvement in the child's activities that require transportation, and the parent who makes the best cookies for the Monday bake sale at school will take on this activity even when the child was in the care of the other parent over the weekend. Reduced financial resources often require that parents collaborate to maintain an adequate standard of living for the children. PCs should take into consideration whether parents are sufficiently mature to engage properly in this form of collaboration.

Direct and Indirect Hardships

When family resources are limited, children may experience both direct and indirect hardships that affect both their physical and psychological well-being. After a thorough analysis of key research studies in this area, Yoshikawa et al. (2012) concluded that the negative impact of family poverty on children's and youth's mental, emotional, and behavioral health is well established. For instance, according to McLeod and Shanahan (1993), economic hardship increases the overall risk of psychological and behavioral problems among children. For instance, a child's health may be compromised as a result of an inadequate diet or an impoverished environment (Slack & Yoo, 2005). Additional studies have shown that family income remains a reliable predictor of student achievement. Taylor (2005) reported that students who live in poverty are more likely to underachieve than their peers from middle- and high-income families and, in general, are at a higher risk of not completing school altogether.

Given that children of parents who divorce are at risk of having negative outcomes in relation to their parental conflict and that poverty also has negative effects on children, children of both divorced and low-income families are at double jeopardy for negative outcomes. The negative effects of divorce on children may be exacerbated given the already-unstable physical and psychological situation that may result from living in a disadvantaged environment. PCs are in a good position to facilitate services or the use of preventive measures that address areas of risk for parents and children. For instance, PCs can assist in the identification of community programs or volunteers to help the children with homework; sport, recreational, artistic, and cultural activities; mentoring; and other such activities of enrichment, which have been found to be protective factors for children and youth (Resnick, 2000; Sibley & Etnier, 2003).

Compromised Parenting Skills

These stresses associated with poverty have been noted (Chilman, 1991) to increase parents' vulnerability to depression, irritability, and explosiveness in their parenting relationships as well as negatively affect children's cognitive and behavioral development (Berger, Paxson, & Waldfogel, 2005). Research indicates that economic well-being may affect the way a parents manage their children (McLoyd, 1998). Specifically, McLoyd (1998) suggested that chronic stressors such as single parenthood, life stress, financial concerns, and the constant struggle to make ends meet affects parents' mental health and in turn diminishes their capacity to provide a sensitive and supportive parenting style. Another study (Mistry, Vandewater, Huston, &

McLoyd, 2002) reported that among low-income families, distressed parents reported feeling less effective and capable in disciplining their children and they were observed to be less affectionate in their parent–child interactions. PCs can help parents find ways to alleviate stress and augment their parenting skills through diverse and creative interventions as well as referrals for specific services. For instance, parenting skills can be strengthened with the use of adequate models of single parenting (real or virtual), parenting groups, modeling to the parents healthy child-related decision-making skills, and providing psychoeducation on child management and bonding activities. Moreover, protective factors for the children, such as a sense of connectedness to adults, social skill development, healthy beliefs and clear family standards for behavior, opportunities for involvement in the school and community, rewards and recognition for prosocial performance (Resnick, 2000), and overall quality of out-of-home caregiving (Blair & Raver, 2012) may need to be strengthened when parents' parenting skills are at risk.

Higher Stresses and Demands for Caregivers May Cause Increased Conflict

Some authors have suggested that the intensity of the conflict between separated or divorced parents is greater among low-income families (e.g., Edin, Kefalas, & Reed, 2004). The quality of the relationships between nonmarried parental figures from low-income populations has also frequently been described as poor and tumultuous. For instance, some studies have revealed that the impact of unemployment often yields significant psychological consequences for both men and women. According to Belle (1990), feelings of inferiority, inadequacy, depression, and frustration are prominent among men and women of low-income status. As noted above, Chilman's (1991) study yielded similar findings, noting that mothers and fathers in circumstances of economic deprivation were more vulnerable to depression, irritability, and explosiveness in their parenting. PCs can use this knowledge to understand parents who may seem overly stressed and explore whether this is related to their socioeconomic burden rather than particular personality pathology, and help them find resources to help alleviate their stresses and lift their spirits.

Lack of Access to or Use of Community Services

Another area in which reduced financial resources greatly affect a family's quality of life is in obtaining third party services. Research indicates that low-income families have more difficulty accessing external resources and support services for many issues, including their physical and mental health (e.g., DeNavas-Walt, Proctor, & Smith, 2011). Children in poor families often do not get help because the services are unavailable, inaccessible, or too costly (Boyle & Offord, 1988). For example, in the United States, children living in poverty are more likely to not have health insurance than the general population. The percentage of uninsured children in the 2010 U.S. Census was 15.4% for children living in poverty, as compared with 9.8% for children in the general population (DeNavas-Walt et al., 2011).

Financial constraints, limited resources available for lower income families, long waiting lists in settings that offer low-fee services, and the unavailability of certain sophisticated services at low fees combine to potentially make the burden of seeking services an insurmountable one for parents already stressed by the relationship dissolution and its consequences. Sometimes, it is not enough to simply make the referral; it also becomes part of the PC's job to case manage and seek out the third party services, set up the appointments, and arrange the transportation for the child to and from the appointments. In cases where parents are not abdicating their responsibility but accepting needed help and learning how to do it independently in the future, these case management services from the PC can make a great difference for a child.

Cultural variables often present barriers to seeking services. Members of racial/ethnic minority groups have been reported as having a negative perception regarding seeking and staying in mental health or substance abuse treatment (Ammar et al., 2005). In fact, many members of cultural minority groups may present with a general mistrust of authority figures and service providers. These perceptions stem from historical and current events, such as slavery, persecution, systematic racism, police profiling, and overall discrimination, that have occurred in the lives of these cultural groups. This mistrust of authority figures in turn influences the families' likelihood of seeking and complying with treatment (Boyd-Franklin, 2003). In these cases, the PC can become a bridge until parents and service providers adjust their alliance. Overall, the PC can work to ensure that the parents feel in control and heard and at the same time informed about their options. It is important to note other cultural barriers that may affect access to external resources. Some of these barriers include, but are not limited to, the stigma associated with seeking mental health services and the view that services outside of their natural support system or kinship group is shameful and indicative of defeat and powerlessness (Leong, Wagner, & Tata, 1995).

Complications in daily life due to external limitations contribute to some coparenting problems and can explain the specific parenting values and coping strategies that had contributed to the conflict. For instance, a parent's ability to take free time from work to pick up or drop off a child with the other parent can enormously influence his or her parenting practices and satisfaction with the parenting role. What may constitute common practice for some families—a parent picking up a child up from school or day care for their scheduled time together—can be a nightmare for families with economic hardships in which a parent might work have to late, cannot take time off from work, needs to take public transportation, and/or is also caring for other children or an elderly parent. As an example, Maria had two jobs and finished working on Fridays at 8:00 p.m. Her children, Pedro and Luis, ages 8 and 10, spent a week with each parent and were exchanged on Fridays after school. Maria asked her boyfriend and also her mother to pick them up, but her ex-husband objected to both. Lacking money for a babysitter or sufficient knowledge of community resources, Maria felt at a loss as to what to do and was feeling pressured to agree to her ex-husband's demand that she pick them up on Saturday at his home, which meant cutting into her time with the boys. In this situation, the PC helped the parents find a community resource—in this case, a soccer camp—that would keep the children until 8:30 p.m., when Maria was able to pick them up. When trying to implement a custody plan that has been ordered from a menu of options without taking into consideration the specific needs of high-conflict families with limited economic means represents a challenge for PCs. Parents should not have to sacrifice time spent with their child because of hardships in getting to their place of employment. An adequate custodial arrangement ideally takes into consideration the extent to which that arrangement is going to interfere with the parents' working obligations and personal responsibilities.

In another example, the parents had a travel time of 3 hours between their houses and, because of financial limitations, neither of the parties could afford to move or leave their current job. Much of the impasse for these parents centered on the issue of travel and involved instances of intense arguments during exchanges. Thus, the PC negotiated the details of the pickup/dropoff with the children's day care, and both maternal and paternal grandmothers were engaged to assist with exchanges, making it easier for the parents and saving them time, money, personal contact, and physical energy. This arrangement also increased the reliability and promptness of pickup/dropoff because there were more people involved in the process. This strategy also modeled a way the PC made use of the parents' interpersonal resources to alleviate the conflict.

As illustrated in this example, an important strength of low-income parents is often the amount of support they receive from extended family or their own created family made up of close friends. It is often the case that these social supports pick a side in the case of separation, and this may demonize them in the eyes of the other parent. When this happens, there is a loss of a precious resource for the family and the children. It is worthwhile for the PC to spend time dealing with the negative feelings parents may have regarding the intervention of extended family members and friends, in order to pave the way for this resource to be useful for the benefit of the children and parents alike. This may be considered a drastic departure of protocol for some PCs who are accustomed to working only with the parents; however, part of the evolution of the field of parenting coordination is the recognition that the individual parents can go only so far and that anything that can help empower parents and push the process forward should be explored.

SEXUAL AND GENDER IDENTITIES

U.S. society has come a long way in terms of the cultural and legal recognition that, as affirmed by APA (2009), "same-sex sexual and romantic attractions, feelings, and behaviors are normal and positive variations of human sexuality regardless of sexual orientation identity" (p. 121). Sexual orientation is neither an obstacle nor a weakness regarding a person's social functioning or parenting functioning. APA has published several public statements regarding the policy of the organization regarding sexual orientation, parents, and children (APA, 1995, 2004, 2012c). In the 2004 statement, the organization asserted that "research has shown that the adjustment, development, and psychological well-being of children is unrelated to parental sexual orientation and that the children of lesbian and gay parents are as likely as those of heterosexual parents to flourish" (p. 10). Courts in many states now recognize that a parent's sexual orientation has nothing to do with his or her fitness as a parent and that sexual orientation per se is not a basis to deny or restrict custody or visitation. A number of state appellate courts (e.g., *Damron v. Damron*, 2003) have held that the sexual orientation of a parent is not a factor in determining custody unless it has been demonstrated to actually harm the child.

PCs who work with LGBT parents need to keep in mind that a child's optimal development is influenced more by the nature of the relationships and interactions within the family unit than by the particular structural form that unit takes (APA, 1995). When PCs are willing to examine their own particular values regarding LGBT parents, they are better able to keep in check any potential biases. For instance, it is important to avoid using heterosexual standards for same-sex couples, such as assuming that one parent played a more nurturing role with the children and the other played a more instrumental role. In fact, LGBT couples parenting together have been noted to divide the labors of parenting fairly evenly (Chan, Brooks, Raboy, & Patterson, 1998; Johnson & O'Connor, 2002).

Conflict may show up in relation to a parent objecting to the other parent's homosexual lifestyle or negative comments of the biological mother against the nonbiological mother, or disparaging comments regarding the other parent and her or his new partner's social gender role conformity (adherence to cultural norms defining masculine and feminine behavior), or implications for the children regarding having same-sex parents. Some studies have noted that when there is heterosexism and stigmatization in a community, children of same-sex parents may be teased and that this interferes with their ability to maintain friendships (Huggins, 1989; Tasker & Golombok, 1995). In all these situations, the PC may want to promote a nonjudgmental attitude and let parents (and, if necessary, other professionals involved in the case) know that children seem to cope quite well when having to understand and explain their family structure to peers or teachers (Perrin, 2002).

At times, the conflict among coparents may be related to aspects related to the children's origin. If the children were adopted, or conceived by one partner in a previous heterosexual relationship, or were born from donor insemination or with assistance of a surrogate, one parent may feel more or less legitimate than the other and use this argument as ammunition against the other parent. In these situations, the PC may need to educate the parents about the significant damage to the child the airing of these issues may cause because they question the child's legitimacy and may cause the child to question whether he or she is "worthy" of parental care.

A related issue is when bisexual or previously heterosexual parents enter a same-sex relationship after the dissolution of a heterosexual relationship. Many lesbians and gay men come out many years after they have been married to a person of the other sex (Buxton, 2005). The implications of this shift for the children and the ex-partner may lead to increased conflict regarding access to and involvement with the children. In addition to education for the parents and children to correct misinformation and prejudice, APA (2012b) standards urge PCs to actively pursue the elimination of discrimination based on sexual orientation in matters regarding access to the children in cases of relationship dissolution. PCs are in a position to facilitate the education of the other parent, the children, family, and community regarding the scientific literature that asserts that children raised by homosexual parents and those raised by heterosexual ones do not differ with respect to the factors that matter: self-esteem; anxiety; depression; behavioral problems; performance in social arenas (e.g., sports, school, and friendships); use of psychological counseling; and mothers' and teachers' reports of children's hyperactivity, unsociability, emotional difficulty, or conduct problems (APA, 1995).

Unique issues for bisexual parents during coparenting may arise in many ways; for instance, societal discrimination against bisexual individuals can also be expressed by gay and lesbian people. Many people do not regard bisexuality as a legitimate sexual orientation and believe that it is a temporary situation or a sign of mental health problems (APA, 2012c). These types of attitudes may appear in the other parent or their children, the family, and community. In addition to education, PCs must be vigilant against discriminatory treatment of the caregivers or children and advocate for the elimination of this situation whenever it exists.

RELIGION

Conflicting religious beliefs among parents sometimes come to the PC's attention. Courts normally make decisions regarding the religion in which a child will be raised and do not concern themselves with the content and value of particular religious beliefs. Neither should the PC be concerned about this when working with parents with different religious beliefs. However, sometimes a parent may argue that the religious practices of the other parent are harmful to the child. For instance, a parent may argue that a father who is a Jehovah's Witness and has been taking the children with him door to door to proselytize during their shared weekends is engaging in harmful behavior. At other times, a parent may argue that the religion of the other parent is imposing restrictions on the other parent's lifestyle, parenting practices, or freedom, such as the case with religions that involve special diets or lifestyle changes and the other parent is expected to support their children in those practices. Of note is that, depending on their age, children may be able to articulate their preference (see Chapter 9, this volume, for a more detailed discussion of involving children in the parenting coordination process). There are cases in which a parent who has converted to the religion of the other parent converts back to his or her original religion after the relationship dissolves, and this changes the assumptions the court should use to make decisions regarding the child's religious practice. In these cases, the issue may be outside the PC's scope of authority and the PC, parents, and their legal representatives may need to go back to court to resolve the issue.

PCs may be able to intervene in issues such as conflict regarding what church, synagogue, or temple the child should attend, child-sharing time during religious holidays, or when there is conflict regarding how to specifically provide religious education to the children. PCs can help also in cases in which a religious parent makes comments to the children that a nonbeliever or nonpracticing parent is going to go "straight to hell" or that the religion of the other parent is wrong. In cases in which the parents may have decided to raise the children in both religions, one parent may put pressure on the children to reject the other parent's religion. There may even be cases in which a parent disagrees on religious values such as repentance, forgiveness, and faith; or of how to handle events such as deaths and births in the family. The PC may need to address these issues by providing education to the parents regarding the need to respect differences, the harm that it may cause the children to be alienated from one parent because of religious differences, the importance for their sense of belonging to the children of following all family and cultural traditions, and the importance of keeping private thoughts that may appear disparaging of the other parent. Just as with any other issue of dispute, the PC should focus on communication to find commonalities and negotiate differences.

In many cases, the PC may help solve practical disputes by being creative and promoting flexibility. For instance, the PC can help parents consider whether to separately celebrate the holidays of their religion or to choose one religion that both of them will celebrate and support its practice. In addition, the parents might decide to celebrate the major holidays in a secular way, with the gift giving, shopping, and festivities; but take away the religious meaning behind the symbols, or even draw traditions from different cultures and regions of the world and incorporate them into their own innovative holiday celebration.

The benefits of belonging to a religious community is also something the PC should take into account. For instance, African American churches have historically provided an important social network of support for its members (Caldwell, Greene, & Billingsley, 1994). Connection to more than one religious community is inherent to the multicultural society of the United States, and the children's exposure to religious and spiritual differences among the family members is something to celebrate. When assessing any specific religious concerns, PCs must observe whether they are superficial attempts to justify controlling or restrictive strategies against the other parent or are indeed valid concerns. Taking a child to religious services during access periods is very different than dictating education, diet, and lifestyle. Sometimes parents may need to be reminded that neither parent should pretend to monopolize the religious identity of the children at the expense of undermining the children's relationship with the other parent (Van Praagh, 1997).

NONTRADITIONAL FAMILY STRUCTURE

The tradition of a mother and a father who, after a period of living together as a married couple, are divorced and share joint custody of their children is no longer the norm. Single-parent families, unmarried parents, stepparents, and extended family caregivers are much more common today than they were two generations ago (Patterson & Hastings, 2007). In addition, family situations often change, and many children live in more than one type of family during the course of their childhoods. Many couples who share custody of their children were never married, and some never lived together. Extended family members may also be a party in the custody dispute, such that a paternal grandmother and a mother may become the primary custodians after the death of the father, or an uncle and an adoptive mother share custody. Extended family members are often important caregivers and attachment figures for the children and can provide a healthy, nurturing environment for the children. The perspective that children will be harmed if they are not raised by a father and a mother has not been substantiated in studies that have looked at children who have multiple adults in a parenting role, whether they are grandparents, other family members, or friends (Silverstein & Auerbach, 1999; Stacey, 1996).

In terms of legislation, the rules governing the determination of legal parenthood have changed and have become at times detached from biological considerations and at other times focused on diverse genetic considerations. An emerging area of inquiry has risen regarding the regulation of known sperm donors' rights and responsibilities regarding their children (McDonald, 2009), as well as the parenting rights of surrogate mothers, as they interact with the best interest of the child in mind (De Alcantara, 2010). Divorced parents with an adoptive child who had an open adoption are another form of family constellation PCs may encounter. PCs should be prepared to understand the particular dynamics of any of the diverse family structures they encounter.

Another situation happens when, by choice or circumstance, a father may be largely absent from his child's life for several years, whether because he did not know of the child's existence or was absent because he was abroad, in prison, or had problems of his own (e.g., substance abuse or mental illness). The reintegration of this parent into the child's life may create significant tension. For instance, some states' welfare system have an aggressive means of tracking down absent parents to pay child support, which may lead a parent to litigate for shared time with the child after being largely absent and uninvolved in the child's life. When a person previously unknown to the child comes into the picture to share custody, the PC is required to assess and address the issues of attachment and incorporate interventions that promote the bond with the children as necessary. Consider this example: Marcus was absent through most of his 5-year-old son's life because he was incarcerated and did not want his son to visit him in prison. After Marcus's release, he petitioned for and obtained a shared custodial arrangement, and the PC was asked to fine-tune the details of a progressively greater plan of time sharing. Through the referral and assistance of an parent–child attachment specialist, the PC was able to work with the parents a plan to both preserve existing attachments and smoothly introduce Marcus into his son's life. Both parents were educated about the potential benefits of the change while also recognizing their concerns and fears. For instance, information regarding the benefits of the father's role in the child's development is relevant to single mothers who do not want the father involved, and some fathers need to learn about the nature of the child's mother resistance to his efforts to have a role in the child's life. In the case of Marcus, the PC's intervention validated both parents' experiences, lessened the mother's unwillingness to allow Marcus back into the child's life, and helped Marcus gain more realistic and appropriate expectations with regard to this new family dynamic.

In many parenting coordination cases, social discrimination may fuel the conflict between parents, or among parents and other family members, as well as within the community, for both parents and children. PCs should assess these issues in order to prevent acts of prejudice toward family members and take steps to help parents eliminate or diminish the impact of discriminative actions toward the children. PCs also should remind parents that research (Amato & Rivera, 1994; Biglan, Flay, Embry, & Sandler, 2012) has made clear that children do best when they have a consistent, caring relationship with at least one responsible adult and that fewer behavior problems occur when parents experience less stress and had low interparental conflict (Chan et al., 1998).

DISABILITY

Disability is a comprehensive term that includes a broad array of different impairments, functional limitations, and barriers to participation in community life (World Health Organization, 2011). Disabilities can encompass mental health conditions; health problems; and sensory, mobility, communication, and neurological impairments (APA, 2012a). Psychologists often have received limited formal training regarding how to work with people with disabilities other than mental health ones, so PCs may need to increase their knowledge base and awareness of the factors that modify the experiences and perceptions of persons with disabilities. Consistent with APA's (2012a) guidelines on assessment and interventions with persons with disabilities, it is important that PCs examine their own beliefs and emotional reactions toward disabilities and how these influence their work (Guideline 2), increase their knowledge and skills (Guideline 3), and acquire information regarding the federal and state laws that support and protect parents with disabilities (Guideline 4, pp. 45–47).

The Americans With Disabilities Act of 1990 (ADA) and the ADA Amendments Act of 2008 prohibit discrimination against individuals on the basis of disability. ADA explicitly states that persons with disabilities have the same right as anyone else to bear and raise children and that disability alone cannot be used to deny child custody, unless the disability prevents the parent from exercising care and control. However, parents with disabilities face a great deal of discrimination and stigma, as do, by association, their partners, ex-partners, and children (Olkin, 1999).

It is important that PCs hold the view that disabled individuals' self-esteem, self-image, and internalization of the disability directly relate to the acceptability and integration of the disability into the family (Olkin, 1999).

Thus, a PC working with a family in which one or both parents have a disability should not make any assumptions regarding limitations to their parenting roles. A study of fathers with spinal cord injury (Buck & Hohmann, 1982) did not find any association between the fathers' disability, or severity of the disability, and maladjustment in children when compared with a control group matched on sex, fathers' age, and socioeconomic factors. Moreover, the children of fathers with a disability reported significantly more positive attitudes regarding love, pride, and respect than the children in the control group. The PC's ability to depathologize the disability and focus on functions rather than limitations will greatly help support parents in their parenting role.

Parents with disabilities face significant social barriers, including their own self-perception as well as societal integration. PCs need to understand and assess the complexity of those needs and strengths. They should familiarize themselves with the array of legislative and service entitlements to which persons with disabilities have access in the United States and about which the parents may not know, or may have not been able to successfully navigate in the past. PCs may want to help a parent directly or indirectly obtain the information and services that will help her or him work around the limitations caused by the disability in the parent's personal life and in the parenting role, and help the children find a healthy accommodation.

A related issue is when parents share custody of a child with a disability. PCs with a mental health education background are in a unique position to understand and manage a child's special needs as well as to coordinate a team of professionals—including medical, educational, psychological, and others—to be involved with the child's case. In these cases there is often an array of needs and demands that may give rise to significant confusion and disagreement among parents regarding the fulfillment of those demands, the coordination of a consistent environment that is responsive to the child's treatment needs, and the diverse perspectives that parents may have in terms of how they perceive and treat the child. PCs can help alleviate for parents the stress and confusion caused by the complexity of these issues and help them find a routine that works for all.

CONCLUSION

Parents from diverse racial, cultural, religious, and other backgrounds are vulnerable to extenuating circumstances that are draining, coupled with the unnecessary stress of social discrimination and their minority status in the milieu of the dominant host culture. PCs must continually recognize, reinforce, and utilize the strengths and resilience that parents derive from their ethnic, cultural, or religious values, in environments that are often hostile, instead of solely focusing on deficits. The key message of this chapter is that PCs need to acquire knowledge about the issues that matter to the parents and children with whom they work, including their ethnic background, native language, traditions, religion, immigration and acculturation experiences, sexual orientation, and/or disability. Just like any family, parents from families with nontraditional backgrounds require education on legal concepts, redefining the family unit, child development, conflict resolution, healthy parenting styles, and the effects of divorce on their children, but they need this information to be tailored to their unique circumstances. When parents' cultural values conflict with developmental guidelines or the best interest of the child, they should be educated about how their children can thrive in the host culture. Ultimately, bringing cases back to court or having to exercise the PC's mandated reporting guidelines may be necessary in extreme cases in which ethnical, cultural, religious, or other factors intersect with a parent's personality pathology that could threaten a child's well-being.

REFERENCES

Alkire, S. (2007). The missing dimensions of poverty data: Introduction to the special issue. *Oxford Development Studies*, *35*, 347–359. doi:10.1080/13600810701701863

Amato, P. R., & Rivera, F. (1994). Well-being in early adulthood. *Journal of Marriage and the Family*, *56*, 1031–1042. doi:10.2307/353611.

American Psychological Association. (1995). *Lesbian and gay parenting: A resource for psychologists*. Retrieved from http://www.apa.org/pi/lgbt/resources/parenting.aspx

American Psychological Association. (2002). Ethical principles of psychologists and code of conduct. *American Psychologist*, *57*, 1060–1073. doi:10.1037/0003-066X.57.12.1060

American Psychological Association. (2003). *Guidelines on multicultural education, training, research, practice, and organizational change for psychologists*. Retrieved from http://www.apa.org/pi/oema/resources/policy/provider-guidelines.aspx

American Psychological Association. (2004). *APA policy statement on sexual orientation, parents and children*. Retrieved from http://www.apa.org/about/policy/parenting.aspx

American Psychological Association. (2007). *APA guidelines for providers of psychological services to ethnic, linguistic, and culturally diverse populations*. Retrieved from http://www.apa.org/pi/oema/resources/policy/provider-guidelines.aspx

American Psychological Association. (2009). *Lesbian, gay, bisexual and transgender persons & socioeconomic status*. Retrieved from http://www.apa.org/pi/ses/resources/publications/factsheet-lgbt.aspx

American Psychological Association. (2010). *Ethical principles of psychologists and code of conduct (2002; amended June 1, 2010)*. Retrieved from http://www.apa.org/ethics/code/principles.pdf

American Psychological Association. (2012a). Guidelines for assessment and intervention with persons with disabilities. *American Psychologist, 67*, 43–62. doi:10.1037/a0025892

American Psychological Association. (2012b). Guidelines for the practice of parenting coordination. *American Psychologist, 67*, 63–71. doi:10.1037/a0024646

American Psychological Association. (2012c). Guidelines for psychological practice with lesbian, gay and bisexual clients. *American Psychologist, 67*, 10–42. doi:10.1037/a0024659

Americans With Disabilities Act of 1990, Pub. L. 101–336, 42 U.S.C. § 12101, et seq.

ADA Amendments Act of 2008, Pub. L. 110–325.

Ammar, N., Orloff, L., Dutton, M., & Hass, G. (2005). Calls to police and police response: A case study of Latina immigrant women in the USA. *International Journal of Police Science and Management, 7*, 230–244.

Aponte, J. F., & Barnes, J. M. (1995). Impact of acculturation and moderator variables on the intervention and treatment of ethnic groups. In J. F. Aponte, R. Y. Rivers, & J. Wohl (Eds.), *Psychological interventions and cultural diversity* (pp. 19–39). Needham Heights, MA: Allyn & Bacon.

Belle, D. (1990). Poverty and mental health. *American Psychologist, 45*, 385–389. doi:10.1037/0003-066X.45.3.385

Bemak, F., Chung, R. C.-Y., & Pedersen, P. (2003). *Counseling refugees: A psychosocial cultural approach to innovative multicultural interventions*. Westport, CT: Greenwood Press.

Berg-Cross, L., & Zoppetti, L. (1991). Person-in-culture interview: Understanding culturally different students. *Journal of College Student Psychotherapy, 5*, 5–21. doi:10.1300/J035v05n04_02

Berger, L. M., Paxson, C., & Waldfogel, J. (2005). *Income and child development*. Fragile Families and Child Wellbeing Study Working Paper No. 2005-16-FF. Retrieved from http://www.fragilefamilies.princeton.edu/ffpubs.asp

Berry, J. W., & Kim, L. (1988). Acculturation and mental health. In P. R. Dasen, J. W. Berry, & N. Sartorius (Eds.), *Health and cross-cultural psychology: Towards applications* (pp. 207–238). Newbury Park, CA: Sage.

Biglan, A., Flay, B. R., Embry, D. D., & Sandler, I. N. (2012). The critical role of nurturing environments for promoting human well-being. *American Psychologist, 67*, 257–271. doi:10.1037/a0026796

Blair, C., & Raver, C. C. (2012). Child development in the context of adversity: Experiential canalization of brain and behavior. *American Psychologist, 67*, 309–318. doi:10.1037/a0027493

Boyd-Franklin, N. (2003). *Black families in therapy*. New York, NY: Guilford Press.

Boyle, M., & Offord, D. (1988). Prevalence of childhood disorder, perceived need for help, family dysfunction, and resource allocation for child welfare and children's mental health services in Ontario. *Canadian Journal of Behavioural Science, 20*, 374–388. doi:10.1037/h0079940

Brewer, M. B., & Brown, R. J. (1998). Intergroup relations. In D. T. Gilbert & S. T. Fiske (Eds.), *The handbook of social psychology* (4th ed., Vol. 2, pp. 554–594). New York, NY: McGraw–Hill.

Bronfenbrenner, U. (1977). Toward an ecology of human development. *American Psychologist, 32*, 513–531. doi:10.1037/0003-066X.32.7.513

Buck, F. M., & Hohmann, G. W. (1982). Child adjustment as related to severity of paternal disability. *Archives of Physical Medicine and Rehabilitation*, 63, 249–253.

Buxton, A. P. (2005). A family matter: When a spouse comes out as gay, lesbian or bisexual. *Journal of GLBT Family Studies, 1*, 49–70. doi:10.1300/J461v01n02_04

Caldwell, C., Greene, A., & Billingsley, A. (1994). Family support in Black churches: A new look at old functions. In S. L. Kagan & B. Weissbourd (Eds.), *Putting families first: America's family support movement and the challenge of change* (pp. 137–160). San Francisco, CA: Jossey-Bass.

Chan, R. W., Brooks, R. C., Raboy, B., & Patterson, C. J. (1998). Division of labor among lesbian and heterosexual parents: Associations with children's adjustment. *Journal of Family Psychology, 12*, 402–419. doi:10.1037/0893-3200.12.3.402

Chilman, C. (1991). Working poor families: Trends, causes, effects, and suggested policies. *Family Relations*, 40, 191–198.

Chin, J. L. (1994). Psychodynamic approaches. In L. Comas-Diaz & B. Greene (Eds.), *Women of color: Integrating ethnic and gender identities in psychotherapy* (pp. 194–222). New York, NY: Guilford Press.

Damron v. Damron, ND 166, 670 N.W. 2nd 871 (2003).

Daum, K. (2007). *The APA Parenting Coordination Program: A project of the American Psychological Association, Argosy University/Washington DC, and the Superior Court of the District of Columbia*. Doctoral clinical research project, Argosy University, Washington, DC.

De Alcantara, M. (2010). Surrogacy in Japan: Legal implications for parentage and citizenship. *Family Court Review*, 48, 417–430. doi:10.1111/j.1744-1617.2010.01320.x

DeNavas-Walt, C., Proctor, B. D., & Smith, J. C. (2011). *Income, poverty, and health insurance coverage in the United States: 2010*. Retrieved from http://www.census.gov/prod/2011pubs/p60-239.pdf

Duncan, G. J., & Hoffman, S. D. (1985). A reconsideration of the economic consequences of marital dissolution. *Demography, 22*, 485–497. doi:10.2307/2061584

Edin, K., Kefalas, M., & Reed, J. (2004). A peek inside the black box: What marriage means to low-income unmarried parents. *Journal of Marriage and Family*, 66, 1007–1014. doi:10.1111/j.0022-2445.2004. 00072.x

Elkin, M. (1987). Joint custody: Affirming that parents and families are forever. *Social Work, 32*, 18–24.

Gershoff, E. T., Aber, J. L., Raver, C. C., & Lennon, M. C. (2007). Income is not enough: Incorporating material hardship into models of income associations with parenting and child development. *Child Development, 78*, 70–95. doi:10.1111/j.1467-8624.2007. 00986.x

Guttfreund, D. G. (1990). Effects of language usage on the emotional experience of Spanish–English and English–Spanish bilinguals. *Journal of Consulting and Clinical Psychology, 58*, 604–607. doi:10.1037/0022-006X.58.5.604

Hague Convention on the Civil Aspects of International Child Abduction. (1980). Senate Treaty Doc. 11, 99th Cong., 1st Sess. 9.

Hays, P. (2008). *Addressing cultural complexities in practice: Assessment, diagnosis, and therapy* (2nd ed.). Washington, DC: American Psychological Association. doi:10.1037/11650-000

Huggins, S. L. (1989). A comparative study of self-esteem of adolescent children of divorced lesbian mothers and divorced heterosexual mothers. *Journal of Homosexuality, 18*, 123–135. doi:10.1300/J082v18n01_06

International Organization for Migration. (2004). *International Migration Law No. 1: Glossary on migration*. Retrieved from http://publications.iom.int/bookstore/free/IML_1_EN.pdf

Johnson, S. M., & O'Connor, E. (2002). *The gay baby boom: The psychology of gay parenthood*. New York, NY: New York University Press.

Johnston, J. (1994). High-conflict divorce. *Children and Divorce, 4*(1), 165–182.

Kelly, J. B., & Emery, R. E. (2003). Children's adjustment following divorce: Risk and resilience perspectives. *Family Relations, 52*, 352–362. doi:10.1111/j.1741-3729.2003.00352.x

Lederach, J. P. (1995). *Preparing for peace: Conflict transformation across cultures*. Syracuse, NY: Syracuse University Press.

Leong, F. T. L., Wagner, N. S., & Tata, S. P. (1995). Racial and ethnic variations in help-seeking attitudes. In J. G. Ponterotto, J. M. Casas, L. A. Suzuki, & C. M. Alexander (Eds.), *Handbook of multicultural counseling* (pp. 415–438). Thousand Oaks, CA: Sage.

McDonald, E. (2009). Sperm donor or thwarted father? How written agreement statutes are changing the way courts resolve legal parentage issues in assisted reproduction cases. *Family Court Review, 47*, 340–355. doi:10.1111/j.1744-1617.2009.01258.x

McGill, D. W., & Pearce, J. K. (2005). American families with English ancestors from the colonial era: Anglo Americans. In M. McGoldrick, J. Giordano, & N. Garcia-Prieto (Eds.), *Ethnicity and family therapy* (3rd ed., pp. 520–533). New York, NY: Guilford Press.

McLeod, J., & Shanahan, M. (1993). Poverty, parenting, and children's mental health. *American Sociological Review, 58*, 351–366. doi:10.2307/2095905

McLoyd, V. C. (1998). Socioeconomic disadvantage and child development. *American Psychologist, 53*, 185–204. doi:10.1037/0003-066X.53.2.185

Mistry, R. S., Vandewater, E., Huston, A., & McLoyd, V. (2002). Economic well-being and children's social adjustment: The role of family process in an ethnically diverse low-income sample. *Child Development, 73*, 935–951. doi:10.1111/1467-8624.00448

Olkin, R. (1999). *What psychotherapists should know about disability*. New York, NY: Guilford Press.

Patterson, C. J., & Hastings, P. D. (2007). Socialization in the context of family diversity. In J. E. Grusec & P. D. Hastings (Eds.), *Handbook of socialization: Theory and research* (pp. 328–351). New York, NY: Guilford Press.

Perrin, E. C. (2002). Coparent or second parent adoption by same-sex parents. *Pediatrics, 109*, 341–344. doi:10.1542/peds.109.2.341

Resnick, M. D. (2000). Protective factors, resiliency, and healthy youth development. *Adolescent Medicine, 11*, 157–165.

Shibusawa, T. (2005). Japanese families. In M. McGoldrick, J. K. Pearce, & J. Giordano (Eds.), *Ethnicity and family therapy* (3rd ed., pp. 339–348). New York, NY: Guilford Press.

Sibley, B. A., & Etnier, J. L. (2003). The relationship between physical activity and cognition in children: A meta-analysis. *Pediatric Exercise Science, 15*, 243–256.

Silverstein, L. B., & Auerbach, C. F. (1999). Deconstructing the essential father. *American Psychologist, 54*, 397–407. doi:10.1037/0003-066X.54.6.397

Slack, K., & Yoo, J. (2005). Food hardship and child behavior problems among low-income children. *Social Service Review, 79*, 511–536. doi:10.1086/430894

Stacey, J. (1996). *In the name of the family: Rethinking family values in the postmodern age*. Boston, MA: Beacon Press.

Tasker, F., & Golombok, S. (1995). Adults raised as children in lesbian families. *American Journal of Orthopsychiatry, 65*, 203–215. doi:10.1037/h0079615

Taylor, J. (2005). Poverty and student achievement. *Multicultural Education, 12*(4), 53–55.

Van Praagh, S. (1997). Religion, custody and child's identities. *Osgoode Hall Law Journal, 35*, 309–378.

Willemsen, E., & Willemson, M. (2000). *The best interest of the child: A child's right to have stable relationships must be central to custody decisions*. Retrieved from http://www.scu.edu/ethics/publications/iie/v11n1/custody.html

Wolsko, C., Park, B., Judd, C. M., & Wittenbrink, B. (2000). Framing interethnic ideology: Effects of multicultural and color-blind perspectives on judgments of groups and individuals. *Journal of Personality and Social Psychology, 78*, 635–654. doi:10.1037/0022-3514.78.4.635

World Health Organization. (2011). *World report on disability*. Retrieved from http://www.who.int/disabilities/world_report/2011/en/index.html

Yoshikawa, H., Aber, J. L., & Beardslee, W. R. (2012). The effects of poverty on the mental, emotional, and behavioral health of children and youth: Implications for prevention. *American Psychologist, 67*, 272–284. doi:10.1037/a0028015

11

PARENTING COORDINATION AND DOMESTIC VIOLENCE

GISELLE A. HASS

In this chapter, I address how parenting coordinators (PCs) can navigate the problems that arise when there is violence among family members with whom they are working. Intimate partner violence (IPV), as well as exposure to violence or abuse of children, is an important social and psychological problem, and PCs who work with abusers and victims have significant ethical and professional responsibilities. PCs need to remember that high-conflict relationships are not the same as domestic violence and that working with abusers and victims involves a significant risk that their decisions can harm, rather than help, clients. PCs should have specialized training so that their interventions in cases of family violence, abuse, and coercion are based on a thorough knowledge of the complex issues that play a role in such cases.

In its report on violence and the family, the American Psychological Association (APA) Presidential Task Force on Violence and the Family (1996) stated that psychologists "play an important role in helping to

http://dx.doi.org/10.1037/14390-012
Parenting Coordination in Postseparation Disputes: A Comprehensive Guide for Practitioners, S. A. Higuchi and S. J. Lally (Editors)

promote violence-free families" (p. 111). Because psychologists, as mandated reporters of violence, have been trained to identify risk in many settings and situations, psychologist PCs are in a unique position to identify—and, with further training, properly assess—the complexity of violent acts and interactions that may affect their parenting coordination work with a family. APA's (2012) parenting coordination guidelines clearly state that "parents who have a history of prior or current domestic violence, also commonly referred to as intimate partner violence, may present substantial safety risks or power imbalances, and may not be appropriate for Parenting Coordination" (p. 67). Having to focus primarily on safety concerns can derail the parenting coordination process.

PCs must also be alert to the possibility that one or more family members may try to use them as another weapon of abuse and control. This means that PCs must routinely screen clients for a history of domestic violence and decide whether the current risks can be safely managed in the PC process. For this to occur, it is important that PCs know about the research regarding family violence, in particularly research regarding domestic violence in situations of separation and divorce, parental alienation, trauma literature, and child maltreatment.

BACKGROUND

APA (1996) defined *family violence and abuse* as comprising the following:

> acts of physical abuse, sexual abuse, and psychological maltreatment; chronic situations in which one person controls or intends to control another person's behavior, and misuse of power that may result in injury or harm to the psychological, social, economic, sexual, or physical well-being of family members. (p. 3)

The abusive behavior can take many forms: physical (grabbing, pinching, pushing, shoving, strangling, punching, assaulting), sexual (rape, pressuring and threatening for sex, public fondling, pornography), psychological (intimidation, threats, causing fear, harassment, stalking, dominating decision making), endangering children (threatening to kidnap, expose to violence, take custody of, deport, or harm the children), economic (trying to make a person financially dependent), destruction of property and harm to pets (Ganley, 1989), immigration-related abuse (threatening to call immigration authorities, threatening to have the partner deported, or refusing to support a visa application; Hass, Dutton, & Orloff, 2000), and emotional (isolation from family and friends, put-downs and name calling, spiteful inaction, ridiculing, blaming; Browne, 1987). The behaviors that make up each one of these groups have been extensively described in the literature of domestic violence, but the central feature that defines a behavior as abusive is the function of that behavior. This means that one or even several abusive behaviors such as those described above, or mutual disrespect and verbal conflict, taken out of context may not necessarily appear to be abusive until its proper meaning is elucidated as being a tool to exert control by one person over another (M. A. Dutton, 1992).

At the Wingspread Conference on Domestic Violence, the Association of Family and Conciliation Courts (AFCC; Ver Steegh & Dalton, 2008) addressed the contradictions in research and philosophical positions among practitioners and researchers of domestic violence in order to develop an operational framework for the family court system. The agreement reached at this conference highlights the problem that using a "rigid and simplistic categorization of complex family situations . . . (may lead to) mischaracterization of violence based on inadequate assessment" (Ver Steegh & Dalton, 2008, p. 25). Understanding that the phenomenon is much more complex than originally believed, a new reading of the research in domestic violence led to the establishment of four different patterns (Graham-Kevan & Archer, 2003; Holtzworth-Munroe, 2005; Johnson & Ferraro, 2000; Johnston & Campbell, 1993; Kelly & Johnson, 2008): (a) separation-instigated violence (SIV), (b) conflict-instigated violence (CIV), (c) violent-resistance violence (VRV), and (d) abusive–controlling violence (ACV).

Separation-Instigated Violence

SIV includes situations of violence (e.g., destruction of personal property) that occur in a couple with no history of power and control issues or of violence in the relationship or other settings prior to the separation. Violence shows up as an atypical form of loss of control and is associated with the humiliating or traumatic events that led to the separation or with the separation itself. There are often only one or two episodes, and the partners do not report coercive or controlling behavior. This type of violence may be carried out by both men and women (Johnston & Campbell, 1993; Kelly & Johnson, 2008).

Conflict-Instigated Violence

CIV is also called *situational couple violence* (Kelly & Johnson, 2008). This is the type of violence in which power, coercion, and control are not central to the dynamic, and it is initiated at similar rates by both sexes. Violence may have occurred as a result of conflicts escalating out of control and in which one or both partners were violent toward the other. An important characteristic of this type of violence is that partners are not afraid of one another. It includes forms such as pushing, shoving, and grabbing, in which serious injuries are not common. This type of violence decreases over time and with age, and it often stops after the separation (Gelles & Straus, 1988; Holtzworth-Munroe, 2005; Jaffe, Crooks, & Bala, 2005; Kelly & Johnson, 2008; Ver Steegh, 2005).

Violent-Resistance Violence

This type of violence has been called *self-defense* and includes the use of violence for self-protection when the other person is using force as part of a pattern of coercive control (Johnson & Ferraro, 2000). The person uses violence to control a situation, sometimes to prevent imminent serious harm, rather than trying to exert control over the other person. A person who has been battered in a previous relationship may use physical violence to establish that abuse will not be tolerated with the current partner (Frederick, 2001). This group includes women in shelters as victims of abuse who killed their batterers (Jaffe, Johnston, Crooks, & Bala, 2008).

Abusive–Controlling Violence

ACV, also called *coercive controlling violence* (Kelly & Johnson, 2008) and *intimate terrorism* (Johnson, 2008), is what has been known for years as *classical battering*. This type of violence is characterized by intimidation, coercion, control, and emotional abuse. There is a pattern of unilaterally dominating the other partner through fear. Often there is severe physical and sexual abuse, and abuse across different dimensions, such as economic and child abuse. Victims of ACV are at very high risk following separation and in contested-custody cases. Injuries to victims are more frequent and more severe, and the risk of lethality is present. Denial, minimizing, and blame are perpetrators' most common excuses. When violence is severe and chronic, there is a higher likelihood that the abuser has a severe personality disorder (D. Dutton, 2007; Johnson, 2008). This type of violence is primarily perpetrated by men, but there are also reports of female perpetrators in married, cohabiting, and lesbian relationships (Jaffe et al., 2005; Johnson & Ferraro, 2000).

ACV must be distinguished from SIV, as sometimes what seems like an isolated violent act or violence instigated by the separation is only the first manifestation of coercive control. When there is a history of one partner exercising power, control, and fear over the other (i.e., ACV), there is often an escalating risk of harm at the time of separation. This is true regardless of whether there is a history of physical violence. As the victim tries to leave the abuser, or discloses the family secret of abuse, the abuser may feel a loss of power and control. The abuser may even show sweeter, kinder, more conciliatory behavior toward the victim, particularly in front of lawyers, courts, and PCs. PCs must be alert to suspiciously defensive and inflexible, as well as flexible or overly compliant, attitudes of the abused parent, which may actually be fear responses to open or subtle control or threats. When there has been violence in a family, and the balance of power is not equal among the parents, one parent may tend to make decisions based solely on safety concerns, and this may not serve either the parent's or the children's needs.

Although categories of violence are helpful, they have certain limitations, and some types of violence cannot be neatly placed into a category, in particular when substance abuse and/or mental illness is involved. Just as with any classifications, reliance on these categories also runs the risk that the PC will oversimplify a complex phenomenon and shortcut the screening process. In addition, sufficient research regarding these dynamics, to determine their progress and stability over time and across relationships, has not yet been conducted. However, the establishment of these four types of domestic violence has resulted in a marked improvement in the ability of professionals and courts to manage cases that involve a history of domestic violence. Although these classifications have forced the revision of research data that assumed domestic violence was a monolithic phenomenon, there remains a long way to go in terms of acquiring sufficient empirical evidence.

DOMESTIC VIOLENCE AND PARENTING COORDINATION

In an ideal world, a PC will receive a referral of a case that has been already evaluated by a custody evaluator, court officer, attorney, or judge and in which a custody order or temporary order was issued that takes into consideration all risk factors. When the court has determined that a case does involve domestic violence or abuse and has issued orders to provide safety to the victims (e.g., orders of protection, supervised visitation, or court-mandated treatment for the abusive parent[s]), PCs should respect this judicial finding and not minimize it on the basis of their own independent reassessment of the underlying facts. In reality, during the period when parents first approach the court to resolve a custody conflict, there may be myriad confounding factors that make the picture of potential risk unclear or inaccurate. Research has documented that allegations of domestic violence or child abuse are not unusual during separations that require judicial intervention (Johnston, Lee, Olesen, & Walters, 2005). Determining the accuracy of those allegations is difficult for the courts because domestic violence occurs inside the privacy of the family, and a lack of concrete evidence is not unusual even in severe cases. In some cases, interparental difficulties that lead to divorce stem from a history of physical, sexual, or emotional abuse by one partner toward the other or toward the children. In other cases, a person who has suffered severe psychological violence may believe that physical violence will be given greater weight by the court and thus make those allegations. For different reasons, including fear of having his or her concerns dismissed, a person may also misrepresent or exaggerate actual experiences of IPV or his or her own role in it. Most common is the fact that in many cases the nature and extent of the violence are concealed, denied, or minimized because of fear. In sum, it may be very hard to determine the existence of domestic violence during custody litigation.

Although custody evaluators who have been trained in the evaluation of domestic violence in custody cases should be able to identify it and recommend appropriate custody plans, many cases have not had a well-trained custody evaluator, or even a custody evaluation at all. In some cases, the violence may commence after the court has made a custody determination, or it may begin or be revealed after the issue was assessed. There could also be cases in which coercive controlling domestic violence was identified but a joint custody order was issued nonetheless. The laws of a majority of states include presumptions against joint custody in cases where there is a finding that intrafamily violence has occurred (American Bar Association Commission on Domestic Violence, 2008). In addition, the detrimental effects on children placed in the custody of an abusive parent have been well documented (H. Cong. Res 172). In spite of this, a preference for joint custody and cooperative coparenting may incline some courts to minimize the role of domestic violence in custody decisions and parenting plans (Dragiewicz, 2010).

In either situation, the PC's ethical and professional responsibility is to evaluate the presence of domestic violence and use this information to inform his or her practice. Allegations of IPV, as well as child abuse, need to be taken seriously from the very beginning, and without bias. A conscientious screening should provide the PC with a good understanding of the family's past and current situation regarding domestic violence and its current risk of continued violence or coercion.

To maintain the integrity of the PC role and avoid double roles or entering into areas outside one's competency, PCs should refer cases for assessment of specialized issues revealed in the screening as necessary (e.g., anger management or batterer evaluation; substance abuse; victim assessment; or specific psychological, social, academic, or medical evaluations for family members). This information will help the PC better understand the different dimensions to take into consideration when making a determination of the type and function of domestic violence involved in the case and the implications of that violence.

Once the PC has obtained training in domestic violence—including the differentiation of types, level of risk, and impact to the victims—he or she can use interviews as well as reviews of court documents, collateral documents, basic assessment measures, and expert assessments to obtain an initial picture of the current situation regarding violence and abuse in the family. Once violence has been identified, through screening, as an issue, the PC may decide either that the picture is clear enough to proceed or that the case is too ambiguous and the information too entangled and thus requires a referral to a mental health evaluator with expertise in domestic violence and any collateral issues (e.g., parental alienation, substance abuse) for an in-depth evaluation.

PCs need to take signs of domestic violence seriously, not only because of ethical and professional mandates but also because of the serious long-term consequences for the family members and the parenting coordination process. The following points, made by Jaffe et al. (2008, pp. 501–504), summarize the research regarding parent–child relationships and family styles when domestic violence is present and are important to take into consideration:

- Spousal abuse does not necessarily end with separation of the parties.
- In extreme cases, domestic violence following separation is lethal, especially in the case of more abusive relationships (ACV).
- Perpetrators of domestic violence are more likely to be deficient, if not abusive, as parents.
- Individuals who have a pattern of abusing their partners (ACV), and those who commonly resolve conflicts using physical force (CIV), are poor role models for children.
- Abusive ex-partners (ACV) are likely to undermine the victim's parenting role.
- Abusive ex-partners (ACV) may use family court litigation as a new forum to continue their coercive controlling behavior and to harass their former partner.
- Diminished parenting capacities often occur among victims of domestic violence.
- A victim's behavior under the stress of abusive relationships (ACV) and during the aftermath of a stressful separation (SIV) should not inappropriately prejudice the residential or access decision.
- Victims of abusive relationships may need time to reestablish their competence as parents and need the opportunity to learn how to appropriately protect and nurture themselves and their children.

When there is a history of ACV and a current dynamic of coercive control, the PC most probably will not be able to work with the parents at all, or at least not in the manner in which the coordination is usually conducted.

This is because perpetrators of abusive and controlling domestic violence frequently seek to assert control over the victim through the use of threats and physical aggression. Even when the physical violence and abuse stops, abusers may use the children as pawns and may be intimidating and inflexible as coparents. In such situations, it can be difficult, if not impossible, for PCs to use the multitude of mediation, collaboration, and dispute resolution skills at their disposal.

These collaboration tools, which are so useful in many high-conflict families, can instead become weapons manipulated by a coercive parent. By their very nature, parenting collaboration tools depend on increasing the parents' mutual sense of trust and fair dealing—something that cannot be relied on in cases with a history or risk of domestic violence and a dynamic of coercion. Not the least of these concerns is that in these situations the PC also becomes a target for the abuser, and a great deal of time and energy are lost in managing the abusive parent in order to maintain one's professional and personal integrity. The safest thing for PCs to do, assuming they feel prepared and comfortable working with cases that involve domestic violence, is to screen cases carefully, refer ACV cases back to the referring court or to experts, and accept only those cases in which, in spite of past or current conflict (usually CIV and SIV), parents are able to use parenting coordination services safely and productively. Both novice and experienced PCs will also benefit greatly from having a seasoned mentor with whom to discuss the case and who can offer a second opinion.

SCREENING FOR DOMESTIC VIOLENCE

The APA parenting coordination guidelines (2012) state, "PCs carefully determine whether a specific case involving past or present intimate partner violence or child maltreatment is appropriate for the PC process, with a particular focus on safety concerns and substantial power imbalances" (p. 67). The ethical obligation of psychologists, and by extension all PCs, is to determine the likelihood that the process of parenting coordination may ignore or facilitate abuse, exploitation, or intimidation of any family member. When a parent seeks to assert control over the other parent, the children, or the PC, through the use of threats and coercion, the process becomes unsafe and counterproductive.

Screening for domestic violence should thus be done in every single case. PCs cannot assume, on the basis of its absence from information provided by the court, the custody evaluation, the attorneys, or the parents, that a screening has been conducted and that violence is not a factor in the case. Identification of the type of violence, its context, and its nuances is the PC's first step toward understanding the complexity of the case so that he or she can determine its suitability to the parenting coordination process. PCs without mental health training who feel unprepared to conduct this screening should refer the case for a professional evaluation. However, with training, PCs should be able to manage this aspect of the role. The factors to assess include the following:

- the frequency, intensity, and recency of the violence;
- the presence of sexual coercion or abuse;
- the existence of nonphysical coercive strategies, including verbal abuse and intimidation, threats, isolation, and financial control;
- the presence of an established history of violence;
- the mutuality of the violence or who the primary perpetrator is;
- criminal activity, substance abuse, or mental health issues;
- the impact on the victim(s);
- the fear one parent may have of the other, the victim's fear of imminent danger, and the victim's vulnerability;
- any history of child maltreatment;
- the extent to which the violence is consistent with a recognized pattern with proven implications for ongoing risk or lethality;
- the ability of family members to participate in the parenting coordination process without fear, coercion, or intimidation; and
- the utility or impact of particular interventions or determinations.

This screening does not have to be exhaustive, but it must look at the different angles of the problem, including abuse by stepparents, children who turned abusive against the vulnerable parent or the abusive parent, and abuse by other family members.

Following certain practices at the outset of the case may help identify productive paths of further inquiry. For instance, the AFCC guidelines specifically state that "in cases of domestic violence involving power, control, and coercion, the PC shall conduct interviews and sessions with the parties individually" (AFCC, Task Force on Parenting Coordination, 2006, p. 12). It is good practice to meet with each parent separately during the first session in order to better assess the individual allegations parents may have against one another. This is a sound ethical practice because each party would be safer in an individual setting to fully disclose a history of violence or coercion in the family, in particular, if it has not been exposed earlier in the process. If the parents meet as a couple, a victim may not feel safe discussing or describing any past or present abuse, harassment, or conflict for fear of retribution, or the abuser may take the opportunity to "rewrite history" and the victim may be too afraid to voice a contradiction.

The AFCC (2006) parenting coordination guidelines offer the following recommendation:

> The PC should review the custody evaluation, other relevant records, interim or final court orders, information from interviews with parents and children and other collateral sources, domestic violence protection orders, and any other applicable cases involving criminal assault, domestic violence or child abuse, educational records, and analyze the impasses and issues as brought forth by the parties. (p. 8)

The goal when studying this information is to elucidate the multiple facets of the dynamic of abuse. It is important to remember that a lack of documents demonstrating the incidence of domestic violence is not proof that it did not exist. Similarly, having evidence of one or a few incidents of physical violence may not contribute greatly to an understanding of underlying coercion, whether it was mutual or there was a primary perpetrator, and the specific types of violence that occurred in the relationship. The presence of violence in the relationship needs to be evaluated within its context because identical violent acts may have different meanings depending on the impact on the victim and the intent of the perpetrator, the individual victims' vulnerabilities and protective factors, and the social and community environment.

Standardized Measures of Domestic Violence

Standardized measures and risk assessment surveys to assess domestic violence may be useful to PCs during a screening. There are numerous inventories and scales that measure different dimensions of domestic violence, such as abusive acts of physical and sexual violence, psychological abuse, and other forms of interpersonal violence. Many of these measures also focus on attitudes toward domestic violence and consequences thereof, including physical injury and psychological impact.

Among the most popular measures available to assess domestic violence is the Conflict Tactic Scales (Straus, 2007) and two other versions of it, the Conflict Tactics Scale—Second Edition (Straus, Hamby, Boney-McCoy, & Sugarman, 1996) and the Conflict Tactics Scale: Parent–Child Version (Straus, Hamby, Finkelhor, Moore, & Runyan, 1998); the Psychological Maltreatment of Women Inventory (Tolman, 1999); the Abuse Observation Checklist (M. A. Dutton, 1992); and the Proximal Antecedents to Violent Episodes Scale (Babcock, Costa, Green, & Eckhardt, 2004). One criticism regarding measures such as these is that they have respondents self-report the violent acts they have experienced (M. A. Dutton & Goodman, 2005; Johnson, 2006) and respondents are not provided an understanding of the dynamic of coercion and control within the relationship. Furthermore,

Donald Dutton (2006) criticized those self-report or structured interview measures because they use information from one partner to confront the other. He believes that such instruments prime clinicians to be biased against alleged abusers and to dismiss their responses as denial or minimization. Another criticism of these measures is that, although they assess the presence of domestic violence, they do not assess motivations and context, do not reliably differentiate among types of violence, and minimally address the role of coercive control. In addition, they are not designed to assess post-separation violence or violence in the parenting coordination process.

An appropriate screening of IPV should address coercive control, which is the key construct that differentiates a pattern of abusive behaviors from those that may be situational and transitory and those that are a tool in the search for and maintenance of power and control over the other person (M. A. Dutton & Goodman, 2005). M. A. Dutton and Goodman (2005) defined the concept of *coercive control* as "a dynamic process linking a demand with a credible threatened negative consequence for noncompliance" (pp. 746–747). Although violence in a relationship makes a partner more vulnerable to coercion, a serious threat can be coercive in the absence of previous physical or sexual violence. In fact, when coercive control is successful the physical violence is less intense or frequent, because it is no longer required to maintain control with an already-submissive victim (Tanha, Beck, Figueredo, & Raghavan, 2009). Therefore, a standardized measure of violent acts may find minimal indications of violence and thus miss the presence of coercive control.

Furthermore, evaluations of IPV need to include a measure of coercive control to accurately differentiate among the different categories of violence described earlier (SIV, CIV, ACV, and VRV) and identify how this dynamic plays out in the conflict related to the custody of the children. PCs need to assess whether one of the parents makes certain demands that are not in the best interest of the children's well-being and requires strict surveillance of the other parent to ensure compliance. For instance, coercive control is often at play when a parent makes child support payments contingent on compliance with certain demands, such as children's calls and visits with that parent.

In some situations, however, the coercion may not be so clear and concrete. The PC should obtain a record of the couple's history to determine whether the agent of coercion has "set the stage" (M. A. Dutton & Goodman, 2005, p. 750), meaning that there were negative consequences to the victim for noncompliance in the past and that thus the threat is successful based on the victim's experience with the abuser. In this case, the victim appraises the threat as a credible risk on the basis of his or her previous experience with the abuser. This helps differentiate a victim of coercion from a parent who is afraid to act or reveal information to the other parent because he or she is afraid of being disliked or displeasing, an overarching personality trait that occurs not only with the ex-partner. In cases where coercion is a powerful tool in the hands of one parent, the other parent will not be free to make his or her own decision. Worth mentioning is that PCs have the ethical duty not to be part of involuntary or unreasonable agreements based on the sole interest of the abuser, although strategic concessions by the vulnerable parent may need to be respected.

Another subtle form of coercion occurs when the abuser uses arguments against the other parent that unfairly exploit his or her vulnerabilities. Often, such vulnerabilities may not constitute a significant parenting weakness or deficit and may include a disability, a history of previous abuse, immigration problems, or a health problem. The abusive partner tries to use this information to manipulate or exploit the situation and in this way obtain the parenting benefits that he or she wants regardless of the best interest of the children.

Popular measures that assess coercive control are the Domestic Violence Evaluation (Ellis & Stuckless, 2006), the Coercive Control Survey (M. A. Dutton, Goodman, & Schmidt, 2005), and the Relationship Behavior Rating Scale (Beck, Menke, Brewster, & Figueredo, 2009). These measures help determine whether one partner has greater control over the other, but they cannot be used in isolation, without formal measures of physical and sexual violence, because do not measure the current risk during the parenting coordination process or in the coparenting process.

Screening of Current Danger and Risk to Victim(s)

One of the overriding concepts PCs should consider when deciding whether a case with a history of domestic violence can be safely managed in parenting coordination is the level of risk to all parties involved. Although worst-case scenario events such as homicide and suicide are rare, they seldom occur without red flags, including a history of previous violence (Campbell, 1992; Langford, Isaac, & Kabat, 1998). Several elements are implicated in the screening of risk. Empirically supported risk factors can be static or dynamic. *Static factors*—for example, past behaviors that are indexes of future risk, such as the number and type of previous criminal offenses (Mossman, 1994)—cannot be modified. *Dynamic factors*, on the other hand, can change over time or with treatment (Hanson & Harris, 2001), such as alcoholism, personality traits, problem-solving skills, or the stress of separation. The predictors of post-separation violence that research has linked to serious harm are sexual assaults; infliction of serious physical injury; and abuser behavior such as drinking, outbursts of anger, jealousy, emotional dependence, and general controlling behavior (Ellis & Stuckless, 2006; Ellis, Stuckless, & Wight, 2006).

Determining the risk helps the PC make a decision about his or her ability to manage the case in the parenting coordination process. Moreover, when the PC is able to identify dynamic risk factors, he or she is in a position to make referrals for the type of services that parents need to reduce the likelihood that these risk factors will play a role in the dynamic of violence and coercion. For instance, a parent can be referred for a substance abuse evaluation and treatment, anger management, psychotherapy, and other such services. The PC can help a parent make progress toward the goals of lifting initial restrictions and achieving greater involvement with the children as the parent becomes more stable and psychologically healthy.

Some of the major standardized instruments that measure risk are the Danger Assessment instrument (Campbell, Webster, & Glass, 2009), the Spousal Assault Risk Assessment Guide (Kropp, Hart, Webster, & Eaves, 1999), and the Ontario Domestic Assault Risk Assessment (Hilton, Harris, & Rice, 2010). These instruments are relatively narrow in scope and were not designed specifically for post-separation violence. They do not take into account specific concerns such as whether there have been threats communicated through the children.

Models of Domestic Violence Assessment in Custody

Recently, there have been interesting attempts to create models that assess the different dimensions of domestic violence and collateral phenomena in order to obtain a picture that will inform the work with these families. These models have risen in relation to custody evaluations. Although personally conducting a comprehensive evaluation of domestic violence may not always be an efficient use of a PC's time and may fall outside the scope of the PC role, it is important for PCs to know about these models in order to refer parents for evaluation if, after the screening, the PC deems that the issues at stake require further clarification.

The *safety first model* (Drozd, Kuehnle, & Walker, 2004) assesses whether the child is safe in a variety of situations, including instances of parents' violence, substance abuse, mental illness, use of credible threats, and other forms of violence in the family. Problems in the relationship between the child and the parents are assessed on the basis of the classifications developed by Kelly and Johnston (2001) and Drozd and Olesen (2004), which delineate the continuum of relationships with both parents, including affinity with one parent and affectional bond with the other, alignment with one parent with little or no emotional bond with the other, alienation consisting of anger and hatred toward one parent while maintaining a close but sometimes unhealthy bond with the other parent, and estrangement in which there is little or no emotion toward one parent while maintaining a relationship with the other (Drozd et al., 2004).

The *potency, pattern, and primary perpetrator model* (Jaffe et al., 2008) differentiates between types of violence and relate them to parenting behaviors. The first factor, *potency*, refers to the degree of severity, dangerousness, and potential risk of serious injury and lethality. This factor pays particular attention to the signs that reveal a tendency for explosive or deadly violence that can appear in a family with no history of violence or other warning signs. *Pattern* refers to the way acts of coercion and domination have combined over time and how they may predict future violence, including post-separation control that may involve the children and continued litigation. The third factor, *primary perpetrator*, aims to distinguish the violence from that which is mutual or involves alternate initiators.

Both of these models provide a systematic structure of inquiry to evaluate the type of violence and the factors to consider in custody evaluations. PCs who refer their cases for these specialized evaluations may obtain in-depth knowledge regarding the risks inherent in the custody decision and parenting plan ordered and either determine the different interventions to reduce risk or reject the case as being unfit for the parenting coordination process.

Mediator's Assessment of Safety Issues and Concerns

The most comprehensive instrument, and one more relevant to the screening of interpersonal violence, is the Mediator's Assessment of Safety Issues and Concerns (MASIC; Holtzworth-Munroe, Beck, & Applegate, 2010), a behaviorally based measure of IPV and abuse that assesses psychological abuse, coercive control, stalking, physical violence (including extreme physical violence), sexual assault/abuse, and fear throughout the relationship and over the past year. It is important to differentiate a past history of violence from current violence and control among ex-partners. The MASIC also asks about risk factors for lethality, such as access to weapons, and reasons for leaving the relationship. In sum, this instrument includes all the major concepts discussed earlier as relevant to the determination of the nature and dynamic of violence among divorced or separated parents.

Because it was intended to be used in court involved cases, the MASIC takes care of forensic concerns, such as not asking a parent about his or her own perpetration of violence so as not to self-incriminate. It consists of a structured interview and checklists that do not require one to have specialized training, and it can be administered during the intake phase of the case. It is not copyrighted and is easily obtainable. The MASIC has not been the subject of empirical validation or reliability studies.

The MASIC also offers procedural changes for mediation based on the level of risk. Although it was created to determine risk in the context of mediation, its procedural strategies to increase safety can be used by PCs.

Some of the accommodations are, for instance, that parents cannot have contact with each other, staggered arrival and departure times for parents, an escort for a parent to and from his or her car, and mediation conducted by telephone or online.

The importance of using a standardized instrument to assess a history of violence and risk lies in the fact that when only an open format interview is used, parents may minimize or rationalize the abuse dynamic and lethality risk. Sometimes, parents may not be in the best position to make the determination regarding how the parenting process may turn into another tool of abuse or of increased risk; however, in some cases victims of IPV are particularly sensitive to the level of risk and their opinion is better informed than the PC's. Having a systematic and comprehensive way of screening domestic violence allows PCs to delve into these important issues and manage their ethical decision of whether to proceed with the case.

Issues of Credibility

The determination regarding the credibility of domestic violence allegations when there is no evidentiary finding and documentation is nonexistent or ambiguous has been the subject of several articles (e.g., Austin, 2000; Bow & Boxer, 2003). The presence of secondary gains and self-interest factors may incline a person to malinger, exaggerate, deny, or become defensive. Austin (2000) proposed a six-factor test to guide clinical decisions regarding the credibility of domestic violence allegations, which, although designed for custody evaluators, may be useful for PCs, because it provides a systematized manner of looking at the data. The six factors are as follows (Austin, 2000, pp. 468–471):

1. objective verification (e.g., police records, medical records),
2. pattern of abuse complaints (timing of the complaint and whether there is a long-term history of abuse),
3. corroboration of credible witnesses (in light of the fact that relatives and friends who have chosen a side in the custody discord may or may not be credible witnesses),
4. absence of disconfirming verbal reports of credible third parties (meaning that relatives and friends fail to rule out the presence of domestic violence),
5. psychological profile and past history of abusive behavior by the alleged perpetrator, and
6. the psychological status of the alleged victim.

PCs should keep in mind that false allegations of abuse are rare (6%; Thoennes & Tjaden, 1990). Allegations of abuse are not raised more frequently in divorce and custody cases than at any other time (Brown, Frederico, Hewitt,

& Sheehan, 2000). Fathers are more likely than mothers to make intentionally false accusations of abuse (21% compared with 1.3%; Bala & Schuman, 2000).

ASSESSMENT OF DOMESTIC VIOLENCE IMPACT

Another factor to weigh when trying to determine the appropriateness of parenting coordination services is the impact of violence on the parties and their children and their needs regarding safety. When there has been a history of IPV, the impact may take many different forms, including trauma, depression, low self-esteem, resentments, stressful memories, emotional alienation, strong dislike, and other emotional experiences. In particular, victims of domestic violence who are depressed and suffering from posttraumatic stress disorder may present poorly in court and be further victimized by the family court, best-interest legal representatives (guardians ad litem, children's attorneys) or custody evaluators (Golding, 1999; Kernic, Monary-Ernsdorff, Koepsell, & Holt, 2005). PCs need to understand the nature of these consequences and how they affect their clients' lives at different levels, in order to proceed in a sensitive and ethical manner. Emotions of loss and resentment that will heal in time need to be differentiated from credible fears or traumatic reactions that would make it impossible for the victim to face the abuser without psychological deterioration. Knowledge regarding the impact of the violence on the family is particularly helpful when the children have been traumatized, because parents need to modify their parenting practices to promote healing and safety.

The assessment of the impact of domestic violence, child abuse, and coercive control on family members regarding the experience of, or exposure to, domestic violence can begin with the initial interview and be aided by gleaning the evidence of the parties' functioning in different areas, such as school, work, and social environments. The issue is to understand whether there has been a marked decline in functioning related to conflict or violence before or after separation. PCs who suspect psychological trauma in a client may want to refer the client for evaluation or psychotherapy. When one or more parties in the family have been traumatized, PCs need to integrate this knowledge among their goals and interventions for the family.

The Substance Abuse and Mental Health Services Administration (n.d.) issued a statement urging providers of public services to become informed about trauma. Delivery of services may need to be modified on the basis of an understanding of the vulnerabilities of or triggers for trauma survivors that traditional service delivery approaches may exacerbate. Without conducting psychotherapy, which is outside the scope of the PC's role, PCs may inform their interventions from the literature on trauma to address the consequences of trauma in the individual and facilitate healing. For instance, this can be achieved by not forcing visitation with the abuser when children were traumatized by abuse they have suffered or witnessed and not pursuing direct contact when one party fears the other until those emotions are worked through. This philosophy encourages service providers to understand that there is a relationship between substance abuse, depression, eating disorders, anxiety, and symptoms of trauma, such that a parent who has been victimized by the other may present with some of these problems, but they are linked to the abuse and are likely to abate when the parent feels safe and receives treatment. If PCs are well informed about this connection, they can go beyond focusing on symptom management to promote an emphasis on skill building and emotional growth. The perspective that trauma is an organizing experience that forms the core of an individual's identity, rather than a single discrete event (Harris & Fallot, 2001), allows the PC to make recommendations and modifications that lead to healing, recovery, and repair.

IMPLICATIONS OF THE DOMESTIC VIOLENCE SCREENING FOR PARENTING COORDINATORS

The outcome of a domestic violence screening by the PC, or a comprehensive assessment of domestic violence by another professional, should clarify whether credible allegations of domestic violence are found and whether the case can be safely managed in parenting coordination. The information obtained should provide a fit with one of the four subtypes of IPV reviewed earlier in this chapter and provide other relevant factors to take into consideration and, with this information, the PC can decide whether to exclude the case from the parenting coordination process. PCs also use the information gathered to determine whether they need to decline a domestic violence case because they do not have the expertise, resources, or procedures in place to manage coercive tactics and the imbalance of power and control, even if it does not reach the level of ACV. PCs are strongly advised to not accept a case until they have fully screened it.

If the PC obtains credible evidence that there is ongoing violence in a family, then mandated reporters such as psychologists and other mental health professionals have a professional duty to inform the appropriate authorities of suspected incidents of self-risk or a threat to another person, as well as of child abuse or neglect, that meet mandatory reporting standards for their jurisdiction. In the same vein, if coparenting is not in the best interest of the children and a parenting plan for shared custody has been issued, PCs should raise this concern with the court.

The information from a screening can also help determine the type of coparenting collaboration and management of relationships that would best fit the needs of the family. PCs should evaluate all the information obtained with regard to their ordered or agreed-on role to make sure their authority is defined very clearly or to ensure that their role is limited to helping the parties comply with court orders rather than establishing a coparenting engagement. It is also important to evaluate the parenting plan and make sure it is sufficiently comprehensive so as to minimize implementation problems or misinterpretations. The PC may want to request that the order or agreement for his or her appointment allows for regular or as-needed court status conferences or reports so that the judge may monitor the parties, bring greater levels of accountability and authority to the process, and review violations.

PCs should assess the appropriateness and practicality of trying to implement a custody arrangement or parenting plan vis-à-vis the emotional and physical safety of the children and parents. There may be occasions when, after evaluating all the available information and conducting the screening, the PC believes the parenting plan as ordered is unworkable or that the parents would be unable to coparent even if all known and available measures for safety are used. This may happen in cases in which a proposed coparenting arrangement creates unsafe physical or emotional conditions for the children and the potential for greater abuse or manipulation. PCs may receive cases in which the custody arrangement or parenting plan may have been court ordered, or may have been stipulated to by the parties, without all the necessary information to assess its safety provisions. In other cases, new conditions may require a change of initial presumptions and, with that, a change in safety provisions. It is outside the PC's purview to make changes to the custody order or to alter significantly the conditions of access, but sometimes safe and efficient services cannot be provided within certain frameworks. In such cases, the PC may consider not taking the case or terminating the process if it has already been initiated. PCs should know the statutory definition of domestic violence in the jurisdiction(s) where they practice, because this information may be useful to justify rejecting a case.

It is important that a PC does not feel forced to work with a parenting arrangement that does not provide safety for all family members. The court may have to review the case to find a different temporary arrangement that best fits the safety needs of the family before a coparenting plan is attempted. It is important that the PC remember that the continuum of parenting arrangements include coparenting, parallel parenting, supervised exchange, supervised contact, and no contact (Jaffe et al., 2008). Each of these arrangements should be fit to specific circumstances between the parties and the children, taking into consideration their special resources and pattern of violence.

Kelly (2011) recommended the following general notions. Situational couple violence—if minor and infrequent, and if the violence has stopped—may be handled effectively in parenting coordination within certain parameters, such as neutral transition sites, avoidance of face-to-face meetings, and other safety precautions. SIV can also be managed through parenting coordination, if there was only one violent act, the parent acknowledges the abusive behavior and sought out treatment or help to avoid repeating it. ACV is, in almost all cases, inappropriate for parenting coordination. Such cases should be referred to expert domestic violence resources that can offer protection and safety to the victim and specialized perpetrator treatment for the abuser while the court or parties address their custody litigation over time.

The decision to accept a case with a history of domestic violence also depends on the PC's training, experience, and background. The vulnerable mental and emotional states of parents involved in high-conflict litigation when there is a history of domestic violence makes it difficult for them to adhere to and maintain appropriate boundaries. Instead, strong emotions and impulses often overwhelm the parties, making their needs or disagreements seem very urgent (Johnston & Roseby, 1997). Therefore, these cases demand clear boundaries early on and maintenance of those boundaries throughout the PC process. Deutsch, Coates, and Fieldstone, (2008) noted that, aside from the need for boundaries to preserve the working relationship, limit setting is also needed and that such limit setting provides models of appropriate behavior for the parents. These cases also require careful documentation, scrupulous investigation and follow-up, a great deal of patience, and an ability to remain nonjudgmental and professional. Abusive parents may make the PC the new target, creating acrimony with the PC, and threatening or actually reporting complaints regarding the PC to their lawyers, the courts, licensing boards, or a professional associations (see Chapter 7, this volume, for a more detailed discussion of this). These cases may test the PC's resilience and increase the risk of professional burnout (Boyan & Termini, 2005).

PARENTING COORDINATING MODIFICATIONS FOR CASES WITH RISK ISSUES

When a PC decides to accept a case in which there are issues of risk for interpersonal violence, the parenting coordination process needs to be modified. In particular, the PC's functions of negotiation, mediation, and arbitration can be difficult to implement when one party does not feel safe to participate freely because of fear, trauma, or coercion. As Beck and Raghavan (2010) noted, "If one party is being coercively controlled, non-coercive negotiations are likely impossible" (p. 557). Tailoring one's services to potential issues of risk was recommended in APA's (2012) parenting coordination guidelines: "The scope of parenting coordination interventions may need to be significantly limited or modified in some cases, with an emphasis on monitoring parties' adherence to court orders and facilitating safe implementation of the court orders and parenting plans" (p. 67). Ver Steegh and Dalton's (2008) report from the Wingspread conference, which was further expanded by Jaffe and colleagues (2008, p. 509), noted that the following five priorities should be used as a guide when interests conflict:

1. protect the children from violent, abusive, and neglectful environments.
2. protect the safety and well-being of the victim parents (under the assumption that they will be better able to protect their children);
3. respect the right of adult victims to direct their own lives, thereby recognizing the state limitations regarding parental rights;
4. hold perpetrators accountable for their abusive behavior in the context of court proceedings, and have them acknowledge problems and seek help; and
5. allow children access to both parents, if safe (implement the least restrictive plan that most benefits children with the least amount of risk).

The way this list works is that when achievement of all five priorities is not possible, the priorities lower on the list need to be abandoned until the risk of abuse is resolved. PCs are also warned to keep in mind the long-term life of the case and that some measures may be implemented in the short term with the goal of working toward relaxing those restrictions as the case progresses satisfactorily.

Modifications in the parenting coordination process to ensure the safety of all family members may need to be implemented by the PC; however, the lack of research regarding the management of domestic violence in parenting coordination significantly limits the analysis of specific recommendations at present. Fieldstone, Carter, King, and McHale (2011) surveyed all PCs practicing in Florida. The data analysis included a principal-components factor analysis that classified the clients into three major groups: (a) Triangulation (parents who placed the child at the center of the conflict), (b) Cooperative Dialogue (parents who were able to support the child's positive relationship with the coparent), and (c) Destructive Conflict (in which animosity was particularly volatile and led to a breakdown of communication). Although Fieldstone et al. (2011) did not directly study management of domestic violence, the interventions with the Destructive Conflict clients provided information relevant to domestic violence situations. The survey revealed that when PCs with a mental health background worked with Destructive Conflict clients, they tended to use the following four types of interventions: (a) holding less frequent first meetings with both parents, (b) typically holding sessions with each parent separately, (c) more coaching of negotiation skills, and (d) more frequent meetings with the children involved in the case.

On the basis of their clinical experience, Boyan and Termini (2005) recommended the following safety measures for conjoint meetings when parents display anger or have a history of domestic violence. These measures can be combined in different ways: caucus or shuttle sessions, videotaped sessions, bringing someone to wait in the waiting room, bringing someone to sit in the session with them without that person participating, having the vulnerable parent sit with free access to the door or sit closer to the PC, and having one parent arrive and leave before the other parent. The authors recommended that safety measures be established before work with the parents commences. These measures are helpful only if they serve to support the parents and do not compromise the autonomy of the vulnerable parent to freely participate in the process.

In addition to Fieldstone et al.'s (2011) findings and recommendations by clinicians (Boyan & Termini, 2005), the literature on custody evaluations and mediation, parenting coordination training, and clinical experience passed through informal channels contains useful information that PCs should consider when modifying parenting coordination services. The following are some of these recommendations:

- Respect the injunctions (e.g., restraining orders). If the court has issued a restraining order, the PC should work within this framework instead of asking the court to make an exception and allow the parties to meet for parenting coordination sessions.
- Excuse parents from mandated parenting education groups that focus on coparenting and decreasing conflict.
- Establish and maintain precautions, such as removal of weapons before meetings; a provision forbidding the use of alcohol, narcotics or other substances while with the children; presence of a third person during exchanges; use of a neutral public place during exchanges; or use of a safe exchange facility, such as a police station.
- Consider temporary orders of emergency parenting plans for the short term when the time share as ordered presents high risks.
- Focus on enforcement of the judge's order and implementation of the parenting plan through monitoring and follow-up to ensure compliance with orders. The PC's entire role may be limited to this focus in difficult cases.

- In addition to follow-up, request, if necessary, periodic review hearings or status reports for ongoing judicial monitoring.
- Make referrals to community resources and services, such as perpetrator treatment programs, anger management, victim services, supervised access centers, mental health services, and substance abuse services. Ensure that other experts brought into the case have the information they need and are qualified to handle the demands of their task. It is important that those service providers collaborate with the PC in terms of shared goals and case management so that PCs are aware of attendance and progress in those programs to make sure the goals are moving forward and achieved.
- Work and coordinate with attorneys, advocates, teachers, and other professionals involved with the family to encourage safety measures in all these settings and at all levels.
- Focus on setting in place protocols and procedures that ensure compliance with the details of the order, and reduce or eliminate opportunities for abuse to occur.
- Have more regular and direct contact with these parents to monitor the dynamic closely and identify any escalating risk, as well as the readiness of vulnerable family members to accept greater involvement with the abusive parent without retraumatization.

PARALLEL PARENTING

Worthy of special mention is the technique of *parallel parenting* (Stahl, 2000; Sullivan, n.d.), the process whereby the parents parent their children at different times and have little or no direct interaction with each other.

When parents do not get along, are uncomfortable or intimidated in each other's presence, prefer not to deal with each other, or have an order of protection, then a parenting plan that eliminates opportunities to interact and have conflict with each other is in the child's best interest. The intervention is somewhat counterintuitive in nature, in that the PC's role is to help these parents disengage while simultaneously helping them learn to work together. Parents work independently in that each parent is responsible for the decisions about the child during the time that the child is in that parent's household. Each parent receives the information about the child, such as school notices, report cards, and medical notes, independently. The goal is to disengage the parties from the conflict itself and avoid opportunities for abuse or quarrels. This option allows the PC to assume a role that will avoid a coparenting model that is inappropriate to the safety of the parties. Because in parallel parenting the parents are unable to hold each other accountable, the PC needs to pay close attention to the quality of their parenting skills.

According to Sullivan (n.d.), in parallel parenting nothing is assumed and the parenting plan has to spell out everything. PC should encourage the relationship among parents to be businesslike, impersonal, and civil. Each meeting conducted with the parents, whether individually or together, is public and formal, scheduled by appointment at a mutually convenient time. Third parties are allowed to be present in these meetings. The PC or the parent initiating the request sends a summary of the understanding reached, from which the other parent confirms or disconfirms this understanding. The schedule is written down in detail and placed on a calendar. Nothing is left open to interpretation, and there is no flexibility in scheduling. See Chapter 7, this volume, for a thorough discussion of working with difficult clients.

PARENTING COORDINATOR MONITORING OF PROGRESS

Jaffe and colleagues (2008) recommended that when restrictions are placed on a parent there should also be explicit goals and behavioral criteria necessary to graduate from such restrictions, a review of progress, and a means of monitoring. Finally, although there is concern that the risks outweigh the benefits in parenting coordination cases with a history of domestic violence (Martindale, 2007), there are significant benefits in many cases. PCs have greater control over the process than parents with a history of conflict in terms of enforcing orders, addressing rule-breaking behavior, identifying subtle undermining behaviors, disengaging parents, and focusing on the children's protection. Given the limited resources courts have to closely monitor these cases, PCs who are well trained in domestic violence can function as a bridge between the parents in order to protect the best interests of the children. The PC should exercise caution in deciding, for each case, whether the benefits of proceeding with parenting coordination will outweigh the risks.

CONCLUSION

As I have illustrated in this discussion of domestic violence in parenting coordination, the complexity of this issue is formidable. The lack of research and literature regarding the management of domestic violence in parenting coordination leaves room for idiosyncratic interventions, which can be dangerous and misguided. In addition, although the published PC guidelines (AFCC, Task Force on Parenting Coordination, 2006; APA, 2012) address this matter, there is room for varying interpretations. This is of great importance because cases that involve domestic violence may include the risk of injury or death, and even small missteps can heighten risk. In addition, PCs hold a great deal of power and authority, and thus they need to be careful to not replicate a situation of greatly unbalanced and oppressive control over the family. The safety and physical, sexual, and emotional well-being of family members has to be balanced with the limits of the PC's role and the parents' civil rights. Because of this, the importance of a PC's experience and training in dealing with families exhibiting domestic violence and child abuse cannot be underestimated.

It is encouraging to see that, since the Wingspread conference in 2008 (Ver Steegh & Dalton, 2008), more and more attention has been given to domestic violence, and an increasing number of publications are discussing the issue of domestic violence in family court, with greater clarity and uniformity being achieved. The specialized practice of parenting coordination will profit from this movement and continue to grow more responsive to new developments in the field, leading to heightened awareness of the safety needs of the parties involved in these custody battles. In the coming years, greater study and awareness of domestic violence should lead to the development of more well-defined standards of practice for parenting coordination cases that confront this issue.

REFERENCES

American Bar Association Commission on Domestic Violence. (2008). Child custody and domestic violence by state. Retrieved from http://www.americanbar.org/content/dam/aba/migrated/domviol/docs/Custody.authcheckdam.pdf

American Psychological Association. (1996). *Report of the American Psychological Association Presidential Task Force on Violence and the Family*. Washington, DC: Author.

American Psychological Association. (2012). Guidelines for the practice of parenting coordination. *American Psychologist, 67*, 63–71. doi:10.1037/a0024646

Association of Family and Conciliation Courts, Task Force on Parenting Coordination. (2006). Guidelines for parenting coordination. *Family Court Review, 44*, 164–181. doi:10.1111/j.1744-1617.2006.00074.x

Austin, W. G. (2000). Assessing credibility in allegations of marital violence in the high-conflict child custody case. *Family Court Review, 38*, 462–477. doi:10.1111/j.174-1617.2000.tb00585.x

Babcock, J. C., Costa, D. M., Green, C. E., & Eckhardt, C. I. (2004). What situations induce intimate partner violence? A reliability and validity study of Proximal Antecedents to Violent Episodes (PAVE) Scale. *Journal of Family Psychology, 18*, 433–442. doi:10.1037/0893-3200.18.3.433

Bala, N., & Schuman, J. (2000). Allegations of sexual abuse when parents have separated. *Canadian Family Law Quarterly, 17*, 191–241.

Beck, C. J. A., Menke, J., Brewster, K. O., & Figueredo, A. J. (2009). Validation of a measure of intimate partner abuse with couples participating in divorce mediation. *Journal of Divorce & Remarriage, 50*, 295–308. doi:10.1080/10502550902766399

Beck, C. J. A., & Raghavan, C. (2010). Intimate partner abuse screening in custody mediation: The importance of assessing coercive control. *Family Court Review, 48*, 555–565. doi:10.1111/j.1744-1617.2010.01329.x

Bow, J. N., & Boxer, P. (2003). Assessing allegations of domestic violence in child custody evaluations. *Journal of Interpersonal Violence, 18*, 1394–1410. doi:10.1177/0886260503258031

Boyan, S. M., & Termini, A. M. (2005). *The psychotherapist as parent coordinator in high-conflict divorce: Strategies and techniques*. New York, NY: Haworth Clinical Practice Press.

Brown, T., Frederico, M., Hewitt, L., & Sheehan, R. (2000). Revealing the existence of child abuse in the context of marital breakdown and custody and access disputes. *Child Abuse & Neglect, 24*, 849–859. doi:10.1016/S0145-2134(00)00140-X

Browne, A. (1987). *When battered women kill*. New York, NY: Free Press.

Campbell, J. C. (1992). If I can't have you, no one can: Power and control in homicide of female partners. In J. Radford & D. E. H. Russell (Eds.), *Femicide: The politics of woman killing* (pp. 99–113). New York, NY: Twayne.

Campbell, J. C., Webster, D. W., & Glass, N. (2009). The danger assessment: Validation of a lethality risk assessment instrument for intimate partner femicide. *Journal of Interpersonal Violence, 24*, 653–674. doi:10.1177/0886260508317180

Deutsch, R., Coates, C., & Fieldstone, L. (2008). Parenting coordination: An emerging role. In C. Coates & L. Fieldstone (Eds.), *Innovations in interventions with high conflict parents: Clinical practice* (pp. 187–223). Madison, WI: Association of Family and Conciliation Courts.

Dragiewicz, M. (2010). A left realist approach to antifeminist fathers' rights groups. *Crime, Law and Social Change, 54*, 197–212. doi:10.1007/s10611-010-9253-6

Drozd, L. M., Kuehnle, K., & Walker, L. (2004). Safety first: A model for understanding domestic violence in child custody and access disputes. *Journal of Child Custody, 1*, 75–103. doi:10.1300/J190v01n02_04

Drozd, L. M., & Olesen, N. (2004). Is it abuse, alienation, and/or estrangement? A decision tree. *Journal of Child Custody, 1*, 65–106. doi:10.1300/J190v01n03_05

Dutton, D. (2006). Domestic abuse assessment in child custody disputes: Beware the domestic violence research paradigm. *Journal of Child Custody, 2*, 23–42. doi:10.1300/J190v02n04_02

Dutton, D. (2007). *The abusive personality: Violence and control in intimate relationships* (2nd ed.). New York, NY: Guilford Press.

Dutton, M. A. (1992). *Empowering and healing the battered woman*. New York, NY: Springer.

Dutton, M. A., Goodman, L., & Schmidt, R. J. (2005). *Development and validation of a coercive control measure for intimate partner violence final technical report*. Document 214438, U.S. Department of Justice, Washington, DC.

Dutton, M. A., & Goodman, L. A. (2005). Coercion in intimate partner violence: Toward a new conceptualization. *Sex Roles, 52*, 743–756. doi:10.1007/s11199-005-4196-6

Ellis, D., & Stuckless, N. (2006). Domestic violence, DOVE, and divorce mediation. *Family Court Review, 44*, 658–671. doi:10.1111/j.1744-1617.2006.00117.x

Ellis, D., Stuckless, N., & Wight, L. (2006). Separation, domestic violence, and divorce mediation. *Conflict Resolution Quarterly, 23*, 461–485. doi:10.1002/crq.150

Fieldstone, L., Carter, D. K., King, T., & McHale, J. P. (2011). Training, skills, and practices of parenting coordinators: Florida statewide study. *Family Court Review, 49*, 801–817. doi:10.1111/j.1744-1617.2011.01415.x

Frederick, L. (2001). *Effective interventions in domestic violence cases: The context is everything*. Battered Women's Justice Project. Retrieved from http://www.bwjp.org/files/bwjp/articles/Effective_Interventions_Context_is_Everything.pdf

Ganley, A. (1989). Integrating feminist and social learning analysis of aggression: Creating multiple models for intervention with men who battered. In P. Caesar & L. Hamberger (Eds.), *Treating men who batter* (pp. 196–235). New York, NY: Springer.

Gelles, R. J., & Straus, M. A. (1988). *Intimate violence: The definite study of the causes and consequences of abuse in the American family*. New York, NY: Simon & Schuster.

Golding, J. M. (1999). Intimate partner violence as a risk factor for mental disorders: A meta-analysis. *Journal of Family Violence, 14*, 99–132. doi:10.1023/A:1022079418229

Graham-Kevan, N., & Archer, J. (2003). Intimate terrorism and common couple violence: A test of Johnson's predictions in four British samples. *Journal of Interpersonal Violence, 18*, 1247–1270. doi:10.1177/0886260503256656

Hanson, R. K., & Harris, A. (2001). A structured approach to evaluating change among sex offenders. *Sexual Abuse, 13*, 105–122.

Harris, M., & Fallot, R. D. (Eds.). (2001). *Using trauma theory to design service systems: New directions for mental health services*. New York, NY: Jossey-Bass.

Hass, G., Dutton, M. A., & Orloff, L. E. (2000). Lifetime prevalence of violence against Latina immigrants: Legal and policy implications. *International Review of Victimology, 7*, 93–113.

H. Con. Res. 172, 101st Cong. (1990). Retrieved from http://niwaplibrary.wcl.american.edu/reference/additional-materials/family-law-for-immigrants/custody/H.Con.Res-172-on-Domestic-Violence-and-Child-Custody-10-26-1990.pdf/view

Hilton, N. Z., Harris, G. T., & Rice, M. E. (2010). *Risk assessment for domestically violent men: Tools for criminal justice, offender intervention, and victim services*. Washington, DC: American Psychological Association. doi:10.1037/12066-000

Holtzworth-Munroe, A. (2005). Male versus female intimate violence: Putting controversial findings into context. *Journal of Marriage and Family, 67*, 1120–1125. doi:10.1111/j.1741-3737.2005.00203.x

Holtzworth-Munroe, A., Beck, C. J. A., & Applegate, A. (2010). The Mediator's Assessment of Safety Issues and Concerns (MASIC): A screening interview for intimate partner violence and abuse available in the public domain. *Family Court Review, 48*, 646–662. doi:10.1111/j.1744-1617.2010.001339.x

Jaffe, P. G., Crooks, C. V., & Bala, N. (2005). *Making appropriate parenting arrangements in family violence cases: Applying the literature to identify promising practices*. Family, Children and Youth Section Research Report No. 2005-FCY-3E, Department of Justice Canada, Ottawa, Ontario, Canada.

Jaffe, P. G., Johnston, J. R., Crooks, C. V., & Bala, N. (2008). Custody disputes involving allegations of domestic violence: Toward a differentiated approach to parenting plans. *Family Court Review, 46*, 500–522. doi:10.1111/j.1744-1617.2008.00216.x

Johnson, M. P. (2006). Conflict and control: Gender symmetry and asymmetry in domestic violence. *Violence Against Women, 12*, 1003–1018. doi:10.1177/1077801206293328

Johnson, M. P. (2008). *A typology of domestic violence: Intimate terrorism, violent resistance, and situational couple violence*. Boston, MA: Northeastern University Press.

Johnson, M. P., & Ferraro, K. L. (2000). Research on domestic violence in the 1990s: Making distinctions. *Journal of Marriage and the Family, 62*, 948–963. doi:10.1111/j.1741-3737.2000.00948.x

Johnston, J. R., & Campbell, L. E. G. (1993). A clinical typology of interparental violence in disputed custody divorces. *American Journal of Orthopsychiatry, 63*, 190–199. doi:10.1037/h0079425

Johnston, J. R., Lee, S., Olesen, N. W., & Walters, M. G. (2005). Allegations and substantiations of abuse in custody-disputing families. *Family Court Review, 43*, 283–294. doi:10.1111/j.1744-1617.2005.00029.x

Johnston, J. R., & Roseby, V. (1997). *In the name of the child: A developmental approach to understanding and helping children of conflicted and violent divorce*. New York, NY: Free Press.

Kelly, J. B. (2011, August). Core training in parenting coordination. Pre-conference institute held at the 119th Annual Convention of the American Psychological Association, Washington, DC.

Kelly, J. B., & Johnson, M. P. (2008). Differentiation among types of intimate partner violence: Research update and implications for intervention. *Family Court Review, 46*, 476–499. doi:10.1111/j.1744-1617.2008.00215.x

Kelly, J. B., & Johnston, J. R. (2001). The alienated child: A reformulation of parental alienation syndrome. *Family Court Review, 39*, 249–266. doi:10.1111/j.174-1617.2001.tb00609.x

Kernic, M. A., Monary-Ernsdorff, D. J., Koepsell, J. K., & Holt, V. L. (2005). Children in the crossfire: Child custody determinations among couples with a history of intimate partner violence. *Violence Against Women, 11*, 991–1021. doi:10.1177/1077801205278042

Kropp, P. R., Hart, S. D., Webster, C. D., & Eaves, D. (1999). *Spousal assault risk assessment guide*. Toronto, Ontario, Canada: Multi-Health Systems and B.C. Institute Against Family Violence.

Langford, L., Isaac, N., & Kabat, S. (1998). Homicides related to intimate partner violence in Massachusetts. *Homicide Studies, 2*, 353–377. doi:10.1177/1088767998002004002

Martindale, D. (2007). The false promise of parenting coordination. *The Matrimonial Strategist, 25*(8). Retrieved from http://www.lawjournalnewsletters.com/issues/ljn_matrimonial/25_8/news/149128-1.html

Mossman, D. (1994). Assessing predictions of violence: Being accurate about accuracy. *Journal of Consulting and Clinical Psychology, 62*, 783–792. doi:10.1037/0022-006X.62.4.783

Stahl, P. M. (2000). *Parenting after divorce*. San Luis Obispo, CA: Impact.

Straus, M. A. (2007). Conflict Tactic Scales. In N. A. Jackson (Ed.), *Encyclopedia of domestic violence* (pp. 190–197). New York, NY: Taylor & Francis.

Straus, M. A., Hamby, S. L., Boney-McCoy, S., & Sugarman, D. B. (1996). The revised Conflict Tactic Scales (CTS–2): Development and preliminary data. *Journal of Family Issues, 17*, 283–316. doi:10.1177/019251396017003001

Straus, M. A., Hamby, S. L., Finkelhor, D., Moore, D. W., & Runyan, D. (1998). Identification of child maltreatment with the Parent–Child Conflict Tactic Scales: Development and psychometric data for a national sample of American parents. *Child Abuse & Neglect, 22*, 249–270. doi:10.1016/S0145-2134(97)00174-9

Substance Abuse and Mental Health Services Administration. (n.d.). *Trauma-informed care and trauma services*. Retrieved from http://www.samhsa.gov/nctic/trauma.asp

Sullivan, M. (n.d.). *Parallel parenting plans*. Retrieved from http://www.californiaparentingcoordinator.com/2007/06/22/parallel-parenting-plans/

Tanha, M., Beck, C. J. A., Figueredo, A. J., & Raghavan, C. (2009). Sex differences in intimate partner violence of coercive control as a motivational factor for intimate partner violence. *Journal of Interpersonal Violence, 25*, 1836–1854. doi:10.1177-0886260509354501

Thoennes, N., & Tjaden, P. G. (1990). The extent, nature, and validity of sexual abuse allegations in custody/visitation disputes. *Child Abuse & Neglect, 14*, 151–163. doi:10.1016/0145-2134(90)90026-P

Tolman, R. M. (1999). The validation of the Psychological Maltreatment of Women Inventory. *Violence and Victims, 14*, 25–37.

Ver Steegh, N. (2005). Differentiating types of domestic violence: Implications for child custody. *Louisiana Law Review, 65*, 1379–1431.

Ver Steegh, N., & Dalton, C. (2008). Report from the Wingspread Conference on Domestic Violence and Family Courts. *Family Court Review, 46*, 454–475. doi:10.1111/j.1744-1617.2008.00214.x

12

COLLABORATION WITH ATTORNEYS

MARGARET J. McKINNEY, LINDA A. DELANEY,
AND ALAN NESSMAN

This chapter reflects our perspective, which is based on our many years of experience as family lawyers working with parenting coordinators (PCs) in divorce cases in Maryland and District of Columbia courts. In this chapter, we present our view on how lawyers can best collaborate with PCs. This perspective may reflect the particular ways that PCs are appointed and used in MD and DC courts, including the fact that most PCs are psychologists or other mental health professionals.[1]

It often takes a team of professionals to help a family navigate the process of separation and divorce. Attorneys are duty bound under the law and the profession's ethical rules to be the "captain of the ship"—charting a course, navigating through choppy waters, and ultimately landing the client safely on shore. They are required to help their clients decide whether

[1]Our viewpoint is just one in a sea of opinions. Our goal in this chapter is to provide a perspective on the parenting coordination process to which PCs might not otherwise be privy and to prompt a dialogue between attorneys and PCs.

http://dx.doi.org/10.1037/14390-013
Parenting Coordination in Postseparation Disputes: A Comprehensive Guide for Practitioners, S. A. Higuchi and S. J. Lally (Editors)

to pursue litigation or some form of alternative dispute resolution, weigh the costs and benefits of such options, and assist the client throughout the process. With this charge comes grave responsibility. Particularly when child custody is involved, the attorney's advice necessarily influences the course of the client's and the children's lives for years, if not decades.

Thus, clients hold their attorneys accountable as the key professionals with whom they engage to work during this very difficult time. The attorney's parenting coordination recommendation is particularly high stakes in nature; probably no other mental health intervention provides the court an ongoing eyewitness to clients' credibility, reliability, and parental judgment as well as their ability to comply with a process and to communicate with the other parent. There may be no other mental health professional better situated than a PC to assist both attorneys and clients with finding and meeting the best interest of the children. In short, the PC has considerable power over the outcome of both the case and the family's postseparation adjustment. Hence, the attorney should and must do all he or she can to make the parenting coordination process work for his or her client.

The important backdrop for any parenting coordination process is the attorney–client relationship. Throughout the case, the attorney advises the client on every material decision that might affect the outcome.[2] The attorney–client relationship subordinates all others for the emotional reason that in the midst of divorce and custody proceedings, parents are likely the most vulnerable they have ever been in their lives; parents often feel that the attorney is the one professional whose primary allegiance is to them (despite what we note in the next section). Finally, the attorney is typically the one who first recommends using a PC and who remains the main influence over the client on all issues.

PCs should consider the impact of the attorney–client relationship on their work. For example, if the attorney and the PC disagree, the client will often turn to the attorney for a final opinion, even on parenting issues. This can often be problematic, but it is understandable. When parents place their children's future in the hands of an attorney, the "custody case"—real or potential—is always looming in the background. Its ultimate outcome is the overriding focus for both the attorney and client; the parenting coordination process is just one piece of the puzzle.

In sum, for the parenting coordination process to be effective, the PC must get comfortable with the fact that the parents will turn to their attorneys throughout the parenting coordination process to get a first or second

[2]This relationship is particularly reinforced and made insular by confidentiality protections afforded by the attorney–client privilege. No such privilege exists in the parenting coordination process, as noted elsewhere in this chapter.

opinion on just about any issue. The parenting coordination process is most successful when both the attorney and the PC operate under the assumption that they are working in tandem to serve the best interest of the child. When the attorney and the PC see each other as allies working toward the same ultimate goal, they can more easily work together to get the parents to constructively coparent.

THE ATTORNEY AND THE PARENTING COORDINATOR'S SHARED OVERARCHING GOAL: THE BEST INTEREST OF THE CHILD

The legal standard for determining legal and physical custody is "the best interest of the child."[3] This mirrors the best-interest-of-the-child goal of the PC.[4] Thus, the attorney and the PC should be working toward the same relatively objective goal.[5]

Because this standard is an objective one, and only indirectly involves the client, determining the best interest of a child often requires an independent analysis from the parent's view of "how things should be." Most nonlawyers think that the attorney is bound to zealously advocate for his or her client without regard to the merits of the client's position. In a custody case, however, the attorney cannot ethically advocate for a client's position if he or she knows that that position is not in the child's best interest. In that situation, the attorney must educate the client as to how a judge is most likely to view the evidence and how that judge will determine the child's best interest. Increasingly, such evidence includes testimony from a custody evaluator, a PC, and sometimes from a mental health professional who specializes in families of divorce, all of whom are informed by the psychological and social science literature.

Here again, the attorney and the PC can serve the family best by working together. For example, if the client has an inflexible, uninformed, or misguided notion regarding the best interest of the child, the attorney can consult with or refer to the PC. Likewise, if the client is unresponsive to the PC, the PC can use the attorney to reach the client. When reasonable people can differ

[3]Reams of writing exist on the "best interest of the child" standard. For a historical analysis, including citations of the 50 states' statutes on the best interest standard, see Lewis and Wilson (2011). For the history of the best-interest standard from ancient Greece to modern-day America, see Kohm (2008).
[4]For example, the American Psychological Association's (2012) guidelines for parenting coordination note that "the underlying principle of the PC intervention is a continuous focus on children's best interests by the PC in working with high-conflict parents and in decision making" (p. 64). Similarly, Guideline VI of the Association of Family and Conciliation Courts' (2006) guidelines for parenting coordination provides that a PC "shall assist the parties in reducing harmful conflict and in promoting the best interest of the children consistent with the roles and functions of a PC" (p. 168).
[5]For the purposes of this chapter, this standard is assumed to be an objective one, that is, subject to a determination different from the views of the parents.

on a parenting issue, the attorney can support the PC's mediator role. Finally, when the PC takes a position that may implicate a financial or other unrelated issue unknown to the PC, the attorney can inform the PC so that he or she understands the interrelatedness of key issues and their impact on the child.

Tension Between the Attorney and the Parenting Coordinator

Two factors create an inherent tension between the attorney and the PC. First, the attorney is always aware that the PC could be a powerful and influential potential witness in a custody proceeding. Second, the attorney must watch how the PC conducts the process to ensure that it is both neutral and fair. As noted previously, the PC can provide critical, neutral, and direct evidence on issues central to the court's custody determination. In many respects, a PC is far superior to a custody evaluator because often the PC will have witnessed the parents long enough to understand how they will coparent, how they will make decisions, and how they will handle day-to-day caretaking. Because of this valuable testimony, one of the parents, or the judge, may ask the PC to testify at a hearing at which custody will be decided or reconsidered.

Conversely, the PC may be aware that the lawyer may be cross-examining him or her at some future hearing. Because of these inherent tensions, some attorneys view a PC as a potential adversary and some PCs do not welcome attorney involvement and shy away from legal proceedings.

We submit that this is not the way to resolve the tension. Instead, the PC should embrace the attorney's involvement, remembering that the latter may be the best ally for getting a recalcitrant parent to cooperate in the PC process. In addition, the attorney provides a useful, if not vital, perspective on the background that led to the appointment and identification of the legal issues in dispute.

Similarly, the attorney must appreciate the pivotal role of the PC. The PC provides the central piece of evidence supporting a client's position, or even the reason why there is no trial at all (if the PC convinces an attorney that his or her client's position is not well founded, the litigation may disappear due to settlement or the client dropping his or her claim). Most important, PCs exist for the children, whose voices are often lost in the chaos of divorce litigation. Attorneys must respect the PC on all these fronts and work with them to effect the most constructive course for their clients.

One potential issue affecting PC–attorney conflict is ex parte communication: the PC communicating with just one parent's attorney without the other attorney. Some PCs permit it and some do not. We believe that such ex parte communication is not only a good thing but also that it is practically required for a successful parenting coordination process. The guidelines set forth by the Association of Family and Conciliation Courts' Task Force on

Parenting Coordination (2006) permit ex parte communication between a PC and the parties or their attorneys "if specified in writing in the order of appointment, PC agreement or stipulation" (p. 170). This frees the PC to work clinically with the parents and use the attorney as reinforcement. The PC can speak openly and honestly with the attorney about the client without having to reveal the same to opposing counsel. This allows the attorney and PC to work privately together to address and, it is hoped, correct problems the parent is having. It is important, however, that the PC strive to ensure balanced communication with both sides (e.g., a comparable number of ex parte communications with each side).

We also recommend that the PC have periodic, substantive bilateral meetings with both lawyers to discuss ongoing issues, recommendations, and decisions. These meetings can be held in person or by phone and may be initiated by the attorneys or the PC. In addition, there are times when the PC will find it helpful to meet with one parent along with his or her attorney. Both the attorney and PC have a duty to strive for a fair and collaborative process in pursuit of the same goal. For that process to succeed, the PC and attorney must recognize the value that each brings to the process and welcome the other's involvement.

Recalcitrant Attorneys

Some attorneys are hesitant about the parenting coordination process; they are either new to or skeptical of parent coordination, are less focused on psychological issues, or they simply do not pay attention to the custody issues in the case. When faced with this type of attorney, the PC must take on the challenge of reaching out to and educating him or her. The PC should call the attorney, outline the issues at hand, explain the operating framework for the process, and raise any compliance issues. In particular, the PC must educate the attorney about any issues the PC believes may be having a negative impact on the child.

In an ideal situation, the attorney wants this information for the sake of the child. However, even if the PC senses that the attorney is not child centered or is disinterested in the parenting coordination process, the PC can assume that the attorney would welcome any information about his or her client that would hurt the client in court. Attorneys typically welcome the chance to help their clients "get with the program" and avoid the prospect of unfavorable testimony or reports in court.

Nevertheless, a PC must understand that the attorney has the last word when it comes to advising the client. In an ideal parenting coordination process, the PC and the attorney will be on the same page. When this is not the case, the PC must do what is necessary for the child's best interest by working hard to educate the recalcitrant attorney.

IMPLICATIONS OF A PARENTING COORDINATOR'S REFUSAL TO TESTIFY OR INABILITY TO BE CANDID ON THE STAND

Some excellent PCs have chosen to work only with parents who agree, in writing, not to call the PC as a witness in litigation. PCs certainly have a right to condition their engagement this way, but doing so may seriously limit a parent's ability to resolve serious custody issues that may arise in the course of the parenting coordination process.

Parenting coordination was created as a mental health intervention to assist families in the context of separation and divorce. Although its primary purpose was to reduce parental conflict, it was also designed and understood to be, in part, the court's window into the litigants' parenting for purposes of making a custody determination. As noted above, this direct evidence of the parents' ability to coparent and care for the children, provided by a qualified and neutral mental health professional, can be indispensable.

A PC who will not testify may prolong conflict and negative engagement, prevent resolution, and, in worst case scenarios, inadvertently block crucial evidence pertaining to a child's well-being from reaching the judge. The PC may have witnessed, and be virtually the only nonfamily witness to, a pattern of significant negative parental judgment and behaviors that negatively affect the child. Thus, a PC who refuses to testify denies a judge the complete picture, which may lead to a less informed custody decision that could be harmful to the child.

A similar concern arises when a PC agrees to testify but waters down or minimizes negative information that he or she has revealed to an attorney privately. The attorney may have filed a motion to change custody based on negative information from the PC about the other parent and based on the PC's support of that motion. If the PC then softens, dilutes, or changes his or her actual negative opinion on the witness stand, this likewise may result in a poor custody determination that is based on inaccurate information.

THE PARENTING COORDINATOR AS A FACT WITNESSES OR EXPERT WITNESS

There are two types of witnesses at trial: (a) *fact witnesses* and (b) *expert witnesses*. A fact witness testifies because he or she has firsthand knowledge of relevant facts at issue in the case; an expert witness testifies because of special expertise or knowledge that will assist the court in interpreting the facts of the case. Some witnesses are identified as both fact and expert witnesses, although for psychologists acting as PCs, serving as both would present multiple role issues (see Guideline 5a, American Psycological

Association, 2012). Courts differ regarding the status of PCs as witnesses. For example, in Maryland, a relatively new rule on parent coordination (Md. Rule 9-205.2[h][2], 2012) expressly states that PCs may not testify as experts.

Does it matter whether PCs may testify as an expert witness (as opposed to merely testifying as a fact witness)? In our view, it does not. The primary benefit to the court of a PC is the PC's factual knowledge and related opinions about the level of conflict between the parents, the parents' ability to communicate, the parents' compliance with the process, and their respective parental judgment. We have been successful in having PCs present fact testimony about these subjects as well as the specific facts, theory, and clinical experience that forms the basis of the opinion. For example, the following is a portion of a typical direct examination of a PC:

Attorney: Can you tell the court your assessment of the conflict between the parties?

PC: There was high conflict.

Attorney: When you say "high conflict," what do you mean?

PC: In the literature, the amount of conflict between parents is usually measured on a continuum. High conflict usually consists of . . .

Attorney: Describe the conduct to which you are referring in this case.

PC: The parties were in conflict during each and every session. They did not agree on what the needs of the children were and therefore had numerous disputes ranging from what type and amount of mental health care was necessary to what extracurricular activities were appropriate for which child. They could not be civil. They could not subordinate their own adult feelings for each other to work together for the children most of the time.

This sample testimony demonstrates that the essential information/evidence can be admitted when the PC testifies as a fact witness. What the court ultimately needs is a factual understanding of the relevant conduct of the parties sufficient to determine custody. A PC fact witness can provide this through his or her factual experience with the parties.

MAINTAINING A COMPREHENSIVE AND SUBSTANTIATED RECORD

PCs will often hear a lawyer say, "That's great, but I need it in writing!" When involved in the litigation process, the legal *record* includes the PC's notes and correspondence, and the attorneys will be relying on and deciphering each word the PC writes. To provide the necessary record, we recommend that PC follows professional guidelines (see Guideline 6; American Psychological Association, 2012) as well as the following three recommendations:

1. Make sure your note-taking is contemporaneous with parent coordination sessions. Take notes during your session, or immediately thereafter. If the judge scrutinizes your findings and recommendations, your testimony will be appear more reliable and credible if you can testify that your notes were made at or near the time the conversations took place.
2. Try to capture statements in the words of the parents. Identify the issues raised by each parent and the response of the other parent. For example, if Mom raises the issue of wanting to get the child into mental health therapy, and Dad opposes it, be sure to capture the data that are articulated as the basis for their positions. In this example, if Mom mentions that she is in favor of mental health therapy based on the suggestion of the child's teacher, and Dad says he opposes this based on an article he read on the Internet, that information becomes relevant in the custody dispute.
3. Put all recommendations and binding decisions in writing and provide the basis for them. Putting your recommendations and decisions in writing minimizes the chances of misunderstanding and disagreements later. Also, if you provide the basis for your decision, the attorneys and the parents will know why the decision was made, and the parent has a clearer guide for improving his or her behavior in the future. For example, your recommendation and supporting basis might state, in part, as follows:

> The child may continue in therapy in as long as Mom engages in meaningful and appropriate consultation with Dad. This recommendation is based on Mom's history of understanding and meeting the child's needs, consulting with appropriate professionals to determine what is in the child's best interest, and her demonstrated track record of engaging in meaningful consultations with Dad regarding the child.

CONCLUSION

Our message as attorneys to PCs is this: We need you to help our clients, we rely on you to gather the relevant information and develop sound recommendations, we support the work you do and recognize the tensions inherent in your position, and we expect to work collaboratively with you and stay involved in the parenting coordination process. In return, we ask that you understand your role in the big picture, including realizing that a custody case is potentially always looming. We also ask that you stay open to testifying in court.

Not every custody case is right for parent coordination, but when it is appropriate, most attorneys understand, or should understand, that this multidisciplinary approach is likely the best opportunity for the family to move forward in the most constructive and child-centered way.

REFERENCES

American Psychological Association. (2012). Guidelines for the practice of parenting coordination. *American Psychologist, 67*, 63–71. doi:10.1037/a0024646

Association of Family and Conciliation Courts, Task Force on Parenting Coordination. (2006). Guidelines for parenting coordination. *Family Court Review, 44*, 164–181. doi:10.1111/j.1744-1617.2006.00074.x

Kohm, L. M. (2008). Tracing the foundations of the best interests of the child standard in American jurisprudence. *Journal of Law and Family Studies, 10*, 337–376.

Lewis, H., & Wilson, M. (Eds.). (2011). Child custody, visitation and termination of parental rights. *The Georgetown Journal of Gender and the Law, 12*, 449–492.

Md. Rule 9-205.2(h)(2) (2012). Retrieved from http://www6.montgomerycountymd.gov/Content/CircuitCourt/Court/FamilyDivision/PDF/MD_Rule_9_205_2.pdf

IV

THE FUTURE OF PARENTING COORDINATION

13

CHARTING THE CHALLENGING PATH TOWARD ESTABLISHMENT OF PARENTING COORDINATION'S EFFICACY

DEBRA K. CARTER AND STEPHEN J. LALLY

In this chapter, we review the preliminary research on parenting coordination, examining both initial studies that describe what parenting coordinators (PCs) are doing in their practices as well as the limited research on the effectiveness of parent coordination. In addition, because the parenting coordination process uses interventions drawn from mediation and parenting education, we examine the efficacy of divorce mediation as an alternative dispute-resolution process and discuss divorce parenting education (DPE) programs. Finally, we offer suggestions about where future research needs to be focused.

RESEARCH ON PARENTING COORDINATION

Research on parenting coordination is still in the early stages. Early studies and surveys were limited by small samples and low response rates; however, the outlook is improving. Researchers have begun to focus not only

http://dx.doi.org/10.1037/14390-014
Parenting Coordination in Postseparation Disputes: A Comprehensive Guide for Practitioners, S. A. Higuchi and S. J. Lally (Editors)

on parenting coordination but also the efficacy of DPEs, and although more work is needed, the results so far have pointed to the efficacy of both.

Surveys on the Nature of Parenting Coordination

Although the process of parenting coordination has been described by various authors in different forums over the past decade (Association of Family and Conciliation Courts [AFCC], Task Force on Parenting Coordination, 2003; Beck, Putterman, Sbarra, & Mehl, 2008; Carter, 2011; Coates, Deutsch, Starnes, Sullivan, & Sydlik, 2004; Fieldstone, Carter, King, & McHale, 2011; Fieldstone, Lee, Baker, & McHale, 2012; Hayes, 2010; Hayes, Grady, & Brantley, 2012; Henry, Fieldstone, & Bohac, 2009; Kirkland & Sullivan, 2008; Mitcham-Smith & Henry, 2007; Parks, Tindall, & Yingling, 2011), only recently has there been an effort to describe the nature of the practice of parenting coordination in more detail (i.e., who is providing this service and what those individuals actually do in their practices). Kirkland and Sullivan (2008) attempted to answer the first question in a survey of 54 PCs who were identified either from the AFCC directory or were attending the annual AFCC symposium. The majority of the respondents were psychologists (44%), with social workers (19%) and professional counselors (15%) being the next most frequently identified profession, followed by attorneys (11%) and bachelor's level PCs (11%). They were an experienced group of professionals (with an average of 18 years of practice, and 8 years of PC practice) who devoted an average of 40% of their practice to PC work (range: 5%–70%). All of the respondents indicated that they conducted their work under legally sanctioned circumstances (a court order or mutually signed consent decree), and most relied on court orders (80%). Kirkland and Sullivan also collected information from the respondents about the information included in written PC agreements (e.g., terms of service, disclaimers about the PC's role, confidentiality), the nature of the initial evaluation (e.g., whether psychological testing is used), fees (e.g., both the amount and how the fees are split), mode of meeting (e.g., place, joint vs. individual meetings), and use of collateral interviews. Kirkland and Sullivan also reported that only 11% of the respondents had encountered formal complaints, something they attributed to the fact that a majority of their PC respondents had grievance policies in their parenting coordination agreements.

Beck et al. (2008) interviewed the 11 professionals who were listed on the PC roster for Pima County, Arizona, to gather information about who provided the services and what roles and goals they perceived for their PC practice. Approximately half of the professionals came from a mental health background (three psychologists, two mediators/counselors, and one social worker) and half were attorneys (three had JDs, and two had both JDs and master's degrees in counseling). Most of the PCs used a mediation model of intervention (73%), with a judicial model (55%) and counseling model (27%) of intervention used less frequently, and cognitive behavioral (9%) and custody evaluation models (9%) used the least often. Beck et al. noted that the attorneys used only the mediation and judicial models, whereas the mental health professionals used more varied intervention models. These disciplinary differences were also noted in the types of contact, with three quarters of the attorneys stating they met face to face with the parents only at the initial meeting or never met with the parents (relying on just telephone contact or e-mails), whereas all of the mental health PCs reported regular face-to-face meetings. Across the sample, the PCs viewed their roles as primarily an authority figure (73%), facilitator and educator (64%), or gatekeeper to the courts (46%). Their goals were system efficiency (82%), facilitative and educative (73%), and authoritative (27%). However, similar to the models of intervention and the types of contact, there were discipline-specific differences in the PCs' perception of roles and goals. Beck et al.'s study helped provide valuable information about how PCs perceive their work; however, it is limited by the size of the sample and what may be situational factors (e.g., the authors opined that low rates of reimbursement were the reason why attorney PCs rarely saw their clients face to face).

Hayes (2010) sought to replicate and expand on Kirkland and Sullivan's (2008) survey of PCs with a sample of PCs in North Carolina. Across five districts in North Carolina, 58 PCs were identified and contacted; 14 of them participated in the survey. The survey included general questions about practice and asked the participants to respond to five vignettes designed to elicit information about the parenting coordination process. The 14 participants included 10 mental health professionals, three attorneys, and one individual with both a law degree and a master's degree in counseling. They had, on average, 24 hours of PC-specific training, had been practicing as a PC for an average of 3.5 years, and had an average of five current parenting coordination cases. The majority reported routine use of telephone and e-mail, with six of the 14 reporting that telephone and e-mail were their primary modes of working with clients. The PCs saw themselves as operating in an enforcement capacity to manage and resolve disputes rather than create new rules, conduct detailed investigations, or burden the court. Hayes noted that the PCs tended to first manage conflict, educate when appropriate, talk to other professionals, and arbitrate minor decisions and only as a last resort refer to the court. Hayes also noted that the PCs preferred manner of working with the court was, to a degree, dictated by their professional background. PCs with mental health backgrounds were more likely to use mediation, education, investigation, and enforcement functions with parents and to refer legal issues back to the parents' attorneys. Attorneys were more likely to use mediation, enforcement, and decision-making functions and less likely to work with parents' attorneys.

A follow-up survey of parenting coordination practices conducted by Hayes et al. (2012) focused on contextual factors that influence the parenting coordination process. The authors used a questionnaire similar to the one used by Kirkland and Sullivan (2008) and Hayes (2010) and surveyed PCs who participated in listservs and online discussion groups to which PCs were known to belong. PCs ($n = 51$) in this research had demographic characteristics similar to those of PCs in other surveys (Beck et al., 2008; Kirkland & Sullivan, 2008; Walker & Hayes, 2006). The majority came from a mental health background (64%); almost one third (28.3%) were attorneys; and they were considered experienced PCs based on the number of cases they had since beginning their practice. Hayes et al. concluded that the most salient contextual factors were formal rules (statutes or local rules), interpersonal characteristics of PC clients (personality disorders, socioeconomic factors), and background characteristics of parenting coordinators (education, experience). Survey results indicated that most respondents' practices were governed by state statutes (64%), whereas 18% followed local rules, and 18% said their practice was not guided by formal legal policies. The authors also found that additional guidance for PC practice came from court orders (80%). Most PCs wanted both a parenting coordination and custody/consent order (53%); one third (33%) worked with just a parenting coordination order; and smaller groups worked with just a custody order (4%) or only the consent of the parties, without any court orders (10%).

Similar to Hayes's (2010) study, Hayes et al.'s (2012) results revealed that most PCs use telephone (53% sometimes/weekly) and e-mail (63% routinely/daily) to communicate with their clients. In addition, they reported methods and frequency of parents' communication with each other and found that most parents use the telephone (53% sometimes/weekly), e-mail (57% routinely/daily), or text messaging (43% sometimes/weekly). This survey had several limitations, including a small sample size and lack of homogeneous samples (most PCs were AFCC affiliated) suggesting that the results may have limited generalizability. However, this study highlights the emerging use of technology in the PC process and, similar to the findings of Fieldstone and colleagues (2011), adds support to the view of parenting coordination as an intervention focused primarily on dispute resolution and education to manage ongoing conflicts. Hayes et al. also raised questions for future research, including understanding how process and contextual factors ultimately affect the goals and outcomes of the parenting coordination process.

Fieldstone et al. (2011) completed a statewide study of Florida PCs around the same time that Hayes and colleagues (2012) were conducting their survey. Fieldstone et al. found that at the commencement of the parenting coordination process, the parties were parents who were contentious, unwilling to compromise, and prone to triangulate their children into their conflict in myriad ways. This survey found that PCs drew on very similar sets of intervention methods and practices in their work with high-conflict cases, including educating coparents about the harmful effect of conflict on children, facilitating resolution of coparenting disputes and changes in parenting plans, introducing the concept of win–win agreements, helping parents establish interactional and communication boundaries for a more effective coparenting relationship, and using attorneys to encourage parents' compliance to court orders. In addition, PCs reported very similar proportions of their casework in which the thrust of the work had ultimately gravitated toward realizing one of three distinctively different aims: (a) developing a *cooperative* coparenting alliance, (b) achieving a functional *parallel* coparenting relationship (in which the parents maintained very limited communication with one another, principally via electronic means), or (c) settling on a fully *disengaged* coparenting relationship (involving no contact at all between parents, with all child-related communication vetted through the PC). Although these findings provide a starting point for understanding the parenting coordination process, the authors noted that data from this study, and inferences drawn from the data, were presented principally for their heuristic value in stimulating follow-up work on effective practices and successful outcomes. Additional limitations include a small sample size ($n = 67$) and the fact that the study did not include outcome measures to shed light on the "micro-events of PC work" that would distinguish successful from unsuccessful cases.

Fieldstone et al. (2012) conducted a study to assess expectations, perceptions, and perceived efficacy of the parenting coordination process from the point of view of family law attorneys, judges, and PCs. They developed a survey that covered 10 main areas of inquiry and used an online survey tool to solicit responses from judges, magistrates, attorneys, and PCs in Miami–Dade county (the fourth largest judicial circuit in the United States and the largest in Florida). Preliminary examination of the items reflecting the perceptions of PCs ($n = 23$) and judges ($n = 17$) indicated a restricted range of variables and, given the smaller size of the samples, the researchers focused primarily on the attorney sample ($n = 94$) to produce a composite of their perceptions. They found that the majority of respondents from each of the three groups indicated that further training in PC would be helpful (judges: 77%, attorneys: 91%, PCs: 91%), particularly in the areas of PC skills and techniques, time-sharing and parenting plans, and court-specific procedures. These researchers also identified an important area of divergent expectancies and ambiguous boundaries in the legal process across the three groups. The solicitation of an opinion on substantial changes in time sharing, which most PCs viewed as a request for a custody recommendation, was regarded as unethical (78%), whereas 71%

of the judges expected that PCs would create a time-sharing schedule. One of the alarming findings was that only 59% of judges indicated that they always checked for safety issues and domestic violence or abuse before considering an order for parenting coordination even though the state statute requires the court to hold an evidentiary hearing to determine whether participants have freely and voluntarily given their consent to participate and whether any safety parameters should be ordered before referring clients to parenting coordination if there has been a history of domestic violence. Adherence to legal protocol was identified as an area warranting further exploration and consideration, including establishment of specific criteria before allowing a PC to testify, domestic violence and abuse screening, and informing participants about the PC's powers and limitations before they become involved with the process. The primary objections to the use of a PC were fees and costs. This study had several limitations, including a lack of geographic diversity (it was administered only to judges, attorneys, and PCs in a single circuit in Florida); changes in practice over the survey period (approximately 5 years) due to the state statute going into effect toward the end of the time the data were collected (October 2009); and the fact that it involved general impressions of the process summarized across all cases with which the respondents had been involved, versus specific issues that arose in individual cases. However, important implications and questions for further study were posited, including the need for greater education about parenting coordination, the issues of PC fees, the need to resolve ethical concerns, the role of legislation, and concerns about use of parenting coordination in cases of domestic violence.

In sum, surveys of PCs are finding that professionals in a variety of disciplines provide the service and that there appear to be some differences in the interventions and goals depending on the professional background of the PC. In spite of some of these variations, there is some consistency in the models used across the different studies. The most recent studies (Fieldstone et al., 2011, 2012; Hayes, 2010; Hayes et al., 2012) have started to provide detailed information about the actual process that occurs during PC sessions. These initial studies suffered from small sample sizes, and it is not clear how much the results reflect idiosyncratic characteristics deriving from the fact that their respondents often comprise samples of convenience. Further replication is needed, with an increasing focus on the nature and process of parenting coordination being administered by the practitioners.

The Efficacy of Parenting Coordination

As noted above, a number of authors (Carter & McHale, 2013; Fieldstone et al., 2011, 2012; Hayes, 2010; Hayes et al., 2012; Henry et al., 2009) have postulated that parenting coordination can reduce the conflict and improve the communication and cooperation between parents, reduce litigation between parents, and ultimately improve the adjustment of children. The Florida Statewide Survey (Fieldstone et al., 2011) also found that PCs, both mental health and legal professionals, believed their casework with families led to beneficial outcomes in the majority of their cases. Although parenting coordination is receiving increasing recognition in state laws and regulations (see Chapter 2, this volume, for a review of these developments) and two major associations have recently published practice guidelines (AFCC, Task Force on Parenting Coordination, 2006; American Psychological Association [APA], 2012), relatively little research has examined the effectiveness of the intervention. Although empirical research of effects of parenting coordination was "practically nonexistent" (Henry et al., 2009, p. 684) only a few years ago, there has been a considerable increase in research in this area in the recent past (Brewster, Beck, Anderson, & Benjamin, 2011; Fieldstone et al., 2012; Hayes et al., 2012), and more is expected as parenting coordination becomes more widespread.

For many years, the only research cited regarding the effectiveness of parenting coordination was an unpublished study conducted by Terry Johnston in northern California in the early 1990s that supported the efficacy of parenting coordination (AFCC, Task Force on Parent Coordination, 2003; Kelly, 2002; Kirkland & Sullivan, 2008). That study reported that the number of court appearances decreased in the year following the appointment of Special Masters (the term for a PC in California). Specifically, the average case ($n = 166$) involved almost six court appearances prior to appointment and less than one (0.22) appearance after the appointment. The report also stated that there was a decrease in conflict between the couples and that the parents expressed satisfaction with the PC. As impressive as these results appear, there was little information about the details of this study, and it was never published in a peer-reviewed journal, only cited by others. However, between 2008 and 2012 the results of four studies providing further support for the efficacy of parenting coordination have been published.

A circuit-wide study of high-conflict cases in Miami–Dade County (Henry et al., 2009) examined numbers of motions filed per couple 1 year before and 1 year after appointment of a PC. The 49 cases reviewed were a convenience sample (based on the amount of material available in court records) drawn from the 88 couples who had been ordered into parenting coordination during 2006. Most of the couples in the study had been married (24.5% were never-married pairs raising shared children), were ethnically (36% Hispanic, 11% Caucasian, 10% African American, and 43% unknown/other) and economically diverse (slightly less than one third were eligible for parenting coordination services free of charge), and their children were generally young (over half were between ages 5 and 12). The authors found that the filing of motions decreased significantly (48.27%) in the year after a PC was appointed. In this study, child-related motions decreased by 75%. Also of interest was that 40% of all non-child–related motions decreased in the year after parenting coordination, leading the authors to suggest that some of the gains parents made in resolving parenting disputes may have applied to other areas as well.

Another study of Miami–Dade County (Fieldstone et al., 2012) found that "most respondents (professionals) portrayed the process to be either very helpful or moderately helpful" (p. 445) and concluded that greater experience in family law and with parenting coordination was related to more positive views of the process. Most attorneys (79%) reported that parenting coordination was helpful to their relationship with their client, and most reporting judges (82%) indicated that they found PCs' reports to be helpful.

Brewster et al. (2011) described a pilot study of a newly implemented parenting coordination program in Pima County, Arizona. The authors followed the first 21 cases that participated in the program for a 2-year period and compared the use of courts and outside agencies via documents in the archived divorce files for the 2 years prior to the appointment of the PC. In the 2-year period after the appointment of the PC there was a significant reduction in the number of legal documents in the files, number of hearings, and the number of changes in the parenting plan. Regarding the latter two, the number of hearings averaged 6.38 per case prior to the appointment of the PC, and then dropped to 1.10 in the 2 years following appointment (an 83% decrease), and the number of changes to the plan showed a similar drop (dropping from 8.83 changes per case to 4.2 changes per case, a 52.5% decrease). There was also a reduction in the use of outside agencies (e.g., Child Protective Services, drug testing, supervised exchange programs). Although nearly one quarter of the couples (23.8%) fired their PC prior to the end of the 2-year postappointment period, Brewster and colleagues examined the number and content of the motions filed for the 16 couples who remained in the program. The number of motions and changes to the plan significantly decreased (a 64.2% and 52.5% decrease, respectively), but the ratio of changes to motions increased. The authors hypothesized that the increase was due to fewer frivolous motions being filed. The content of the motions was also examined, and the authors noted that a significant decrease in motions was evident across four content areas: (a) finances, (b) children, (c) safety issues, and (d) administrative issues. As Brewster et al. noted, this study was limited by its very small sample size as well as the range of variability in the experience and professional training of the PCs.

Additional evidence supporting the efficacy of parenting coordination has been reported in the results from the Parenting Coordination Project based in the Washington, DC's Superior Court (Child Trends, 2010; Lally & Higuchi,

2008). The program began as a project funded by the APA and included the participation of a number of local stakeholders; it is now a permanent program of the court (see Chapter 8 for a detailed description of the development of the project). One of the primary goals of the project was to collect data to assess the efficacy of parenting coordination. The project collected information on children's adjustment (Child Behavior Checklist [CBCL]; Achenbach & Edelbrock, 1983), parents/guardians' communication and conflict (Parenting Alliance Measure [Abidin & Konold, 1999] and Acrimony Scale [Shaw & Emery, 1987]; Emery, 1982; Emery, Matthews, & Wyer, 1990), satisfaction surveys completed by parents, judges, attorneys, and guardians ad litem; as well as information on the frequency and types of hearings involving the project's cases.

Lally and Higuchi (2008) presented the project's preliminary results on the first 16 cases, and a report from Child Trends (2010) included a more comprehensive analysis of the preliminary results as well as data from additional cases (the first 21 seen by the project). The parents' and children's data were collected at entry into the program and later, after at least 6 months in the program. At entry into the program, the parents reported much higher levels of acrimony (mean score of 55.8 for mothers and 54.2 for fathers on the Acrimony Scale) than had typically been found in prior studies of couples engaged in divorce mediation (Emery, Matthews, & Wyer, 1991; Shaw & Emery, 1987). Similarly, the Parenting Alliance Measure, which assessed the couple's ability to work together cooperatively, indicated significant dysfunction (54% of the mothers rated the alliance as problematic or dysfunctional; 86% of the fathers gave a similar rating). Over the first 6+ months of the program, both acrimony and alliance scores improved; however, this improvement did not reach a level of statistical significance. This analysis, and much of the data from the project, was hampered by small sample size and, at times, missing data, which affected the authors' ability to statistically assess the change. Similarly, the results of the measures of children's adjustment (CBCL) found only a few significant changes. Specifically, fathers noted a reduction in rule breaking for younger children (ages 1.5–5 years) and a reduction in affective, anxiety, and posttraumatic stress problems for the older children (ages 6–18). Mothers also noted a reduction in anxiety problems in that older group. Across the multitude of scales of the CBCL, most (but not all) scales showed changes in a positive direction during time in the program but, except for the specific scales noted above, these changes were not statistically significant.

Satisfaction surveys were completed (Child Trends, 2010; Lally & Higuchi, 2008) by judges, other concerned professionals (attorneys, guardians ad litem), and parents at the end of the couples' first year in the program. Overall satisfaction was quite high for the judges (3.8 on a scale of 4), and they noted improvements in specific areas (e.g., parents' communication and conflict, children's well-being, information provided to the court). Qualitative comments mirrored the ratings (e.g., "You helped to resolve the most difficult case in my calendar for 2006, Thank you"; see Lally & Higuchi, 2008, for additional examples). The overall ratings by other professionals were more moderate (2.7 out of 4) and may have reflected the unique influence of a specific case within this small sample of professionals ($n = 6$) as well as some ambivalence about the parenting coordination process from attorneys accustomed to adversarial litigation (see Lally & Higuchi, 2008, for further details). The parent satisfaction surveys were not interpretable because of missing data (only two parents completed the surveys). The most robust data from the project came out of the analysis of court outcomes for 19 of the cases. There was a statistically significant decrease in the number of court activities per month (decreasing from 17.53 to 6.7), the percentage of cases in which contempt orders were filed (reduced from 37% to 5%), and instances in which participants were found to be in contempt of court (reduced from 16% to 0%). Also, the percentage of cases that were resolved without a court order significantly improved (from 0% to 32%). The number of emergency hearings per month evidenced a decrease after the appointment of the PC (from 0.1 to 0.02); however, this decrease was not significant. Overall, the program provided support for the efficacy for parenting coordination, but the small size of the sample and missing data limit the strength of the conclusion.

In sum, the results of this first generation of outcome measures for parenting coordination provides strong support that PCs reduce the number of court hearings and motions filed. It is notable that this finding was found across different jurisdictions, and across ethnically and economically diverse parents, and was true for court-based programs as well as PCs in private practice. As Brewster et al. (2011) noted, this success is not universal and, in their study, nearly one quarter of the parents fired their PC before the end of the study's 2-year period. Beyond the reduction in absolute number, there is evidence from these studies that the PC's impact is focused on particular types of motions and hearings. Specifically, parenting coordination has led to fewer frivolous (Brewster et al., 2011) and child-related motions (Henry et al., 2009), fewer contempt findings and emergency hearings (Child Trends, 2010), and an increase of resolution of cases without court order (Child Trends, 2010). The results from the District of Columbia program (Child Trends, 2010; Lally & Higuchi, 2008) have also provided some preliminary support for improvements in parents' level of conflict and cooperation (both from direct measures and judges' ratings) and support (albeit more equivocal) for improvements in the children's adjustment (both from parents' ratings on the CBCL and judges' ratings). However, this first generation of efficacy research is marred by small sample sizes and provides only indirect measures of PC efficacy, specifically whether PC is having a positive impact on parents' behavior and children's adjustment.

The issue of access to parenting coordination and community-based services for parents who do not have the resources to afford these services outside of the court-based program has also been examined. In 2000, the American Bar Association's Family Law Section (Elrod & Ramsey, 2001) recognized the need for parenting coordination in high-conflict cases and recommended that such a process be available through the court's case management or service delivery program, especially for parents who cannot afford a community provider.

Support for Parenting Coordination From Related Social Science Research

Although carefully controlled clinical trials have yet to be completed on parenting coordination as an alternative dispute-resolution process, some conclusions can be drawn from social science research in related fields. To assess the foundation of parenting coordination as an effective intervention for high-conflict parents, the effectiveness of divorce mediation as an alternative dispute-resolution process and the potential benefit of DPE programs should be formally examined. From the empirical studies on these processes, one can infer that specific interventions and methodologies used in these processes may have similar effects when used in parenting coordination.

Research on the Effectiveness of Mediation in Domestic Relations Cases

Mediation is a task-oriented, time-limited alternative dispute-resolution method whereby parties meet with a neutral person and isolate the disputed issues, consider options and alternatives, and reach a consensual settlement (Beck & Sales, 2001). Mediation was first used in domestic relations cases in the 1960s as an alternative to litigation, and its use increased greatly in the intervening years and now is mandated in many states. Even though parenting coordination has been viewed as an alternative to mediation for high-conflict families, PCs use in their work many of the techniques and processes of mediation. Evidence of the efficacy of mediation with families is indirect support for elements of the work conducted by PCs.

The most robust support for the effectiveness of divorce mediation comes from a large-scale longitudinal study involving randomized trials of mediation and adversary settlement (Emery, Matthews, & Kitzmann, 1994; Emery, Sbarra, & Grover, 2005). Emery et al. (1994, 2005) have found that mediation produced several important and sizable differences relative to adversary settlement in terms of benefits for postseparation family relationships. For example, in a 12-year follow-up study, they found evidence of increased contact between nonresidential parents and their children as well as improvement in the quality of the parent–child relationship. In addition, they found that the increase in contact between children and nonresidential parents did not increase parental conflict and that there were benefits for the relationship between the parents themselves.

Reviews of the literature on effectiveness of divorce mediation on parent and child psychological adjustment has not produced the same uniformly positive results. Kelly (1996), in her review of divorce mediation research, reported that neither parent nor child psychological adjustment was affected in a statistically meaningful manner by mediation, but she also noted that these findings were not surprising given the brevity of mediation interventions. Emery and colleagues (1991) found no differences in psychological well-being in comparing mediation and adversary settlement groups immediately after dispute resolution and 1 year later (Emery et al., 1994). They did find that reduced parental conflict predicted improved psychological adjustment among children 18 months after dispute settlement (Kitzmann & Emery, 1994). Unfortunately, results from a longitudinal study (Emery et al., 2005) also found no group differences in the mental health of parents or children 12 years after dispute resolution based on whether they mediated or proceeded with adversary settlement.

These researchers and others have suggested that mediation might improve mental health outcomes if packaged with other effective interventions that specifically target psychological outcomes such as parenting or children's groups (Pedro-Carroll & Alpert-Gillis, 1997; Wolchik et al., 2002). Results from research suggest that improved psychological adjustment in children and adults may require longer term interventions, specifically those that target psychological outcomes, lending support to the potential value of parenting coordination and the necessity of including these ingredients in the parenting coordination process.

Emery and colleagues (1999) sought to identify the potentially modifiable aspects of family relationships that are most important to children's mental health in divorce and concluded that there are four such variables: (a) an authoritative relationship with at least one parent, (b) mild parental conflict or conflict that does not involve the children, (c) economic stability, and (d) a good relationship with the other parent. These researchers (Emery et al., 1994, 2004) also focused on primary ingredients in mediation versus adversary settlement that are responsible for producing positive results: cooperation, education, and businesslike boundaries. They drew a distinction between "active ingredients" and "elements" of mediation, noting that their work did not show specifically the mechanism (elements) that allows the ingredients to work effectively.

A parenting plan or detailed custody arrangement provides structure that is consistent with Emery et al.'s (2005) notion of a formal, businesslike relationship. It is designed to help parents disengage from a conflicted relationship (see

Chapter 7, this volume) and establish a successful conflict resolution framework (Carter, 2011). A comprehensive parenting plan not only specifies time-sharing arrangements and decision-making responsibilities for children but also includes a system for child-focused communication and problem-solving techniques. Emery et al. (2005) emphasized the need for parents to view their parenting plan as a living agreement and considered it a success, not a failure, when parents returned to mediation to update and change their agreement using cooperative negotiation methods. In their 12-year follow-up study, they found that parents who mediated made more changes in their agreement in comparison to parents in the adversary settlement group: "Parents who mediated flexibly accommodated important changes in their own and their children's lives" (Emery et al., 2005, p. 28). Drawing on this support for establishing a detailed but flexible parenting plan lends additional endorsement for a central role of parenting coordination: helping parents negotiate modifications to their parenting plan without litigation and prolonged conflict. These modifications may be necessary as children's needs change and family dynamics evolve and parents strive to establish and maintain a successful coparenting framework.

Zuberbuhler (2001), in her study of random assignment into mediation, found that it was more difficult for parents to cooperate once they had moved too far down the litigation path. Emery (2004) suggested that the "most important benefit of mediation is that it keeps parents from following an adversarial route, one that can cause severely strained relationships to deteriorate further, perhaps irreparably" (p. 34). Parents using parenting coordination services may have already followed an adversarial legal route and often need sensitive and intensive interventions over an extended period of time if the ruptures in their coparenting relationship are to be sufficiently repaired for relatively healthy functioning as a parenting unit. These findings suggest that parents and children may benefit from parenting coordination interventions that occur relatively early in the separation and divorce process in the hope of preventing deterioration of the relationship between the parents and between each parent and child.

Research on Divorce Parent Education Programs

Although parenting coordination differs from parent education in several important ways (i.e., duration, strategies used, and court oversight), parenting education is a key component of parenting coordination. Therefore, evidence of its efficacy provides indirect support for the efficacy of parenting coordination. DPE programs vary considerably in content (Braver, Salem, Pearson, & DeLusé, 1996; Geasler & Blaisure, 1999), teaching strategies (Bowers, Mitchell, Hardesty, & Hughes, 2011; Wolchik, Sandler, Winslow, & Smith-Daniels, 2005), length of program (Arbuthnot, Kramer, & Gordon, 1997; Fackrell, Hawkins, & Kay, 2011; Kramer & Washo, 1993; Shifflett &

Cummings, 1999), targeted participants (Braver, Griffin, & Cookston, 2005; Cookston & Fung, 2011; Forgatch & DeGarmo, 1999; Gilman, Schneider, & Shulak, 2005; Stolberg & Garrison, 1985; Wolchik et al., 2005), timing of attendance (McIntosh & Deacon-Wood, 2003), and outcome measures (Sigal, Sandler, Wolchik, & Braver, 2011). In most of the programs, parent satisfaction is high, and there is modest evidence that they are effective (Fackrell et al., 2011; Pollet & Lombreglia, 2008). However, analyses of the extant research has yielded mixed results, and some researchers (Sigal et al., 2011) have suggested that "the lack of convincing evidence of program effects is due to methodological limitations in the evaluations" (p. 135) rather than program ineffectiveness.

Many parent education programs teach parents how to coparent more cooperatively with their former partner in an effort to avoid the detrimental effects of interparental conflict (Pollet & Lombreglia, 2008). Program curricula vary but generally focus on understanding children's adjustment to divorce and the importance of low-conflict, cooperative parenting after divorce (Braver et al., 1996; Geasler & Blaisure, 1999). DPEs vary considerably in the amount of instruction hours and aims of the program. In a meta-analysis involving review of 28 studies, Fackrell and colleagues (2011) looked at differences in "dosage" between court-mandated, court-affiliated, and non-court–affiliated programs. They found that most court-mandated programs had less than 3 hours of instruction, whereas nearly all court-affiliated programs (voluntary attendance) involved 10 or more instruction hours. The non-court–affiliated programs' instruction hours fell somewhere in the middle (between 4 and 9 hours). The aims of these preventive interventions also varied, with most of the mandatory programs being targeted to both parents and described as "brief information programs," whereas the multisession, skill-building interventions were generally voluntary and focused on specific groups, such as primary residential parents (Pollet & Lombreglia, 2008; Wolchik et al., 2005). Brief information programs are the most widely available (Pollet & Lombreglia, 2008) and target residential parents (usually mothers) because they are seen as change agents for improving children's postdivorce adjustment.

Two recent reviews of postdivorce parenting education programs (Fackrell et al., 2011; Sigal et al., 2011) concluded that DPEs had a significant but modest positive effect. In evaluating the programs, the authors made distinctions between different aspects of parenting and improvements in child outcomes. Sigal and colleagues (2011) specifically highlighted as factors that influence each other and influence child well-being the "dynamic interrelationships" among the level of conflict, cooperation between the parents, the quantity of time each parent spends with the children, and the quality of parenting provided by both parents. The two most consistent findings in their review were that (a) the quality of parenting by both the residential and nonresidential parent was significantly related to children's postdivorce adjustment outcomes and (b) parents can be taught to improve the quality of their parenting (Dawson-McClure, Sandler, Wolchik, & Millsap, 2004; DeGarmo & Forgatch, 2005; Wolchik et al., 2000, 2002). However, Fackrell and colleagues (2011) cautioned that child outcomes were primarily by parent reports rather than direct measure or observation and that there was a lack of randomized control trials.

There is some evidence that the mixed results of DPE program effectiveness on child well-being may be related to the length of the intervention (i.e., brief vs. multiple sessions). For example, two reviews conducted in 2004 and 2005 found no short-term parent education programs to have an effect on child well-being (Goodman, Bonds, Sandler, & Braver, 2004; Wolchik et al., 2005). Others found some positive outcomes (Arbuthnot & Gordon, 1996; Kramer & Washo, 1993; Shifflett & Cummings 1999), but their efficacy was questioned on the basis of the design of the program evaluations and lack of effect on child outcomes (Wolchik et al., 2005).

In programs of longer duration (e.g., 10 sessions), however, there is strong evidence that improvement in quality of parenting leads to improvement in child outcomes. In one of the most rigorously evaluated programs using large samples (the New Beginnings Program), researchers found reduced levels of externalizing problem behaviors among children of participating parents shortly after divorce (Wolchik et al., 2000) and 6 years after the intervention (Goodman et al., 2004; Wolchik et al., 2002, 2005). Specifically, children had more positive outcomes in terms of mental health, substance use, academic outcomes, and sexual behavior than those in the randomly assigned control group (Wolchik et al., 2009). Other programs for divorcing or separating parents conducted in experimental settings have also been positively linked with improvements in coparenting and in reducing interparental conflict (Cookston, Braver, Griffin, DeLusé, & Miles, 2007) and child well-being outcomes (Pedro-Carroll & Cowen, 1985; Forgatch & DeGarmo, 1999).

Some DPE programs have also looked at improvements in parent well-being. A meta-analysis of five multicomponent parent education programs found substantial reductions in depressive symptoms in participating mothers of children with developmental disabilities compared with those in control groups (Singer, Ethridge, & Aldana, 2007). These programs included both behavioral training (parenting skills to address children's behavior problems) as well as psychoeducation (teaching psychological skills to cope with feelings of stress). Other programs (Cookston, Braver, Sandler, & Genalo, 2002; Pruett, Insabella, & Gustafson, 2005) have found that parents who participated in the program experienced decreased parental distress and interparental conflict (Pruett et al., 2005) and reported lower anxiety and depression (Cookston & Fung, 2011). According to end-of-program surveys, parents have also credited parent education programs with helping them adjust to the divorce (Pollet & Lombreglia, 2008). The Kids' Turn program, a community-based multiple-session intervention, involves both parents and children and is the only controlled, randomized trial of family education programs for divorcing couples that has been found to reduce interparental conflict (Cookston et al., 2007; Cookston & Fung, 2011). Cookston and colleagues (Cookston et al., 2007; Cookston & Fung, 2011) concluded that participation in Kids' Turn specifically lowered levels of anxiety.

Of the empirically supported correlates of children's postdivorce adjustment that parents control, parenting is the only factor for which replicated, rigorous evaluations have demonstrated that program-induced improvements mediate short- and long-term program effects to improve children's functioning. (Dawson-McClure et al., 2004; Fackrell et al., 2011; Sigal et al., 2011; Wolchik et al., 2002). There is strong evidence that postdivorce parenting by the residential parent (usually the mother) is a critical resilience resource, and interventions that promote effective parenting in divorced families consistently predict children's postdivorce adjustment. Bowers et al. (2011) concluded that many parents need extensive education and support to successfully transition through the divorce process.

Prevention Program Outcomes and Implications for Parenting Coordination

On the basis of evidence from DPE programs and mediation processes, there is reason to be optimistic that parenting coordination interventions that clearly target improvements in parenting variables—in particular, the quality of parenting by both the custodial and noncustodial parent—may lead to improvements in the outcomes of children after divorce. The specific interventions can be derived from programs that have demonstrated efficacy and include the following: a detailed parenting plan or custody arrangement; a structured relationship that promotes more businesslike interactions and effective communication about child-related issues; a system for resolving parenting disputes; a relationship component to educate parents about the impact of high-quality parenting by both parents and of low interparental conflict; a component that builds parents' motivation to strengthen the quality of their parenting and to not undermine the other parent; active skill-building components, which include modeling, role play, and feedback; and a way to help parents self-assess their need for longer term interventions to build their skills for effective parenting and to reduce interparental conflict.

These findings lend support to the need for parenting coordination as an intervention specifically targeted to establish an effective dispute-resolution framework; improve the quality of parenting and coparenting relationships; and, indirectly, to promote positive outcomes for children. It is important to note that the programs that have proven to be most effective involve multiple sessions that are aimed at skill building and include a variety of interventions and teaching strategies that afford parents the opportunity to clarify their understanding of children's needs and to understand the impact of interparental conflict on their children and the importance of quality parenting. This suggests that parenting coordination must include these necessary ingredients if it is to be effective in improving outcomes for parents and children.

Future Research

Although a few surveys are beginning to collect information about what is actually said and done during parenting coordination and the impact of interventions on outcome, there has yet been no rigorous review of the practice of parenting coordination. Such empirical studies are needed to record and analyze PCs' behaviors and communications and their effects on positive outcomes.

The limited body of research on parenting coordination programs points to the need for additional research on their benefits to court services (Coates et al., 2004; Henry et al., 2009; Lally & Higuchi, 2008), the role of children in parenting coordination (Kelly, 2002), which components of parenting coordination are the most effective (Coates et al., 2004; Fieldstone et al., 2011), the impact of parenting coordination services on nontraditional family configurations and children (Henry et al., 2009), improving parental communication and cooperation (Fieldstone et al., 2011), and reducing parental conflict (Lally & Higuchi, 2008). The results of the first generation of research need to be replicated and expanded. It is also important to note that the most effective outcome measures for researchers may at times be at odds with the need to provide services to the parents and be less relevant to the needs of the stakeholders (i.e., courts; Child Trends, 2010).

With parenting coordination still in its infancy and the empirical research in only its first generation, future researchers have the opportunity to gather data that may enable legal and mental health professionals to understand outcome differences and to determine the effectiveness of specific parenting coordination interventions. Some important questions are yet to be answered:

1. Does early parenting coordination intervention lead to better outcomes than appointments later in the separation/divorce process?
2. Is it helpful for a PC to have arbitration (or binding decision-making) authority to resolve parenting disputes? If so, what are appropriate limitations to protect parents' rights?
3. Does parenting coordination lead to more compliance with court orders and less relitigation?
4. Is conflict reduced, and interparental cooperation enhanced, through parenting coordination, compared to couples who do not receive these services?

5. Does parenting coordination improve the quality of parenting for each parent?
6. In what situations are structured coparenting arrangements most effective? When is a parallel parenting arrangement most effective?
7. Does parenting coordination enhance the psychological adjustment of parents and their children?
8. What type of families may benefit most from parenting coordination? Who should be included or excluded, and on what basis?
9. Does parenting coordination save time and money?
10. Is parenting coordination more or less effective after a mediated settlement agreement versus litigated settlement agreement?

Additional methodological challenges are the heterogeneity of interventions and models of parenting coordination. Therefore, an important feature of an evaluation of parenting coordination programs must include a detailed description of what the parenting coordination process entails. This should include, at the least, a detailed description of goals and intervention methodology. If the goals of parenting coordination are not clearly specified, it is not possible for an evaluation to assess whether the program is achieving an intended outcome. A well-constructed program evaluation would involve a clear specification of what parenting coordination is trying to accomplish, a full description of the nature of the interventions that are designed to accomplish those outcomes, random assignment of sufficient numbers of participants to parenting coordination and a comparison condition, and the use of reliable and valid measures of the outcomes.

Empirical studies on outcome, practice, and process are needed to help advance the field of parenting coordination and to determine the utility of the parenting coordination process among the major service interventions offered to clients in need. Research needs to proceed in looking at how, why, and for whom any program or interventions work. Variations in research populations, methodologies, and measures were the norm in early studies on outcome of mediation, making it problematic to generalize about mediation. To the degree that we can learn from past studies on alternative dispute resolution, basic descriptors of parenting coordination research are necessary to provide a framework for assessment outcome measures and promote generalizability of findings.

Studies of parenting coordination interventions ideally will include comparison groups and random assignment to parenting coordination in order to evaluate whether any change observed can be attributed to the intervention rather than other factors, such as the passage of time. If analyzed appropriately, a strong inference can be made that the changes observed in parents and children in the program versus control conditions can be attributed to the effects of the program rather than some artifact.

However, this ideal study of parenting coordination would be labor intensive and costly. Realistically, the next generation of research will involve cobbling together cases across various private practitioners and having court-administered programs include outcome measures within their protocols. A first step would be to organize a research group of practitioners who would articulate common information to be gathered in a standard format (e.g., demographic information, information regarding types of interventions, common outcome measures). Although research is vitally important, legal and mental health practitioners cannot wait for science to catch up to their ongoing cases, because recommendations and decisions need to be made pending the outcome of good research. As a consequence, using the research available and our own experience as legal and mental health practitioners, we are able to draw reasonable conclusions that parenting coordination may be of benefit to families negatively affected by high conflict and a decreased quality of parenting. However, a careful investigation and risk–benefit analysis of each case to determine what, if any, intervention serves the children's best interests is paramount.

REFERENCES

Abidin, R. R., & Konold, T. (1999). *Parenting Alliance Measure: Professional manual.* Odessa, FL: Psychological Assessment Resources.

Achenbach, T. M., & Edelbrock, C. S. (1983). *Manual for the Child Behavior Checklist and Revised Child Behavior Profile.* Burlington, VT: University of Vermont, Department of Psychiatry.

American Psychological Association. (2012). Guidelines for the practice of parent coordination. *American Psychologist, 67,* 63–71. doi:10.1037/a0024646

Association of Family and Conciliation Courts, Task Force on Parenting Coordination. (2003). Parenting coordination implementation issues. *Family Court Review, 41,* 533–564.

Association of Family and Conciliation Courts, Task Force on Parenting Coordination. (2006). Guidelines for parenting coordination. *Family Court Review, 44,* 164–181. doi:10.1111/j.1744-1617.2006.00074.x

Arbuthnot, J., & Gordon, A. (1996). Does mandatory divorce education for parents work? A six-month outcome evaluation. *Family and Conciliation Courts Review, 34,* 60–81. doi:10.1111/j.174-1617.1996.tb00400.x

Arbuthnot, J., Kramer, K., & Gordon, D. A. (1997). Patterns of relitigation following divorce education. *Family Court Review, 35,* 269–279. doi:10.1111/j.174-1617.1997.tb00469.x

Beck, C., Putterman, M., Sbarra, D., & Mehl, M. (2008). Parenting coordinator roles, program goals and services provided: Insights from Pima County, Arizona program. *Journal of Child Custody, 5,* 122–139. doi:10.1080/15379410802070468

Beck, C. J. A., & Sales, B. D. (2001). *Family mediation: Facts, myths, and future prospects*. Washington, DC: American Psychological Association. doi:10.1037/10401-000

Bowers, J., Mitchell, E., Hardesty, J., & Hughes, R. (2011). A review of online divorce education programs. *Family Court Review, 49*, 776–787. doi:10.1111/j.1744-1617.2011.01413.x

Braver, S. L., Griffin, W. A., & Cookston, J. T. (2005). Prevention programs for divorced nonresident fathers. *Family Court Review, 43*, 81–96. doi:10.1111/j.1744-1617.2005.00009.x

Braver, S. L., Salem, P., Pearson, J., & DeLusé, S. R. (1996). The content of divorce education programs: Results of a survey. *Family Court Review, 34*, 41–59. doi:10.1111/j.174-1617.1996.tb00399.x

Brewster, K. O., Beck, C. J. A., Anderson, E. R., & Benjamin, G. A. H. (2011). Evaluating parenting coordination programs: Encouraging results from pilot testing a research methodology. *Journal of Child Custody*, 8, 247–267. doi:10.1080/15379418.2011.620926

Carter, D. K. (2011). *Parenting coordination: A professional guide for family law professionals*. New York, NY: Springer.

Carter, D. K., & McHale, J. (2013). Protecting generational solidarities through interventions with divorcing families: Theory, research and practice. In H. Fulchiron (Ed.), *Solidarity between generations* (pp. 313–321). Paris, France: Bruylant.

Child Trends. (2010). *The Parenting Coordination (PC) Project Implementation and Outcomes Study Report*. Retrieved from http://www.apapracticecentral.org/update/2010/04-29/pc-report.pdf

Coates, C., Deutsch, R., Starnes, H., Sullivan, M., & Sydlik, B. (2004). Parenting coordination for high-conflict families. *Family Court Review, 42*, 246–262. doi:10.1177/1531244504422006

Cookston, J. T., Braver, S. L., Griffin, W., DeLusé, S. R., & Miles, J. C. (2007). Effects of the Dads for Life intervention on interparental conflict and coparenting in the two years after divorce. *Family Process*, 46, 123–137. doi:10.1111/j.1545-5300.2006.00196.x

Cookston, J. T., Braver, S. L., Sandler, I. N., & Genalo, M. T. (2002). Prospects for expanded parent education services for divorcing families with children. *Family Court Review*, 40, 190–203. doi:10.1111/j.174-1617.2002.tb00830.x

Cookston, J. T., & Fung, W. W. (2011). The Kids' Turn program evaluation: Probing change within a community-based intervention for separating families. *Family Court Review*, 49, 348–363. doi:10.1111/j.1744-1617.2011.01376.x

Dawson-McClure, S. R., Sandler, I. N., Wolchik, S. A., & Millsap, R. (2004). Risk as a moderator of the effects of prevention programs for children of divorce: A six-year longitudinal study. *Journal of Abnormal Child Psychology, 32*, 175–190. doi:10.1023/B:JACP.0000019769.75578.79

DeGarmo, D. S., & Forgatch, M. S. (2005). Early development of delinquency within divorced families: Evaluating a randomized preventive intervention trial. *Developmental Science*, 8, 229–239. doi:10.1111/j.1467-7687.2005.00412.x

Elrod, L. D., & Ramsey, S. H. (2001). High-conflict custody cases: Reforming the system for children: Conference report and action plan. *Family Law Quarterly, 34*, 589–606.

Emery, R., Sbarra, D., & Grover, T. (2005). Divorce mediation: Research and reflections. *Family Court Review, 43*, 22–37. doi:10.1111/j.1744-1617.2005.00005.x

Emery, R. E. (1982). Interparental conflict and the children of discord and divorce. *Psychological Bulletin, 92*, 310–330. doi:10.1037/0033-2909.92.2.310

Emery, R. E. (1999). Postdivorce family life for children: An overview of research and some implications for policy. In P. Amato & R. Thompson (Eds.). *The post-divorce family* (pp. 3–28). Thousand Oaks, CA: Sage.

Emery, R. E. (2004). *The truth about children and divorce: Groundbreaking research and advice for dealing with the emotions so you and your children can thrive*. New York, NY: Viking/Penguin.

Emery, R. E., Matthews, S. G., & Kitzmann, K. M. (1994). Child custody mediation and litigation: Parents' satisfaction and functioning a year after settlement. *Journal of Consulting and Clinical Psychology, 62*, 124–129. doi:10.1037/0022-006X.62.1.124

Fackrell, T. A., Hawkins, A. J., & Kay, N. M. (2011). How effective are court-affiliated divorcing parents education programs? A meta-analytic study. *Family Court Review, 49*, 107–119. doi:10.1111/j.1744-1617.2010.01356.x

Fieldstone, L., Carter, D. K., King, T., & McHale, J. (2011). Training, skills, and practice of parenting coordinators: Florida statewide study. *Family Court Review, 49*, 801–817. doi:10.1111/j.1744-1617.2011.01415.x

Fieldstone, L., Lee, M. C., Baker, J. K., & McHale, J. P. (2012). Perspectives on parenting coordination: Views of parenting coordinators, attorneys, and judiciary members. *Family Court Review, 50*, 441–454. doi:10.1111/j.1744-1617.2012.01459.x

Forgatch, M. S., & DeGarmo, D. S. (1999). Parenting through change: An effective prevention program for single mothers. *Journal of Consulting and Clinical Psychology, 67*, 711–724. doi:10.1037/0022-006X.67.5.711

Geasler, M. J., & Blaisure, K. R. (1999). 1998 nationwide survey of court-connected divorce education programs. *Family and Conciliation Courts Review, 37*, 36–63. doi:10.1111/j.174-1617.1999.tb00527.x

Gilman, J., Schneider, D., & Shulak, R. (2005). Children's ability to cope post divorce: The effects of Kids Turn intervention program on 7 to 9 year olds. *Journal of Divorce & Remarriage, 42*, 109–126. doi:10.1300/J087v42n03_07

Goodman, M., Bonds, D., Sandler, I., & Braver, S. (2004). Parent psychoeducational programs and reducing the negative effects of interparental conflict following divorce. *Family Court Review, 42*, 263–279. doi:10.1177/1531244504422007

Hayes, S., Grady, M., & Brantley, H. (2012). E-mails, statutes, and personality disorders: A contextual examination of the processes, interventions, and perspective of parenting coordinators. *Family Court Review, 50*, 429–440. doi:10.1111/j.1744-1617.2012.01458.x

Hayes, S. W. (2010). "More street cop than a detective": An analysis of the roles and functions of parenting coordinators in North Carolina. *Family Court Review*, *48*, 698–709. doi:10.1111/j.1744-1617.2010.01343.x

Henry, W., Fieldstone, L., & Bohac, K. (2009). Parenting coordination and court relitigation: A case study. *Family Court Review*, *47*, 682–697. doi:10.1111/j.1744-1617.2009.01281.x

Kelly, J. B. (1996). A decade of divorce mediation research: Some answers and questions. *Family Court Review*, *34*, 373–385. doi:10.1111/j.174-1617.1996.tb00427.x

Kelly, J. B. (2002). Psychological and legal interventions for parents and children in custody and access disputes: Current research and practice. *Virginia Journal of Social Policy & the Law*, *10*, 129–163.

Kirkland, K., & Sullivan, M. (2008). Parenting coordination (PC) practice: A survey of experienced professionals. *Family Court Review*, *46*, 622–636. doi:10.1111/j.1744-1617.2008.00228.x

Kitzmann, K. M., & Emery, R. E. (1994). Child and family coping one year following mediated and litigated child custody disputes. *Journal of Family Psychology*, *8*, 150–159. doi:10.1037/0893-3200.8.2.150

Kramer, L., & Washo, C. A. (1993). Evaluation of a court-mandated prevention program for divorcing parents: The Children First program. *Family Relations*, *42*, 179–186. doi:10.2307/585452

Lally, S. J., & Higuchi, S. A. (2008). The American Psychological Association Parenting Coordination Project: Development of the project and initial review of the first two years. *Journal of Child Custody*, *5*, 101–121. doi:10.1080/15379410802070435

McIntosh, J., & Deacon-Wood, H. B. (2003). Group interventions for separated parents in entrenched conflict: An exploration of evidence-based frameworks. *Journal of Family Studies*, *9*, 187–199. doi:10.5172/jfs.9.2.187

Mitcham-Smith, M., & Henry, W. (2007). High-conflict divorce solutions: Parenting coordination as an innovative co-parenting intervention. *The Family Journal*, *15*, 368–373. doi:10.1177/1066480707303751

Parks, L. S., Tindall, H. L., & Yingling, L. D. (2011). Defining parenting coordination with state laws. *Family Court Review*, *49*, 629–641. doi:10.1111/j.1744-1617.2011.01398.x

Pedro-Carroll, J. L., & Alpert-Gillis, L. J. (1997). Preventive interventions for children of divorce: A developmental model for 5 and 6 year old children. *The Journal of Primary Prevention*, *18*, 5–23. doi:10.1023/A:1024601421020

Pedro-Carroll, J. L., & Cowen, E. L. (1985). The Children of Divorce Intervention Project: An investigation of the efficacy of a school-based prevention program. *Journal of Consulting and Clinical Psychology*, *53*, 603–611. doi:10.1037/0022-006X.53.5.603

Pollet, S. L., & Lombreglia, M. (2008). A nationwide survey of mandatory parent education. *Family Court Review*, *46*, 375–394. doi:10.1111/j.1744-1617.2008.00207.x

Pruett, M. K., Insabella, G. M., & Gustafson, K. (2005). The Collaborative Divorce Project: A court-based intervention for separating parents with young children. *Family Court Review*, *43*, 38–51. doi:10.1111/j.1744-1617.2005.00006.x

Shaw, D. S., & Emery, R. E. (1987). Parental conflict and other correlates of the adjustment of school-aged children whose parents have separated. *Journal of Abnormal Child Psychology*, *15*, 269–281. doi:10.1007/BF00916354

Shifflett, K., & Cummings, E. M. (1999). A program for educating parents about the effects of divorce and conflict on children: An initial evaluation. *Family Relations*, *48*, 79–89. doi:10.2307/585685

Sigal, A., Sandler, I., Wolchik, S., & Braver, S. (2011). Do parent education programs promote healthy postdivorce parenting? Critical distinctions and a review of the evidence. *Family Court Review*, *49*, 120–139. doi:10.1111/j.1744-1617.2010.01357.x

Singer, G. H. S., Ethridge, B. L., & Aldana, S. I. (2007). Primary and secondary effects of parenting and stress management interventions for parents of children with developmental disabilities: A meta-analysis. *Mental Retardation and Developmental Disabilities Research Reviews*, *13*, 357–369. doi:10.1002/mrdd.20175

Stolberg, A. L., & Garrison, K. M. (1985). Evaluation a primary prevention program for children of divorce: The Divorce Adjustment Project. *American Journal of Community Psychology*, *13*, 111–124. doi:10.1007/BF00905724

Walker, J., & Hayes, S. (2006). Policy, practice and politics: Bargaining in the shadow of Whitehall. In M. S. Herrman (Ed.), *The Blackwell handbook of mediation: Bridging theory, practice, and research* (pp. 99–128). Malden, MA: Blackwell.

Wolchik, S. A., Sandler, I., Jones, S., Gonzales, N., Doyle, K., Winslow, E., . . . Braver, S. L. (2009). The New Beginnings program for divorcing and separating families: Moving from efficacy to effectiveness. *Family Court Review*, *47*, 416–435. doi:10.1111/j.1744-1617.2009.01265.x

Wolchik, S. A., Sandler, I. N., Millsap, R. E., Plummer, B. A., Greene, S. M., Anderson, E. R., . . . Haine, R. A. (2002). Six-year follow-up of preventive interventions for children of divorce: A randomized controlled trial. *JAMA*, *288*, 1874–1881. doi:10.1001/jama.288.15.1874

Wolchik, S. A., Sandler, I. N., Winslow, E., & Smith-Daniels, V. (2005). Programs for promoting parenting of residential parents: Moving from efficacy to effectiveness. *Family Court Review*, *43*, 65–80. doi:10.1111/j.1744-1617.2005.00008.x

Wolchik, S. A., West, S. G., Sandler, I. N., Tein, J.-Y., Coatsworth, D., Lengua, L., . . . Griffin, W. A. (2000). An experimental evaluation of theory-based mother and mother–child programs for children of divorce. *Journal of Consulting and Clinical Psychology*, 68, 843–856. doi:10.1037/0022-006X.68.5.843

Zuberbuhler, J. (2001). Early intervention mediation: The use of court-ordered mediation in the initial stages of divorce litigation to resolve parenting issues. *Family Court Review*, *39*, 203–206. doi:10.1111/j.174-1617.2001.tb00604.x

14

THE FUTURE OF PARENTING COORDINATION

JOAN B. KELLY AND SHIRLEY ANN HIGUCHI

As is evident from the breadth and content of the chapters included in this book, parenting coordination has, over the past 25 years, garnered the attention of family courts, mental health and legal professionals, researchers, and families and become a well-established and beneficial intervention. Parenting coordination integrates a decision-making or more formal arbitration component into the familiar elements of dispute assessment, mediation, focused parent education, communication management, and case coordination. Parenting coordination services are child focused and psychologically sensitive yet authoritative, and many parents with enduring high-conflict and repeated patterns of relitigation have been able, with the assistance of parenting coordinators (PCs), to lower the number of their child-related and parenting plan disputes and reduce their reliance on the adversarial court system.

http://dx.doi.org/10.1037/14390-015
Parenting Coordination in Postseparation Disputes: A Comprehensive Guide for Practitioners, S. A. Higuchi and S. J. Lally (Editors)

The most important achievements in developing and establishing the parenting coordination intervention include

- a continued clarification and broad consensus regarding the role and function of the PC;
- a clear differentiation of the parenting coordination role from the more usual roles of mental health professionals, family lawyers, and mediators involved in separation and divorce practices;
- early national, regional, and local PC trainings and workshops, and early publications describing parenting coordination and providing practice guidance for the hybrid model;
- the development, by two national professional organizations (the Association of Family and Conciliation Courts [AFCC], Task Force on Parenting Coordination, 2006; and the American Psychological Association [APA], 2012) of guidelines for the practice of parenting coordination, including the specialized training and knowledge base needed to undertake the PC role, role definition and practice, ethical issues, and the importance of domestic violence screening to determine whether parenting coordination is appropriate (this topic is discussed in more detail in Chapter 11, this volume);
- the development of state legislation and local jurisdictional rules and procedures establishing the basis for proceeding with parenting coordination practice;
- the extension of parenting coordination into the family court; and
- initial and subsequent research that demonstrated a dramatic reduction in court motions filed by parents who work with a PC.

PARENTING COORDINATION INTO THE FUTURE: CHALLENGES AND ISSUES

In recognition of these achievements in establishing parenting coordination in the United States and Canada, it is timely to consider the future course of this unique service. A number of issues have emerged that need to be addressed if the PC role as originally conceptualized and implemented is to be maintained. These include the need for a continued sharp focus on role definition and the hybrid model, the divergence in views on confidentiality versus nonconfidentiality of parenting coordination, the relationship between PCs and the court system, making services available to increasingly more diverse populations of parents through the expansion of court-based programs, future training needs, continued empirical research, and continued development of state-level legislation and local rules.

Role Definition and the Hybrid Model

As indicated above and in several chapters in this volume, from its inception the PC role has included a decision-making component, most typically available for a circumscribed set of child-related disputes spelled out in the parenting coordination agreement or court order. PCs do not (and should not) have the authority to make decisions in parenting disputes that infringe on judges' exclusive authority to determine physical and legal custody, relocation, or substantial and permanent changes to the parenting time plan. The ability to make appropriate decisions when necessary gives the PC delegated authority with limited scope, an essential component of the model that encourages parents to work more diligently on trying to reach their own agreements with the PC's assistance. Many PCs report that the number of disputes requiring court decisions diminishes over the course of their term of service as parents learn to compromise and reach consensual agreements with the PC's guidance.

For the most part, limited decision-making authority as part of the PC role has been adopted in state and local jurisdictions and in many private consent agreements. Over time, however, as mental health and legal professionals have attempted to establish parenting coordination programs in their jurisdictions, there has been role confusion and, in some cases, a significant dilution of the PC role, which has caused concern (Sullivan, 2013). For example, some legislation has limited and changed the PC role to involve only parent education, mediation, and/or coparenting counseling, with no recommendation or decision-making authority, yet has retained the label *parenting coordination*. This role dilution has sometimes occurred in the process of seeking state legislation for parenting coordination, when objections to PCs making even minor decisions in child-related disputes were raised by the family bar or judiciary. In some instances, these changes were the result of a failure to understand the unique service needs of parents with long-entrenched conflict patterns, or the failure to develop an interdisciplinary, consensual process for drafting legislation that discussed and carefully circumscribed the types of decisions PCs could make. A few states permit PCs to make recommendations to the court rather than decisions; the court reviews and either accepts or rejects the PC's recommendations. This structure assumes that the PC has some authorized capacity included in the stipulation and/or court order to communicate recommendations to the court. If PCs have neither recommending nor decision-making authority as backup and an integral component of the parenting coordination process, it is likely that parents will return often to litigation when disputes cannot be negotiated. On the basis of parenting coordination research demonstrating a significant reduction in motions filed on child (and other) matters, a parenting coordination model without teeth appears to compromise the important goal of helping parents avoid the adversarial system and the associated emotional and financial costs.

In this context, it is useful here to review the characteristics of separated or divorced parents for whom parenting coordination was developed. More often than not, at least one parent, if not both, have long-standing unresolved anger and conflict, demonstrate a consistent inability or unwillingness to discuss child-related disputes, communicate provocatively with their former partners, fail to reach even small agreements with mediation assistance, and do not cooperate or focus on their children's needs. Many have poor insight into their contributions to the conflict, blame others for problems, see no need to change their behaviors, feel highly entitled, and think that rules and court orders do not apply to them. Severe personality disorders are common in one or both parents (see Chapter 7, this volume, for a more thorough discussion of this topic). It is important for the ongoing effectiveness of parenting coordination that there be common agreement not only about the characteristics of parents and relationships that can benefit from parenting coordination but also that specified decision making in child-related and parenting plan disputes be maintained as a core component of the process.

Nonconfidentiality Versus Confidentiality of the Process

Parenting coordination was first established as a nonconfidential intervention, for a number of valid reasons. The primary reason was to provide PCs the formal authority to communicate with the court, either to send recommendations to the court for review, report a pattern of noncompliance, or file decisions and new and revised agreements reached through negotiations with the parents to supplement the court file. As with PCs' decision making, a nonconfidential process provides PCs with another tool that encourages coparental agreement and compliance with court-ordered parenting plans. A nonconfidential model also permits PCs to communicate with the parents' lawyers, therapists, physicians, and other professionals involved in children's lives as needed, as well as with a previous or future PC. When such communication is stipulated or court ordered, parents sign releases provided by the PC in order to talk with these professionals. The absence of confidentiality is (or should be) clearly spelled out in stipulations, court orders, and private consent agreements. Both the AFCC Task Force on Parenting Coordination (2006) and APA (2012) guidelines for the practice of parenting coordination state that the parenting coordination process is generally a nonconfidential one. The absence of confidentiality in parenting coordination does not constitute an unethical practice for PCs because it is described up front as a feature of the model and because parenting coordination, as widely accepted, is not considered to be a form of therapy or counseling.

It has been argued that the parenting coordination process should be confidential because it is described as an alternative dispute resolution process that includes some mediation, which in North America has generally been a confidential process (Parks, Tindall, & Yingling, 2011). There is, however, no overarching confidentiality expectation attached to all "alternative" forms of dispute resolution, as, for example, to judicial settlement conferences or to family court mediation in some jurisdictions. From its inception, the parenting coordination process and model were seen as a step beyond and distinct from the practice of family mediation. Because PCs rely on mediation processes and techniques as important elements and skills in the larger hybrid model does not mean that the parenting coordination process is bound by the traditional constraints of family mediation practice. Mediation clients sign an agreement that specifies confidentiality, among other things, including the fact that nothing will be transmitted about the mediation to any other entity or party in the event of a failure to reach agreements. In contrast, when parents agree to parenting coordination, whether by stipulation, court order, or private consent agreements, the nature of parenting coordination is clearly spelled out as incorporating aspects of education, facilitation, consensus building or mediation, and arbitration or decision making in helping parents settle child-related parenting disputes. These documents clearly state that the parenting coordination process is not confidential and is not psychotherapy, counseling, or legal representation. In states where courts can assign a PC to a case over the objection of a parent, court orders should contain similar language.

The Relationship Between the Parenting Coordinator and the Court System

A related issue is whether there should be a link between the family court and the parenting coordination process. This is important because the PC's connection to the court promotes parent accountability and encourages compliance given the inherent power of the court to enforce the terms of the final parenting plan orders contained in the decree. Experienced PCs agree that the need to report serious parent noncompliance problems is relatively rare. Parents are well aware of this backup enforcement power of family courts, and most parents do comply if reminded. Any reports prepared for the court, other than routine and factual transmissions of agreements, recommendations, and decisions, must be prepared carefully to protect children and parents.

A relationship to the court also provides an avenue for the PC to terminate an inappropriate case, for example, when a parent is too mentally ill or refuses to participate, a child is potentially endangered, violence has occurred, or a parent has refused to pay for services as a way of forcing the PC to terminate the case prematurely (see Chapter 5, this volume, for a more in-depth discussion of how to set up appropriate boundaries at the outset of a parenting coordination case). The court connection also provides an avenue for clients to complain to the court of inappropriate PC behavior or fees. Stipulations and orders in some jurisdictions, such as California, have language and procedures in the stipulation and court order for resolving client grievances against the PC that ultimately rely on the judge for final resolution if other prescribed grievance procedures do not work. These grievance procedures help protect parents and may serve to limit the number of direct complaints to licensing boards.

Making Parenting Coordination Services More Available and Affordable: The Family Court Connection

Parenting coordination was initiated in, and continues to be provided almost exclusively in, the private sector. The need for affordable or low-cost services for parents desiring or needing a PC is a major concern for the parenting coordination field, and few current answers are available at the time of this writing. Parenting coordination work is challenging and stressful, and it requires highly knowledgeable, experienced, and skilled psychologists or other qualified professionals who often have experience in providing forensic services. The high incidence and complexity of disputes regarding children demand considerable attention. Psychologists often charge their customary forensic rates, which are generally higher than psychotherapy fees. Although one PC is considerably less expensive than two family lawyers pursuing litigation, there has been a significant increase in the numbers of unrepresented parents in family courts who can neither afford lawyers after a separation nor a PC in the years after the final decree.

As described in Chapter 8 of this volume, APA, in collaboration with the District of Columbia (DC) Bar, Argosy University, and the DC Superior Court, developed a unique program to provide parenting coordination services to families with limited income. Modeled after traditional legal clinics staffed by law students, the *DC Program*, as it is called, is a model for interdisciplinary collaboration. It provides training for doctoral students, supervised by a licensed psychologist acting as the PC, which allows the program to serve more clients on a pro bono basis. It also creates an infrastructure within the court system to support this innovative service, and it educates judges, lawyers, and families in the family court system about the potential benefits of the parenting coordination intervention.

Many of the cases that come through the DC Superior Court involve pro se (unrepresented) litigants and generally present substantial challenges for family court judges in the context of intense conflict and child custody disputes. The court-based parenting coordination program provides welcome relief for the court system. An additional benefit is that the structure of the family court and the high volume of cases facilitate research on the process and outcome of parenting coordination services.

Future Training Needs for Parenting Coordinators

The delineation of specific training needs in the AFCC Task Force on Parenting Coordination guidelines (2006) and the APA (2012) practice guidelines have established a baseline of psychological and legal knowledge and skills that serves as a template for 1- to 3-day core parenting coordination trainings. Although these core trainings have differed in emphasis and complexity depending on the expertise and interests of the trainers, the parenting coordination model taught and the overall course content have been reasonably consistent. Thousands of mental health and legal professionals have received detailed information about the basics of the parenting coordination model, including the process, ethics, case management, characteristics of high-conflict parents, practice tips, and case examples for group discussion. Participant satisfaction with the content and delivery has been quite high for more than 15 years (C. Walker, AFCC Program Director, personal communication, 2012; first author's review of APA-sponsored parenting coordination workshop evaluations from 2008 to 2011), even though many professionals leave the training with understandable apprehension about the daunting challenges of the PC role and beginning a parenting coordination practice. It is likely that core parenting coordination trainings will continue to offer much the same content, assimilating new research and practice techniques as they emerge.

A central training need for the future is the development of a consensus about the type of content that constitutes advanced parenting coordination training. We should note that parenting coordination is itself a challenging topic for practitioners because it presents an advanced practice model that requires considerable knowledge, skill, and practice experience with high-conflict parents. In this respect, it is similar to obtaining a 5-day divorce and custody mediation training session in order to add mediation practice to one's more typical therapeutic and evaluative services. Parenting coordination is a unique service for psychologists, not just because of its mediation, education, and arbitration components but also because psychologists' parenting coordination practice is guided by highly structured court orders or private consent agreements. High-conflict parents present a continuing series of legal and psychological challenges, for which advanced parenting coordination trainings and consultations with experienced PCs and peer groups are necessary. Well-conceived advanced parenting coordination trainings enable PCs to obtain the relevant continuing education expected in the published guidelines and to sharpen and supplement their core knowledge and skills once they have gained practice experience as a PC. Participants come to advanced trainings with varying backgrounds in clinical and forensic practice, varying degrees of knowledge about the core parenting coordination process, and different levels of experience as a practicing PC. Trainers increasingly can expect a degree of sophistication among advanced training participants who are looking for more complex practice insights and help with difficult cases and issues. Currently, most advanced 1- or 2-day trainings build and expand on content normally provided in the core training, for example, describing in more detail how to manage the unwieldy parenting coordination process and the coparental relationship through specific communication structures and case management, or focusing on strategies for dealing with parents who have severe personality disorders. Other advanced trainings provide specialized components thought to enhance the parenting coordination process, such as the knowledge and skill base for interviewing children in the parenting coordination process, or using current and specific social science research to educate and motivate parents to cease behaviors associated with children's psychological and social adjustment problems.

In the first author's extensive experience as a PC educator and trainer, advanced PCs' evaluations of the formal training sessions they have attended provide useful guidance for the content of future trainings. They often express the need to discuss actual, complex case scenarios constructed by trainers that contain examples of the types of situations PCs manage on a regular basis. One or two detailed case studies, including information from individual or joint sessions, e-mails, and phone calls, might include examples of particularly egregious behaviors (how to manage), uncooperative clients (how to motivate them and when to terminate a case), unsuccessful attempts to mediate a child dispute (when to switch to arbitration), failure to comply with an aspect of the parenting plan (how to handle), a powerful or demanding client (how to stay in charge and maintain a working alliance), inappropriate use of a child as a messenger to express anger toward the other parent (how to sensitize a parent to and build empathy for the child's position), and PC stress (how to prevent burnout).

Training participants also describe the benefits of brief case examples that demonstrate the parenting coordination process from the first e-mail or phone call from a parent about a time-sensitive child dispute that needs to be resolved, gathering information from the parents and the child, and subsequent unsuccessful attempts to reach a consensus or complete mediation. Small group exercises, which include analyzing the dispute, determining whether it falls within the PC's scope of power or domain, deciding whether there is sufficient information from all relevant parties, and then discussing what the PC does next, including any decision or recommendation to be made, also are valuable. Such exercises are illuminating because there is generally more than one way for a PC to proceed, and opinions about what the PC might decide in an arbitration phase often vary widely. Participants also often express the desire to see situations role-played.

Other advanced practice topics might focus on a series of interactions, communications, and challenges with a parent with antisocial or borderline personality disorder, framing questions about how to proceed in each instance. PCs with the authority to make recommendations and decisions must learn to draft their decisions with precision and in anticipation that one or both parents will attempt to exploit any gray areas or unclear, incomplete writing. Other than mediation training and subsequent experience with drafting parenting plans, there is very little in the prior training or experience of a practicing psychologist that provides the knowledge and drafting skills for this exacting task. An advanced training can, for example, promote good drafting skills by presenting the details of a PC's decision or recommendation, with the rationale underlying that decision and then providing feedback about the structure of the document, choice of language, loopholes, omissions, and evident biases that can permeate the language used.

Future Research Needs

As with any new field of practice, over time research questions typically become more specific, and methodologies more sophisticated, as knowledge accumulates and generates more research interest and hypotheses. Early research on parenting coordination focused primarily on parenting coordination demographics and qualifications as well as self-descriptions of the PC's roles, practices, experience, and techniques through the use of online surveys of practitioners identified through listservs and colleagues (see Chapter 13, this volume). Some of these surveys have been limited to a particular jurisdiction, with its own set of laws or local rules describing the PC's role, which limits generalizations about parenting coordination practices at the national level.

The few studies of the efficacy of parenting coordination have been promising, indicating that the number of motions filed regarding disputes are reduced after the parents start working with a PC, compared with the number of motions prior to the PC's term of service. Furthermore, various measures of expenditures of court resources (e.g., judicial time spent, burden on court personnel) all indicate substantial reductions (see Chapters 1 and 13, this volume, for more detailed discussions of research that has focused on parenting coordination issues and efficacy). Although PCs, judges, and lawyers have indicated in a few surveys that parental conflict was reduced following the introduction of the PC, there has been only one study with pre and post measures of different types and intensities of parent conflict, and the results of this study, which focused on the DC Program (see Chapter 8), were limited by a small sample size and missing data. Additional research is needed to answer the question of exactly how effective parenting coordination services are. To date, sample sizes have been small, and not representative, and many findings are anecdotal. One of the weaknesses of these studies has been the failure to specify the nature of the PC's role and the extent of authority given to PCs to make recommendations and decisions. Specifying these variables is important to understanding the context of the study and the outcomes of the parenting coordination intervention, and to making comparisons with other studies of outcomes and client satisfaction.

Future research also can address a number of additional needs. One current broad need is to establish a committee of experienced PC practitioners and researchers, tasked by an interdisciplinary organization such as AFCC, to develop a consistent framework and set of standardized questionnaires for measuring multiple aspects of the PC role, process, and outcomes, to be provided to PCs and parents. This committee could also focus on developing methods for collecting data from a broader based and more representative samples of PCs within a longitudinal framework.

Research that focuses on PCs' role and practices, parenting coordination processes, and parenting coordination outcomes, in both private practice and court-based services, also is needed. Examples of questions that would help clarify PC role and practices include the following:

- Does the PC role include any type of decision making? If so, what or who gave the PC that authority (i.e., legislation, the judge/court, the parents' stipulation or signed private agreement), and over what specific type of child-related and parenting plan disputes?
- Does the PC have the authority to make recommendations to the court, and if so, do recommendations become effective if a parent does not file a motion within a period of time?
- Does the PC record all negotiated decisions between parents, and do recommendations and decisions get sent to the court to become part of an amended final parenting plan decree?
- Does the PC view his or her role as including coparenting counseling, and if so, how is that defined and is it viewed as a form of therapy?

- Does the PC interview children of sufficient age as a routine part of the process to determine their views and ideas? If so, how does the PC use the children's perspectives and desires to help parents settle disputes (see Chapter 9, this volume)?

Parenting coordination process questions might examine questions such as these:

- Is the process completely confidential, partially confidential, or nonconfidential, and why? If it is partially confidential, what things are confidential and what are nonconfidential?
- Are clients always or predominantly seen jointly, individually, or a combination of both?
- Does the PC provide a written summary of all joint meetings for review by the parents?
- Are rules and guidance provided to clients regarding the format, time sensitivity, and language of e-mail communications, and are copies of all e-mails sent to the PC and both parents?
- What percentage of the PC's time is spent using e-mail or the phone to work with parents, as compared with in-person meetings?
- How many parents continue to have a lawyer representing them, how helpful is the lawyer to the parenting coordination process, and does the PC speak with the lawyers?
- What were the total hours per case, and hourly and total fees for the period of time the PC served?

The following are some important outcome issues a PC may wish to consider:

- pre and post assessments of parent conflict over the course of the PC's appointment, using measures of both the frequency and intensity of conflict and differentiating the conflict by content or category;
- children's ratings of conflict, including the extent to which they feel caught in the middle of the conflict, hear parental denigration, or are asked to carry messages from one parent to the other;
- pre and post measures of parent cooperation and parent support as provided by parents and the PC around different aspects of parenting, scheduling, and decision making about the children;
- the number and nature of parent disputes for which the PC made decisions and/or recommendations for the judge's consideration;

- the parents' overall level of compliance with the parenting plan and the PC's recommendations and decisions; and
- client evaluations of multiple dimensions of the PC's services using an established and valid questionnaire to help clarify what aspects of the parenting coordination process parents find useful.

As was true of the path of research in the emerging family and divorce mediation field (Kelly, 2004), research will steadily create and expand a knowledge base about parenting coordination practices, processes, important parent characteristics and interactions, and the various outcomes of the parenting coordination process, all of which can be used to modify and improve the parenting coordination intervention.

CONCLUSION

The future of parenting coordination seems ensured by the widespread acceptance of the hybrid model as evidenced by increased state legislation, practice guidelines published by two prominent national professional organizations; the increasing use of parenting coordination by family courts, family law and mental health professionals, and parents needing relief from the emotional and financial expense of continued litigation focusing on their children; and the evident benefits to children. The quality of future parenting coordination will continue to be enhanced by appropriate training at the core and advanced levels, continued publications focused on ethical and effective practice, and guidance from increasingly sophisticated and relevant research.

REFERENCES

American Psychological Association. (2012). Guidelines for the practice of parenting coordination. *American Psychologist, 67*, 63–71. doi:10.1037/a0024646

Association of Family and Conciliation Courts, Task Force on Parenting Coordination. (2006). Guidelines for parenting coordination. *Family Court Review, 44*, 164–181. doi:10.1111/j.1744-1617.2006.00074.x

Kelly, J. B. (2004). Family mediation research: Is there empirical support for the field? *Conflict Resolution Quarterly, 22*, 3–35. doi:10.1002/crq.90

Parks, L. S., Tindall, H. L., & Yingling, L. C. (2011). Defining parenting coordination with state laws. *Family Court Review, 49*, 629–641. doi:10.1111/j.1744-1617.2011.01398.x

Sullivan, M. J. (2013). Parenting coordination: Coming of age? *Family Court Review, 51*, 56–62. doi:10.1111/fcre.12008

INDEX

ABOUT THE EDITORS

Shirley Ann Higuchi, Esq., is the associate executive director of legal and regulatory affairs for the American Psychological Association (APA). In this role, Ms. Higuchi manages all aspects of a complex agenda focused on developing and implementing legal and regulatory strategies to achieve optimal psychologist participation in the health care field. Topics covered include managed care, class action litigation, state health care reform, Medicaid, professional licensing, scope of practice, confidentiality, telehealth, and parenting coordination. Through her work at APA, Ms. Higuchi has contributed to the field of parenting coordination by offering training workshops, developing practice guidelines, supporting research, and helping launch the Office of the Parenting Coordinator in the District of Columbia Superior Court. Ms. Higuchi is active in the DC Bar, having served on the Board of Governors from 1994 to 2000, as chair of the Bar's Nominations Committee in 2001, and as president in 2003. She recently completed a 6-year term on the Judicial Tenure and Disabilities Commission for the DC Courts. Ms. Higuchi has received several prestigious awards, including the Lever Award, the Honorable Annice M. Wagner Pioneer Award, and the United Planning Organization Community Service Award. In addition to her service to the legal and psychological communities, Ms. Higuchi is chair of the Heart Mountain Wyoming Foundation, which provides education, policy, and research on the experiences of Japanese Americans wrongly incarcerated during World War II. Prior to joining APA, Ms. Higuchi was in private practice with the law firm of Epstein Becker & Green, PC. She received her undergraduate degree from the University of Michigan and her law degree from Georgetown University.

Stephen J. Lally, PhD, ABPP, is a professor in the clinical psychology program at the American School of Professional Psychology at Argosy University, Washington, DC. He is the past president of the National Council of Schools and Programs of Professional Psychology. He received his diplomate in forensic psychology from the American Board of Professional Psychology. Dr. Lally is the past president of the District of Columbia Psychology Association, a former APA Council Representative for DC, and a past member of APA's Committee for Professional Practice and Standards. He has presented and published in the areas of assessment, ethics, and forensic psychology. Dr. Lally has a part-time forensic and clinical practice in the Washington, DC, area.